SABINE R. ULIBARRÍ
CRITICAL
ESSAYS

PASÓ POR AQUÍ
Series on the Nuevomexicano Literary Heritage
Edited by Genaro M. Padilla &
Erlinda Gonzales-Berry

SABINE R. ULIBARRÍ CRITICAL ESSAYS

EDITED BY
María I. Duke dos Santos
& Patricia de la Fuente

UNIVERSITY OF NEW MEXICO PRESS
Albuquerque

Library of Congress Cataloging-in-Publication Data
Sabine R. Ulibarrí : critical essays / edited by María I. Duke dos
Santos & Patricia de la Fuente.—1st ed.
    p.   cm.—(Pasó por aquí : series on the Nuevomexicano
literary heritage)
  Includes bibliographical references.
  ISBN 0-8263-1627-1
  1. Ulibarrí, Sabine R.—Criticism and interpretation. I. Duke
dos Santos, María I., 1939-   . II. De la Fuente, Patricia.
  III. Series: Pasó por aquí.
PQ7079.2.U4Z87   1995
868—dc20   95-19998
                                                                 CIP

First edition

Designed by Linda Mae Tratechaud

CONTENTS

PREFACE

I became acquainted with Sabine Reyes Ulibarrí, the author, in 1978. As I read *Tierra Amarilla* and *Mi abuela fumaba puros*, I was immediately struck by the musicality and rhythm of his prose, by his subtle humor and his love of New Mexico. Then, in 1980, I became acquainted with Sabine Reyes Ulibarrí, the person and the educator, when he accepted my invitation to lecture at East Texas State University (ETSU) and was a guest in my home. I was impressed by his friendly and gentle manner and by his baritone voice, which he used to full advantage as he spoke to a room full of students and faculty members from ETSU and other institutions in the Metroplex (Dallas/Fort Worth) area. His dedication to teaching was evident then as it had been a short time before, when I traveled to New Mexico on a consulting job and visited him at the university. (He was then chair of the department of Modern and Classical Languages.) His commitment to educate New Mexican youth was apparent as I sat in one of his classes and later talked with him in his office. As he said to me during the course of one of our conversations, "I am an educator first, an author second."

During the 1980s, as I read and reread Ulibarrí's works and continued our conversations, I realized there were insufficient research materials to guide the readers of his works, especially since stu-

SABINE R. ULIBARRÍ WITH MARÍA I. DUKE DOS SANTOS IN HIS OFFICE AT THE
UNIVERSITY OF NEW MEXICO.

dents wanted to know more about him, both as a writer and as a
man. Originally I planned to interview him and publish the interview. However, the idea of a critical anthology germinated while I
was visiting my colleague, Patricia de la Fuente of the University
of Texas–Pan American. We decided then to undertake this project,
which we hope will be followed by other collections with additional critical approaches as more of Ulibarrí's works are published.

I traveled to Albuquerque to interview the author on three different occasions, the first one being the longest—an entire week
at his home, which he and his wife, Connie, graciously opened to
me. He picked me up at the airport on a very cold evening. My
plane had been unable to land because of a heavy snowstorm, and

we had flown first to El Paso and then returned to Albuquerque, where we finally landed more than three hours late. I was very concerned about the delay, but when I arrived at the gate, Ulibarrí was there, smiling broadly and concerned only about my safety. He insisted that I wait while he went to get the car, but I began to worry when I realized he was taking too long to return. At last he showed up and explained that it had snowed so much that all the cars were completely covered and he could not find his: they all looked alike. When he had finally found his car, he discovered that the lock on the driver's side was frozen, so he had to open it from the opposite side. After we were both safely inside the car and on our way to his home, we laughed about the whole experience, and he said he would have to write a story about it. His wife was waiting for us, not concerned at all since he had telephoned her from the airport to advise her of my late arrival.

I spent a most interesting and rewarding week with the Ulibarrís. They showed me their family pictures, and we took some photographs, a few of which appear in this volume. Connie took me shopping at Old Town one afternoon and later gave me one of her pieces of jewelry, a small turquoise brooch that I shall always treasure. Their beloved home, which offers a wonderful view of the Sandía mountains, has a sign over the front door that reads, Casa Ulibarrí. It was a most auspicious time for me to be in New Mexico since it was Holy Week, and I associated some of the observances with "Los penitentes," a piece he had written some time back. The second time I visited he was not in very good health, but the third time, in 1992, I was glad to see him well and looking much better. Each time I obtained additional material and new information about his writing and projects. We have also kept in touch over the telephone.

The interview and most of our conversations were conducted in Spanish as Ulibarrí and I sat for long periods at the round kitchen table, his favorite spot, while his wife listened and worked or spent time with their grandson, a frequent visitor. His son and his wife also visited while I was there. I recorded the interview and later sent him a transcribed manuscript for his approval. I also translated it so it could appear in a bilingual format.

SABINE R. ULIBARRÍ WITH HIS WIFE CONNIE AT THEIR HOME IN ALBUQUERQUE.

Patricia de la Fuente met Ulibarrí in March 1991 in Albuquerque. I was chairing a section honoring Ulibarrí at the annual convention of the National Association of Chicano Studies, where she was one of the presenters. Other presenters were Francisco Lomelí, don Luis Leal, and María Herrera-Sobek. Ulibarrí and his wife came to the session and afterward we all adjourned to a restaurant for conversation and refreshments. Later that day Ulibarrí picked me up at the convention site, and I spent an additional two days with him and his wife at their home.

Each of the contributors to this volume had a specific goal: some chose a linguistic approach, some chose to address a particular aspect of Ulibarrí's prose, others focused on his poetry, and still another focused on his essays, a long-neglected yet very important part of Ulibarrí's writings. This volume also contains an annotated bibliography by Teresa Márquez, a librarian who has worked for many years at the University of New Mexico and therefore is very well acquainted with Ulibarrí and his writings. An Appendix containing a small selection of the author's unpublished works is also included.

My sincere thanks to the editors of the UNM Press for their suggestions, Sheila Berg for her superb copy editing of the manuscript, and to Professor Gerald C. Duchovnay for his encouragement and support of this project.

María I. Duke dos Santos

SABINE R. ULIBARRÍ
CRITICAL
ESSAYS

INTRODUCTION

Luis Leal

This collection of critical essays on the literary production of Sabine Ulibarrí represents a valuable addition to the few such collections dedicated to the works of a single Chicano author. Ulibarrí's literary production, composed of poetry, short fiction, and critical essays is examined in these studies from different perspectives and from a variety of critical approaches. No aspect of his work is left out. Especially welcome are the two chapters dedicated to his poetry, an aspect of his literary contributions that critics have neglected. This neglect was perhaps due to the fact that Ulibarrí is mainly recognized for his short fiction. But, as shown by Santiago Daydí-Tolson and Patricia de la Fuente, his two books of poems, *Amor y Ecuador* and *Al cielo se sube a pie*, already contained the principal images and symbols that were to become the core of his fiction; therefore, an examination of his poetry becomes essential for a more complete analysis of his fiction.

Daydí-Tolson's examination of Ulibarrí's spatial imagery contributes significant insights into the poet's creative process and therefore helps the reader to understand not only the author's poetry but also his fiction, since the same type of imagery is found in both genres. This study is complemented by that of Patricia de la Fuente, who approaches Ulibarrí's poetry from a slightly different perspective, that of the presence of female images, with which the

3

poet integrates dreams and reality. As the author himself has stated in the highly informative interview with María I. Duke dos Santos, poetry is what predominates even in his fiction.

Like his poetry, Ulibarrí's critical essays have also been neglected by most critics. This is more understandable, since not all of his work in this field is available in print. It is fortunate that Francisco Lomelí has had access to some of these unpublished manuscripts and has been able to analyze them and prepare a carefully researched study—as far as we know, the first dedicated to Ulibarrí's nonfictional prose.

Since 1971, when he published his first collection of stories, *Tierra Amarilla*, characterized as "golden with the light of youth" by the translator and editor of the bilingual edition, Ulibarrí has become a leading exponent of the Chicano short story. To that first book he has added several others, to which over half of the essays presented here are dedicated. This preference of the critics for his short fiction is understandable, since most of Ulibarrí's contributions to Chicano literature have been in the field of the short story. The varied approaches from which critics have studied this fiction, as the reader will discover, complement each other to give a well-rounded overview of Ulibarrí's art in this difficult genre.

Gene Steven Forrest and Wolfgang Karrer approach the subject from the mythical perspective, Forrest concentrating on the presence of timeless mythical patterns in the stories collected under the title of one of them, "The Condor," and Karrer discovering in the stories of *Tierra Amarilla* old and new approaches to the problems of ethnic identity and communal relations, as manifested in the recurring myth of masculinity.

In her informative study of folklore elements in Ulibarrí's collection of short stories, *Mi abuela fumaba puros/My Grandmother Smoked Cigars*, María Herrera-Sobek examines with keen perception folk motifs, giving particular attention to La Llorona, considered the most widely known folk character among Chicanos and Mexicanos. Contrary to other interpretations of the stories collected by Ulibarrí in that volume, Herrera-Sobek considers them part of the resistance literature that arose during the Chicano movement of the 1960s and 1970s. The overall purpose of the stories, according to her, is to document the harmonious and peaceful lifestyle existing before Anglo hegemony came into full force in New Mexico. This interpretation complements and enriches the available criticism about this popular collection of short stories.

The variety of literary approaches found in the studies here collected and edited by María I. Duke dos Santos and Patricia de la Fuente can be observed in the essays already mentioned, as well as in those by the other contributors. James J. Champion, by means of a computer-aided study, compares the formal aspects of the Spanish language as found in the stories of Ulibarrí, Juan Rulfo, and Gabriel García Márquez; Arnulfo G. Ramírez applies the narratological method, as developed by the critic Mieke Bal, to three short stories selected from different collections, "El caballo mago" from *Tierra Amarilla*; "Mi abuela fumaba puros" from the collection of the same title; and "Amena Karanova" from *El Cóndor and Other Stories.*

Contrasted to the above is the study by Juan Bruce-Novoa, who applies a poststructuralist method (deconstruction) to reveal the paternalistic attitude of a Latino superhero—the protagonist of "El Cóndor"—who leads a revolution in defense of the Indians of Ecuador, where the action of the story takes place.

In spite of the great variety of critical approaches found in this collection of essays on the literary production of Sabine Ulibarrí, the reader will find certain basic rhetorical and theoretical principles and assumptions. They all emphasize the importance that Ulibarrí gives to certain themes: the recovery of a lost idyllic past; the nostalgia for a disappearing world; the use of recollection as the basis of his poetics; the presence of popular lore; and the presence of traditional mythical images used in a realistic context. Most important, this volume contributes to the growing body of Chicano literary criticism, especially to the study of the literary production of one author, an aspect of Chicano literary criticism that has not yet attained the position reached in other ethnic literatures. It is hoped that this collection may stimulate the publication of other volumes dedicated to other authors.

ENTREVISTA CON SABINE REYES ULIBARRÍ

María I. Duke dos Santos

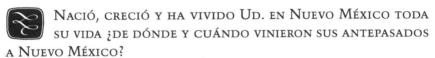 Nació, creció y ha vivido Ud. en Nuevo México toda su vida ¿de dónde y cuándo vinieron sus antepasados a Nuevo México?

Pues no sé. Tengo en mis manos un documento que fue un diario que hizo un capitán, Juan de Ulibarrí, en 1706. Sucedió que el gobernador en Santa Fe lo envió a rescatar a treinta y cinco familias teguas que los apaches de Kansas tenían prisioneras, de esclavos, y él fue y trajo a esas treinta y cinco familias a Nuevo México, e hizo un diario de sus experiencias. Yo no sé si ése sea mi antepasado porque no tengo yo documentos, pero luego, en el siglo XIX aparece otro Juan de Ulibarrí, otro capitán, en el gobierno de Armijo, que era entonces el gobernador mexicano de Nuevo México, y ése es el antepasado que conocemos. La familia directa mía viene de un pueblo que se llama hoy Abiquiú. Era entonces un pueblo fronterizo para proteger a los habitantes del Río Grande de las incursiones de los apaches y de los yutas. De allí mi familia se traslada a Las Nutrias, una ranchería como a unas nueve millas al sur de Tierra Amarilla. Allí compraron catorce mil acres a lo largo del río Las Nutrias, es toda la montaña que está hacia el éste de Tierra Amarilla, y allí establecieron sus haciendas. La familia era toda de ganaderos, y esa sierra la utilizaban para pasteo de verano, porque los Ulibarrí criaban borregas, vacas y caballos. Cuando yo era niño

7

mi papá le vendía caballos a la caballería del ejército de los Estados Unidos. Venían de El Paso, del fuerte que está allí, y había un gran rodeo donde los compradores militares los escogían.

¿VIVÍAN UDS. EN EL RANCHO TODO EL AÑO, O VIVÍAN EN DOS LUGARES?

Vivíamos en el rancho todo el año hasta cuando nos trasladamos a Tierra Amarilla. Entonces compró mi padre una casa allí. Yo nací en Santa Fe porque mi madre fue allí para dar a luz, pero vivíamos en Las Nutrias.

¿PERO SIEMPRE VOLVÍAN AL RANCHO?

Sí. El rancho seguía allí y mi abuela siguió viviendo allí. Mi papá continuaba administrando la hacienda y el ganado, aunque ahora estuviera en Tierra Amarilla, pero había un ir y venir constante entre Tierra Amarilla y Las Nutrias.

¿DE DÓNDE SE ORIGINA EL NOMBRE SABINE?

Bueno, el nombre de mi padre ere Sabiniano Reyes Ulibarrí. El Reyes porque nació el seis de enero—es nombre, no apellido. Cuando los vaqueros tejanos llegaron al norte de Nuevo México, no podían con el nombre "Sabiniano," y ellos le dieron a mi padre el nombre de "Sabine," al parecer por el nombre de un río en Texas. El apodo se le quedó a mi padre y cuando yo nací me dio ese nombre.

DESPUÉS DE QUE FUE A LA ESCUELA EN TIERRA AMARILLA ¿ENTONCES CONTINUÓ PARA LA UNIVERSIDAD?

Sí. Desde que yo era niño siempre se habló en la familia de que yo iba a ser abogado, esa era la ilusión de mi padre y a mí me parecía estupenda la idea, de modo que eso de ir a la universidad no fue una decisión que se hizo de inmediato; eso estaba establecido creo que desde que yo nací.

¿CÓMO LLEGÓ UD. A SER PROFESOR DE LA UNIVERSIDAD?

Cuando yo estaba en el último año de la secundaria, mi padre murió en un accidente. Tenía yo quince años. Entonces mi madre se trasladó a Santa Fe y construyó una casa allí. Mi padre quería que yo fuera a Georgetown, pero no había manera de irme yo a Washington. Irme yo en esos momentos, tan lejos, y dejar a mi madre viuda con tres niños menores en la casa no me pareció justo, de modo que vine a la Universidad de Nuevo México. Antes de eso ocurrió que tenía yo unos primos hermanos que se habían educado en el éste y acababan de graduarse de la universidad. Estaba yo en la secundaria cuando volvieron y me prestaron una cantidad de libros. A ellos les había entrado, como a tanto latinoamericano, el deseo de meterse en la filosofía. Pues cuando yo estaba en la secundaria, estaba devorando libros de filosifía, y entre otras cosas, aunque esto no es filosofía, me leí *El origen de las especies* cuando estaba en el último año de secundaria, y ese libro me fulminó. Considera tú en aquel ambiente, en aquellas circunstancias, en aquel tiempo, las revelaciones de *The Origin of the Species*, pues me lanzaron, me pusieron en órbita, y entonces me puse en dificultades con las monjas, porque andaba yo expresando y diciendo cosas que eran totalmente redicales, para ellas, herejías, y lo que pasó es que yo estaba demasiado joven, demasiado inmaduro para asimilar un libro como ése, pero así fue. Mis primos hermanos me consiguieron una beca en una universidad protestante en el éste; pues yo me iba a ir allí cuando mi padre todavía estaba vivo. Cuando las monjas se dieron cuenta de esto, pues se apresuraron y me consiguieron una beca en Notre Dame. Pues eso me estimuló a mí mucho. Notre Dame era famosa en todo el mundo por su equipo de fútbol, y para mí, un chico fascinado por los deportes, pues ir a Notre Dame era como ir al cielo. Luego la monja me explicó que me daban la beca y tendría que trabajar en el comedor. Eso estaba bien, yo estaba dispuesto a todo, pero después de la beca y después de trabajar todos los días, tenía que pagar 800 dólares, yo no sé si sería por semestre o por el año, pero no importaba. ¿Quién podía poner manos en 800 dólares durante la depresión? Y le dije; "Lo siento mucho hermana, pero ser católico es muy caro y yo no tengo dinero." De modo que eso también determinó que yo viniera acá en vez de irme por aquellos lados.

¿CONTINUÓ LUEGO ESTUDIANTO?

Bueno, aquí estaba yo, un chico fulminado de ambición. Estaba decidido a recibirme de la universidad en tres años, yo no me iba a esperar cuatro, de modo que directamente de la secundaria me vengo a la escuela de verano, luego sigo con el otoño, la primavera, y otra vez la escuela de verano. Y en eso estaba cuando murió mi madre. Tenía yo diez y seis años y tenía tres hermanitos menores que yo, de modo que tuve que abandonar mis estudios para encargarme de los niños. Primero, mis tíos y mis abuelos maternos se habían reunido y cada quien había decidido quién se iba a llevar a quién; nos iban a repartir, y a mí no me pareció eso bien y les dije: "¡No se llevan a nadie, se quedan conmigo!" Y todas estaban dispuestos a decirme "te lo dije." Así que yo llevaba esa responsabilidad a los diez y seis años, pero todo salió bien.

De modo que entonces conseguí un certificado de emergencia, como se llamaban entonces, y me fui a enseñar en las escuelas públicas. Enseñé en un lugar que se llamaba Ranchitos que está entre Riverside y San Juan, una pequeña aldea donde no había escuela, pero un sitio muy cercano a Santa Fe. En mi condado de Río Arriba el superintendente de escuelas era mi primo hermano, el supervisor de escuelas era otro primo hermano, y el jefe del cuerpo de educación era mi tío, de modo que abrieron una escuela allí y fui a enseñar. Ya para entonces tenía diez y siete años, y algunos de mis estudiantes eran de la edad mía. Enseñé allí un año, y luego en el pueblo de San Juan otro año.

Después me fui al Rito, que se llamaba entonces Spanish American Normal School. Enseñé allí dos años y entre tanto la hermana que me sigue se había casado. Yo llevaba aquí en la conciencia una obligación a mi padre, de que iba a Georgetown. Pues cuando mi hermana se casó y pudo encargarse de los dos menores, me fui a Washington y resulta que no pude pagar la matrícula, porque Georgetown era demasiado cara. Pero me matriculé en George Washington University de noche y entré a trabajar para el gobierno de intérprete. Duré allí tres meses, porque la guerra en 1942 estaba a todo dar y yo, que creía que me podría escapar, no me di cuenta de que iba a tener que dormir conmigo mismo, y me empezó a molestar aquello. Yo trabajaba en un edificio con quinientos empleados, de los cuales doce eran hombre y casi todos tenían más de sesenta años o estaban cojos. Me dio vergüenza. Llamo a Connie, porque ya éramos novios, y le pido que se case conmigo. Me vine de Washington, me casé y me alisté en la misma semana.

¿CUÁNTOS AÑOS TENÍA UD. ENTONCES?

Para entonces veinte y dos años, porque enseñé cuatro años en las escuelas públicas.

¿DE MANERA QUE UD. SE ALISTÓ Y SE FUE A LA GUERRA?

Sí. Y pedí combate. Y me costó mucho trabajo mantenerme en ese camino porque donde quiera que iba, pues veían mis credenciales de que tenía universidad, y luego mi "IQ," y querían ponerme a trabajar en una oficina, y les dije: "Yo no entré en el servicio para trabajar en una oficina."

¿CUÁNTO TIEMPO ESTUVO EN EL SERVICIO ACTIVO?

Tres años. Y fíjate que no había terminado la universidad. Volé treinta y cinco vuelos de combate sobre Alemania. Volví y me había ganado muchos puntos. Por el número de viajes de combate que habías hecho te daban equis puntos, por haber servido en ultramar, más puntos. De modo que yo fui uno de los primeros veteranos que salieron. Recibí la Medalla del Aire (Air Medal) cuatro veces, y la Cruz Distinguida de la Aviación (Distinguished Flying Cross).

¿REGRESÓ LUEGO A LA UNIVERSIDAD DE NUEVO MÉXICO?

Sí. Terminé mi B.A. e inmediatamente me dieron un "teaching assistantship." Hice la maestría e inmediatamente me nombraron para enseñar en la universidad. ¿Sabes tú que yo nunca he pedido trabajo en mi vida? Nunca he presentado una solicitud para un trabajo. Entré como instructor, un rango que ya casi ha desaparecido, y luego pedí licencia y me la dieron por tres años para ir a UCLA a hacer el doctorado. Volví después de los tres años para enseñar y trabajar en la tesis.

¿DESDE ENTONCES ESTÁ UD. ENSEÑANDO AQUÍ?

Bueno, me dieron el nombramiento en el año 1950 pero con la excepción de los tres años de licencia, desde el año 1950 hasta ahora he estado en la universidad. Pasé por todos los rangos. De instructor pasé a "assistant professor," después a "associate" y luego a "full professor." Este último lo conseguí hace como veinte y cinco años. En julio de 1990 me jubilé y ahora enseño solamente un curso por semestre.

¿EN QUÉ OTRAS ACTIVIDADES HA PARTICIPADO UD. DURANTE EL TIEMPO QUE HA SIDO PROFESOR EN LA UNIVERSIDAD?

He dirigido programas de la universidad en Quito, Ecuador. Llevé allí dos institutos del NDEA. Fui director de un instituto de año académico, el único en español en todo el país, porque había en el país sólamente dos de año académico, uno en español y uno en ruso. Eso duró tres años. Luego, pues era yo director del instituto de verano de segundo nivel en el extranjero. Es decir, los que iban a mi instituto eran los que habían pasado ya por un instituto aquí en los Estados Unidos, y el segundo nivel era en el extranjero. De modo que era director de dos institutos a la vez, uno de verano y uno de año académico. Luego tuve sabáticos cuando fui a España. Después fui a Quito a establecer el Centro de Estudios Andinos; fui como su primer director. Allí llevábamos estudiantes desde el tercer año de español y estudiantes de postgrado. Por once años llevamos un gran número de estudiantes.

¿CUÁNTO TIEMPO PASÓ EN ESPAÑA?

Déjame ver. En total son cuatro veranos separados y luego un año entero, doce meses.

TENIENDO EN CUENTA TODAS SUS ACTIVIDADES ¿CÓMO ENCUENTRA UD. SUFICIENTE TIEMPO PARA ESCRIBIR?

Hace muchos años que comencé a enseñar seis créditos por semana, es decir, dos cursos, y ése es tiempo completo, porque me han dado a mí libertad para que escriba. Eso hace esta universidad. A los escritores les dan libertad y les reducen el número de horas.

¿HA TENIDO UD. ALGUNA VEZ DIFICULTAD EN PUBLICAR SUS OBRAS?

No. El primer libro mío que se publicó fue *Al cielo se sube a pie*, que es un libro de versos. Yo tenía ficheros llenos de poemas que había escrito, pero no me atrevía a enviarlos a publicar, porque publicar, especialmente versos, es ponerte a la descubierta, es en efecto desnudarte ante el público. En la poesía estás dando confesiones, confesiones íntimas, y te da miedo de que te vayan a entender mal, o te da vergüenza de ponerte al desnudo. Un amigo mío me decía: "¿Por qué no los publicas?" Y me dijo: "Mira, yo voy a México; déjame llevar unos poemas tuyos a ver si te los publican." Y le dije: "Allí están los ficheros, escoge tú." Y él escogió cincuenta y se los llevó a México, donde su publicaron primero. El libro no tuvo mucha difusión pero me dio a conocer. Ya empezaron a comentar mis poemas, de modo que cuando fui al Ecuador y La Casa de la Cultura publicó *Tierra Amarilla*, pues ya fui cobrando más reconocimiento. Ya se me comentaba como poeta y como cuentista, y desde entonces no he tenido ya problema ninguno en publicar.

¿QUÉ LE ACONSEJARÍA UD. A UNA PERSONA QUE QUIERE COMENZAR A ESCRIBIR, QUE VA A COMENZAR SU CARRERA DE ESCRITOR?

Bueno, lo primero que hay que hacer es leer, leer y leer. Para aprender a escribir, primero hay que aprender a leer, porque en la lectura encontrarás en primer lugar inspiración, y encontrarás los modelos, modelos de estilo, modelos de léxico, modelos de punto de vista, de actitudes, de retruécanos, ripios si quieres, tópicos si quieres. Luego hace falta que el futuro escritor tenga ganas de escribir, que sienta la necesidad de escribir. Escribir por escribir no lleva a ninguna parte. Escribir cuando hay una destinación, cuando hay un propósito, un fin, ya ése es buen camino. Si alguien puede contar un cuento, o puede echar un piropo, ya puede hacer versos, ya puede hacer cuentos. Y luego hace falta coraje, atreverse, lanzarse. Una de las cosas más difíciles para los jóvenes escritores, y lo ha sido para mí también, es cómo empezar. Y no hay que buscar un comienzo literario, a eso de literario por literatura hay que huirle. El que se pone a hacer literatura no puede escribir cuentos, ni novelas, ni poemas. El buen cuentista es el que tiene un cuento que contar y lo cuenta. Y puede resultar literario, pero si yo presumidamente digo que voy a hacer literatura, eso es un engaño, eso es una burla. Aún cuando ya tiene uno una idea más o menos definida de lo que quiere decir, no le halla la entrada. Con una poca de experiencia, uno se da cuenta de que la entrada es verdaderamenta fácil, en realidad gratis. Se entra por cualquier parte, por la puerta de enfrente, por la puerta de atrás, o hasta por la ventana. De la manera más sencilla. Si no se sabe precisamente por dónde empezar, pues describir el paisaje, o el sitio donde va a ocurrir algo, y luego introducir al personaje, y después la acción.

¿DATA DESDE HACE MUCHO TIEMPO SU INTERÉS EN LA LITERATURA?

Yo nací y me crie hasta la edad de ocho años en una hacienda, muy aislada. Los vecinos más cercanos vivían a distancia de dos o tres millas, y así crecí, solitario en esa hacienda. Pasaba los días en al campo con mis perros, y las circunstancias abrían las posibilidades del ensueño. La diversión era la fantasía y además mi padre por las noches nos leía obras literarias. Así llegué yo a conocer el *Quijote* desde muy niño, el *Lazarillo de Tormes*, los viejos romances, el *Conde de Montecristo*, Edgar Allan Poe, y te digo esto María, que aquello valía más que lo que vale la televisión ahora. Yo, cuando él nos leía un capítulo, me acostaba llevando la mente y el corazón llenos de fantasía e ilusiones, y todo el día siguiente me lo pasaba especulando, fantaseando sobre qué vendría, y apenas podía esperar a que viniera el siguiente capítulo. Así me introdujo a la prosa. También se contaban cuentos, de modo que yo me crié con esa tradición de contar cuentos oralmente. Pero mi padre era también un declamador de poesía de primera, así es que desde que yo era bien niño, creo que desde que empecé a habar, yo ya estaba aprendiendo poesías de memoria y luego, pues mi padre me lucía con la familia, con los amigos. Me ponía a recitar y yo me convertí en un recitador desde que tenía los seis años; y sabes, María, que esas poesías que aprendí de niño, todavía las sé. Las poesías que aprendí la semana pasada ya se me han olvidado; acaso eso sería un mensaje para los padres y para los profesores, de que hagan a los niños aprenderse poesías de memoria, porque es un regalo que les dura para toda la vida.

Cuando tenía yo ocho años nos mudamos de la hacienda a Tierra Amarilla, donde está situado el asiento del condado, para que yo y mis hermanitos asistiéramos a la escuela. Tuve la buena suerte, que yo entonces no supe apreciar, de estudiar con las monjas. Eran monjas franciscanas del "Midwest," y ellas trajeron a Tierra

Amarilla todos esos conceptos y todos esos valores americanos que están tan arraigados en esa parte de los Estados Unidos, de modo que yo aprendí mucho de ellas. La directora de mi escuela superior tenía doctorado, hablaba siete lenguas. Todas mis profesoras de secundaria tenían maestría, lo cual no se conseguía en ninguna parte de Nuevo México. Ni en Albuquerque, ni en Santa Fe, ni en Roswell, ni en Las Cruces tenían profesoras tan bien educadas como las que tuve yo. Pero claro, entró un conflicto entre ellas y yo por razones disciplinarias y de otro tipo. Fue después cuando quise agradercerles lo que habían hecho por mí. Ellas me involucraron en la literatura americana, y tuve en la secundaria un profesor de español que al pasar los años sigue siendo el mejor profesor de gramática que yo he tenido, y me tocó que fue en Tierra Amarila. Allí se van uniendo corrientes, todas orientadas hacia la literatura, de modo que yo andaba haciendo versos desde muy joven; los cuentos vinieron mucho más tarde, los versos llegaron primero.

Su educación antes de los ocho años ¿fue en la casa?

Sí, sí. Mi papá y mi mamá se conocieron en Las Vegas, New Mexico. Allí tenían entonces una de esas escuelas para entrenar maestros, una escuela normal. Allí se conocieron, aunque ninguno de ellos resultó maestro porque se casaron y a mi papá se le había muerto su padre y a él le encargaron la hacienda. Pero lo que sabía me lo enseñó, me enseñaron los dos, de modo que cuando yo llegué a Tierra Amarilla para empezar la escuela, yo ya estaba leyendo libros, no sólo cuentos, sino libros en español y en inglés.

¿Cuáles diría Ud. que son las influencias principales en su obra?

Bueno, primero viene la influencia de mi padre, porque él era muy dedicado a la lectura, de modo que a través de mis padres, desde muy chico, yo ya estaba metido en la literatura universal, tanto española como latinoamericana, como inglesa, como norteamericana, y también literatura francesa y otras en traducción. Esa es la primera influencia, y acaso mi dedicación a la poesía, eso me vino de mi padre, porque me gustaba a mí declamar, y él lo hacía también. De modo que cuando yo llego a la secundaria ya yo estoy haciendo versos y estoy haciendo ensayos, y cuando vine a la universidad me gradué con dos especialidades, el español y el inglés, un "double major." Para la maestría, la misma cosa, español e inglés. Luego en UCLA mis campos doctorales fueron cuatro: el primero, la literatura peninsular; el segundo, la literatura latinoamericana; el tercero, la literatura portuguesa; el cuarto, la literatura francesa. De modo que mi doctorado es dedicado en total a la literatura.

¿QUÉ OTRAS INFLUENCIAS CONSIDERA UD. IMPORTANTES EN SU OBRA?

Mis lecturas. Desde muy temprano yo tenía predilección por Gustavo Adolfo Bécquer, una predilección por Edgar Allen Poe, y por la novela picaresca. Muchos que han leído mis obras han señalado que hay un elemento picaresco en mis cuentos. También los místicos españoles, junto con Sor Juana Inés de la Cruz.

SE HA DICHO QUE SE NOTA TAMBIÉN LA INFLUENCIA DE JUAN RAMÓN JIMÉNEZ.

Claro. Mi contacto con Juan Ramón es casi totalmente accidental o determinado en total. Una de las dos cosas. Que en mis lecturas yo leía que Juan Ramón era considerado el padre espiritual de todos los poetas de la lengua española en el siglo XX. Yo me leo a Juan Ramón y no me dice nada. Pero yo deliberadamente me dedico a estudiarlo, porque si voy a comprender y a conocer la literatura moderna, debo conocer al padre. Pero mientras iba leyendo se me iba abriendo la obra de Juan Ramón como una flor, y llegué a estimarlo y admirarlo con entusiasmo.

AL LEER SU OBRA SE NOTA QUE INCORPORA UD. ELEMENTOS DE LA RELIGIÓN, DEL RITO CATÓLICO. ¿SUS PADRES ERAN MUY DEVOTOS Y RELIGIOSOS?

Mi abuela era devota y religiosa. Mi papá y mi mamá eran católicos pero llevaban el catolicismo como un manto de seda, no como cilicio; es decir que el catolicismo para ellos era algo cómodo, no eran fanáticos en nada, aunque había por todas esas tierras un fanatismo bastante fuerte. Pero ellos, por haber asistido a la universidad estaban, digamos, emancipados. Homero dijo en un poema suyo: "Yo soy parte de todo lo que he conocido." Y lo que se revela en mis escritos son todas esas experiencias sentimentales, sociales, intelectuales, familiares. De alguna manera o de otra todo eso se filtra en lo que yo esrcibo.

TAMBÍEN SE HA DICHO QUE EL ESPAÑOL QUE UD. EMPLEA EN SUS OBRAS ES UN ESPAÑOL CLÁSICO, CORRECTO EN UNA FORMA CLÁSICA.

Yo creo que a lo mejor es verdad, pero eso no viene solamente de mis estudios. En la sociedad en que yo me movía, Tierra Amarilla, ya te dije que mis padres eran universitarios, y el asiento del condado estaba en Tierra Amarilla, y la Casa de Cortes [courthouse] era el centro social y todos los que trabajaban allí, tesorero, secretario, pues todos eran mis parientes o conocidos. Yo me pasaba de chico jugando en la Casa de Cortes, jugando a los bandidos en la cárcel de veras. Allí jugábamos, allí nos encerrábamos. Una vez me dejaron allí toda una noche y no me podían hallar, los amigos me dejaron encerrado y no dijeron nada y en la casa no sabían dónde estaba. Pero bueno, toda esa gente era culta, que hablaba un español correcto entonces. Luego, pues también me dediqué al estudio del español desde que estaba en la secundaria en Tierra Amarilla.

¿ENTONCES CRECIÓ HABLANDO ESPAÑOL?

Sí. Y el español de Nuevo México en ese entonces era muy superior a lo que es ahora. Se ha desmoronado, se ha destartalado, se ha envejecido, pero entonces era un instrumento vital. Mi abuela no hablaba inglés y las faenas del campo eran todas en español. Mis padres, sin embargo, eran totalmente bilingües.

¿EN LA SECUNDARIA LA ENSEÑANZA ERA BILINGÜE O SOLAMENTE EN INGLÉS?

Era en inglés. Solamente la clase de español era en español. Las monjas que teníamos no hablaban español. Aunque yo seguía devorando libros en español.

¿EN QUÉ IDIOMA SE SIENTE UD. MEJOR ESCRIBIENDO? ¿O LE ES TAN FÁCIL HACERLO TANTO EN INGLÉS COMO EN ESPAÑOL?

Bueno, para escribir mis cuentos y mis versos, español, siempre. Todo lo que he escrito para publicar, de literatura, lo he escrito en español. Después lo traduzco. Otras cosas, como conferencias, eso me sale igual en español que en inglés. Porque yo aprendí las dos lenguas simultáneamente.

¿Pero algo en su espíritu es más español que inglés?

Decían de Mariano José de Larra, que se formó en Francia con una educación clásica, que su estilo era clasicista pero su corazón era romántico. Yo creo que mi corazón es muy español. La orientación mía es el hispanismo. Todos somos hispanos, ya sea puertorriqueños, cubanos, españoles o mexicanos—esa es la belleza de la hispanidad.

¿Diría Ud. que la naturaleza a su alrededor, el campo, el paisaje de Nuevo México, la vida de la ranchería, son aspectos importantes en su obra?

Y la soledad. Porque yo en mis primeros años me pasé tanto tiempo solo, y luego ya mayorcito mi padre me sacaba de la escuela un mes antes de que terminaran las clases porque entonces era cuando volvían las partidas del invernadero, y yo me iba a la sierra y me pasaba los meses del verano en la sierra. Yo he leído que dicen algunos críticos que hay cierto misticismo en mis escritos. Si es que lo hay, y no estoy seguro de que lo haya, no es algo aprendido. Eso es algo que estaba en el aire, en esa soledad, en esa naturaleza, en esa fantasía. Ese amor a la tierra, eso no es cosa mía, es cosa de todos, de esa gente de allá.

¿Y Ud. participaba en los quehaceres del campo?

Sí, desde pequeño, porque esa era una obsesión de mi padre, de que yo fuera hombre, de modo que desde tempranito yo tenía mis tareas.

Muchos de sus cuentos son básicamente de un ambiente rural.

Bueno, la cultura neuvomexicana es una cultura rural, porque todo Nuevo México era rural hasta que vino la segunda guerra mundial. Mira, en 1940 el censo de Albuquerque registró 38,000 habitantes, o sea una pequeña ciudad. Ahora está por medio millón, y todo ese avance ha sido desde la guerra. Pero una cosa extraña ocurrió. Cuando el nuevomexicano, el nativo, sale del campo y se viene a la ciudad ¿adónde va a dar? Al barrio. Y trae al barrio sus costumbres, sus tradiciones. Es como si no hubiera salido del campo.

La familia extendida, las tradiciones de allá del campo, están en el barrio. Viven en el barrio, aislados del resto de la comunidad que es una comunidad dentro de otra más grande. De modo que hay algo campestre y rural en nuestra cultura, aún dentro de la ciudad.

¿CÓMO Y EN QUÉ SE INSPIRA PARA DESARROLLAR LOS PERSONAJES QUE APARECEN EN ESTOS CUENTOS?

No creo que me inspire en desarrollar personajes, porque los que aparecen en esos cuentos son reales, y lo que yo trato de hacer es dibujar al personaje tal y como yo lo conocí, de modo que no estoy creando personajes, estoy trayendo personajes de mi pasado a mis cuentos. Tengo una especie de problema en Tierra Amarilla, en que alguien me dice: "Se te olvidó, Ulibarrí. No fue aquí, fue allá; y no fue él, fue este otro." Y yo les digo: "Miren, yo estoy haciendo cuentos, no historia, y todo escritor empieza de una base real, y su material se basa en los hechos, hechos reales, y él baraja los hechos, como las barajas, hasta que le cae una buena mano, y ésa es la que escribe." Los hechos han sido siempre los mismos, lo que se ha cambiado acaso son las relaciones, o las combinaciones. De modo que yo no estoy creando personajes. En mis cuentos más recientes, donde estoy haciendo cuentos de fantasía, allí sí me veo obligado a crear un personaje, pero en esos cuentos regionales, costumbristas, míos, pues todos ellos salen de mi pasado; son personas que yo conocí.

¿Y HUBO UN VAQUERO COMO EL NEGRO AGUILAR?

Sí, sí. Aunque él no murió de la manera que yo dije que murió, eso lo inventé yo. Pero el personaje era así como lo dibujé. Yo solamente estoy copiando del recuerdo. Pero incluso trato de imitar o recordar el lenguaje característico de los diferentes personajes. No sé si habrás leído ese cuento "Brujerías o tonterías," donde hablo de una bruja de Ensenada que tenía una manera muy peculiar de hablar. Pues yo trato de reproducir el lenguaje de ella como ella lo usaba, no como yo lo usaría.

¿ES "LOS PENITENTES" LO MÁS HISTÓRICO QUE TIENE ENTRE SUS CUENTOS?

Sí, ése casi no es cuento, es casi una narración, un relato. Pero allí tengo un penitente que sí trabajaba para mi papá. Las aventuras y las actividades de ese penitente, ésas no las conocía yo. Tanto de las actividades de la cofradía, de la hermandad, eran para nosotros un gran misterio. Íbamos a verlos los Jueves Santos y los Viernes Santos cuando se azotaban, pero eso era como ir a un espectáculo, a un partido de fútbol, tenía mucho de diversión aquello, porque esa hermandad es bastante secreta, aún para nosotros. Solamente los hermanos saben lo que pasa dentro de las moradas y en sus sacrificios y servicios particulares.

¿Y LA ABUELA ERA LA MISMA MUJER MARAVILLOSA DE SU CUENTO?

Exactamente como yo la recuerdo. Te habrás dado cuenta que el dibujo que hicieron, la ilustración de la abuela que hicieron, pues no corresponde a la abuela que yo describí. Yo dije: "Era recta, alta, esbelta," o algo parecido, y ésta es baja, gorda y rechoncha.

¿CREE UD. QUE HAY CIERTA IDEALIZACIÓN DEL CAMPO EN ESAS HISTORIAS?

Jorge Manrique dice que cualquier tiempo pasado es mejor. Y es posible que sí haya una idealización. Pero no es que yo la intentara. Yo estoy viendo todo ese mundo a través del recuerdo, y el recuerdo suaviza, ennoblece, enriquece la experiencia. A través de los ojos del recuerdo todo parece más bello, más ideal. Y acaso sin querer, eso esté haciendo yo. Yo vivo con una Tierra Amarilla de mi infancia y de mi juventud, y el mundo es risueño y dulce cuando uno es joven. Esa infancia y esa juventud fueron en todo sentido felices, y el mundo visto a través de la sonrisa, la risa y la alegría, pues resulta mucho más atractivo. De manera que es muy probable que sí haya yo idealizado sin quererlo, sin pensarlo, sin contemplarlo. No fue ésa nunca mi intención.

TENGO ENTENDIDO QUE AHORA ESTÁ UD. ESCRIBIENDO UN NUEVO TIPO DE CUENTO FANTÁSTICO, DE IMAGINACIÓN. ¿ES ÉSTA UNA NUEVA DIRECCIÓN?

Sí. No es que haya abandonado el cuento regional costumbrista. Ése es mi camino y volveré a él. Pero a cada escritor le gusta tantear nuevos caminos y éste no sé adónde me lleve, pero lléveme donde me lleve, siempre volveré a los de allá de mi tierra. Una cosa curiosa de la cual no me di cuenta hasta después, es que estos nuevos cuentos me están saliendo más largos que los anteriores, y yo mismo no sabía por qué. Me pregunté, y pensándolo, creo que caí en la clave; es que en esos cuentos regionales yo no tengo que inventar la realidad y no tengo que justificarla, allí está. Pero en estos cuentos de imaginación tengo que inventar la realidad y justificarla, hacerla creíble, y por eso me toma más espacio y resultan los cuentos más largos.

Y ESTOS NUEVOS CUENTOS DE FANTASÍA ¿VIENEN ALGUNOS DE IDEAS QUE UD. OBTUVO EN SUS VIAJES POR SUDAMÉRICA?

Pues en una colección sí, pero ésa no se ha publicado. Anda en el Ecuador buscando editor, pero ésa es una colección de leyendas de Quito, porque Quito está lleno de leyendas, unas de ellas tan llenas de chispa, de alegría y de malicia, y otras que son bien siniestras y terribles. Pues a mí me interesaban solamente las alegres, y primero creí en sólo coleccionarlas y publicarlas, así como las leyendas del Perú, que son tremendas. Y anduve coleccionándolas y de pronto no me satisficieron porque la leyenda te deja un vacío, o varios vacíos; hay mucho que se queda en la sombra. Hay una leyenda en Quito que trata de una casa que llamaban "la casa del toro" y en esa casa estaba la cabeza de un toro. Decían que ese toro venía desde los tiempos coloniales, y la leyenda era ésta: que una chica adolescente despertó de una terrible pesadilla, desesperada, a gritos. Pues bien, los padres descubren que ella había soñado que un toro había entrado en su dormitorio y la quería matar. Pues la apaciguaron. La mamá tuvo que dormir con ella porque el miedo era tanto que no podía dormir. Poco después de eso hubo una corrida de toros en Quito y en esos días tenían las corridas en la plaza central. Le ponían barreras a las calles, las cerraban, y la gente veía la corrida desde los balcones y ventanas de las casas. El día estaba lleno de ilusión, de música, de ruido, de alegría, de risa, y todo Quito estaba allí, incluso el papá, la mamá y la hija. Cuando de pronto aparece un toro y se queda mirando por las gradas como si estuviera buscando a alguien, y el toro no quiso embestir a los toreros. De pronto lo ve la chica y se queda petrificada de susto, y grita: "¡Ése es el toro!" Y se desmayó. Pues la llevaron a la casa y entre tanto el toro anduvo rondando el ruedo hasta que saltó la barrera y se fue corriendo por las calles directamente a la casa de la chica. Llega y la mata. Y allí termina la leyenda. Pero ¿ves cuánto deja a la sombra? No se explica ni justifica por qué, por qué razón, por qué esta chica. Pues yo tomo esa leyenda y le invento una fábula de por qué, y luego el fin. Y eso hice con todas las leyendas que recogí. Porque la leyenda no necesita explicar nada, el misterio basta por sí mismo. Pero en el cuento el lector requiere principio, mitad y fin.

Su libro titulado *El Cóndor y otros cuentos* ¿tiene también tema sudamericano?

Bueno, francamente tiene ese título porque no se me ocurrió otro. Es que el cuento más largo se llama "El Cóndor," y así el editor estuvo de acuerdo en que le llamáramos *El Cóndor y otros cuentos*.

Pero ese cuento es de los indios del Ecuador ¿no?

Sí, pero los demás cuentos no tienen nada que ver con Latinoamérica. Son cuentos de imaginación. A mí se me ocurren ideas, y me divierto cuando estoy escribiéndolos.

¿Entonces el cuento del Cóndor es también pura imaginación?

No. Es que la condición del indio me afectó a mí profundamente. Lo que digo allí, que la primera vez que yo llego a Quito, estoy leyendo el periódico y hay un anuncio de una hacienda que se vende, toda una página. Se hacía lista de los haberes de la hacienda, tantas cabezas de ganado vacuno, tantas de ganado ovejuno, tantos caballos, tantos cerdos, tantas hectáreas de sembrado, tantas de pasto, y al final decía: "doscientos indios." Eso es verdad. Eso te sacude, te estremece, te dan ganas de llorar. Que los indios iban con la hacienda como mercancía, como ganado. Aún en estos cuentos de fantasía entran los elementos reales.

¿Ha pensado Ud. alguna vez en escribir algo basado en sus experiencias de la segunda guerra mundial?

Qué curioso que me preguntes esto, porque precisamente eso estoy haciendo. Tuvieron que pasar más de, bueno, cuarenta y cinco años después de la guerra para que yo me enfrentara con esos recuerdos. Dios es muy bondadoso en la manera que nos hace, porque a medida que vamos viviendo, vamos olvidando todo lo feo de nuestro pasado y vamos recordando sólo lo bello. Gracias a Dios eso hace la vida posible, porque si recordáramos el sufrimiento, el dolor, las frustraciones, las furias, las rabias, las pesadillas de toda la vida, esa vida sería imposible, y gracias a Dios las olvidamos. De modo que esas memorias de la guerra las he tenido yo en la trastienda, allí en un baúl encerradas, y no me han molestado. He vivido muy contento, muy feliz, desde la guerra. Al abrir ese baúl ¿ves cómo me han estremecido otra vez esos recuerdos?

¿Pero sí se van a realizar esos relatos?

¡Oh sí! Ya tengo tres escritos y otros en mente. Déjame decirte cómo hago yo cuentos. Cuando se me ocurre la idea de un cuento, allí me anda zumbando por la cabeza, zumba que zumba, friega que friega. Es un personaje, acaso en busca de autor, como Pirandello. Y un día, el cuento cuaja, y cuando cuaja, entonces me pongo escribir. Y yo escribo un cuento de un tirón, se me va la mano. Acaso me tarde una noche en a escribirlo. Puedo amanecer escribiendo, pero eso no quiere decir que me tarde seis o doce horas escribiéndolo; ese cuento me anduvo allí dentro por mucho tiempo, y cuando me siento a escribir, ya sé adonde voy, lo que no sé es cómo voy a llegar. Tengo que abrirme camino, pero ya mi destinación está fija. Otros escritores se sientan a la máquina y pam, pam, pam, le dan a la máquina, y luego arrebatan el papel y lo botan al cesto y ponen otro. Así sale en las películas ¿no? Para el fin de la escena en la película, pues el cesto, o el suelo, está lleno de papel. Pues acaso eso es lo que yo estoy haciendo, sin saberlo. Y allí donde me anda la idea tomando forma, yo estoy añadiendo, eliminando, borrando, cambiando, alterando, y lo estoy haciendo de una manera entre consciente e inconsciente. Yo no soy escritor profesional, me pongo a escribir cuando me llega la inspiración. Un escritor profesional tiene un régimen, tiene un horario, y se sienta a la mesa de trabajo honradamente un determinado número de horas, día tras día. Lo que sí me ha ocurrido algunas veces es que una vez que me pongo a escribir y que me animo, pues paso de un cuento a otro, porque un cuento parece indicar o llamar a otro; pero horario, ni calendario, o tengo.

AÚN EN SU PROSA HAY MUCHO DE POESÍA. ¿CÓMO INCORPORA UD. EL SONIDO, LA CADENCIA, DENTRO DE SU PROSA?

Creo haberte dicho que yo empecé a hacer versos antes de hacer prosa, y que todavía ahora siempre ando haciendo versos, aunque no los escriba siempre. Es que la poesía para mí es como un manantial; me viene. La poesía para mí es algo natural, y el lenguaje con toda su capacidad de musicalidad y toda su capacidad de insinuación, eso siempre me ha intrigado. Yo juego con las palabras, me divierto con la palabra, ése es un deporte. Escribo yo oralmente, es decir, que yo me estoy escuchando a medida que voy escribiendo, y los valores fonéticos, y los valores musicales de la lengua, para mí son muy atractivos. De modo que yo me digo lo que voy a escribir, y si me suena bien, lo escribo, y si no me suena bien, no lo escribo. Así que no quiero solamente comunicar información. Yo quiero comunicar sensación y emoción, y los sonidos tienen una manera de decir cosas que el significado de la palabra no dice. Mira; palabras como murmullo, susurro, suspiro, son onomatopoéticas porque no sólo nombran la acción sino la demuestran fonéticamente. De modo que hay mucho de onomatopeya en lo mío, hay mucho de aliteración, hay mucho de rimas internas. Hay también ritmo; las frases frecuentemente son cortas, o con deliberada puntuación produzco un cierto ritmo, una cierta cadencia que me suena. A mi oído me suena bien, y así lo pongo. En mi conversación ando siempre jugando con las palabras; es decir, haciendo oraciones, haciendo combinaciones de palabras para producir efectos de cualquier tipo. He publicado dos libros de versos y hace mucho que no publico versos, pero no es porque no los piense, los sienta o los escriba de vez en cuando. Tengo ficheros por todas partes, de versos que no se han publicado. pero acaso escribir poesía, y en español, en Estados Unidos, es escribir sin destino, escribir sin lectores. ¿Quién te va a leer? Aún en los países de habla española los poetas escriben para un público limitado. ¿Quién lee poesía?

De modo que mi avenida de expresión ha llegado a ser el cuento. Así me expreso, así me comunico, así canto.

¿ALGUNA VEZ HA PENSADO EN ESCRIBIR NOVELA?

En muchas ocasiones se me ha ocurrido hacer novela y no lo he intentado nunca, y acaso nunca lo intente. Es que la novela requiere una disciplina, una paciencia que yo no tengo. Es el cuento que es mi avenida de expresión. Y aunque la novela necesita mucha más disciplina, mucha más paciencia, tolerancia, la novela te da más libertad. En una novela tienes tiempo y espacio para moverte, para desarrollar el personaje. Si metes la pata en el capítulo número dos, pues tienes diez y siete capítulos para arreglar la cosa. En el cuento, si metes la pata en la página dos, ya se te fregó el cuento. Es decir, que hay otro tipo de disciplina. El cuento requiere más atención; es poner la mira en el núcleo y no perderlo de vista, porque si te desvías un poquito, ya estás fregado. En la novela te puedes desviar a lo bestia, y a lo largo del camino te enderezas y terminas bien. El cuento lo haces bien, pronto y rápido. Y si no lo haces así, no te resulta. Y acaso lo mío es eso del cuento. Eso de la novela es para otros. Y esto no es para menospreciar la novela. La novela, a mi parecer, es la forma literaria más completa, más profunda y más complicada de todas. Es que la poesía nace más temprano, y en los pueblos primitivos es el canto. Primero nace la música, acaso un tambor, un ritmo, una cadencia, y de pronto a alguien le surge la necesidad de cantar, y surge el canto acompañado de la música, y ya eso es la poesía. Más adelante surge la danza. Esa cadencia, ese ritmo, produce en los oyentes una sensación, y resulta la danza. Todo esto en el mundo primitivo, y aún en ese mismo mundo, en la danza, alguien canta, y un día se le ocurre a alguien contestar al canto de este primero, y éste después vuelve a contestar, y nace el drama. Y a lo largo, en este mismo período, surge el cuento, porque los mayores de las tribus primitivas contaban cuentos para educar a la juventud en los valores, las tradiciones, en las leyendas, en la historia de la tribu. Pero mira cuándo aparece la novela. La primera novela de la historia es el *Quijote*, la primera en el tiempo y la primera en importancia. ¿Y cuándo aparece el *Quijote*? Cuando la cultura española había alcanzado su punto más alto de desarrollo, cuando precisamente empezaba la decadencia, cuando ya el imperio español estaba temblando, estaba para desplomarse. Y si no me crees eso, piensa que la gran novela americana no se ha escrito todavía. No se ha escrito en la América Latina, ni en la América sajona. Al parecer, esa gran novela, la americana, va a nacer, va a surgir en la América Latina. En estos días la mejor novela del mundo se está haciendo en la América Latina, no en la América del Norte, ni en Europa. Pero eso parece indicar que esas culturas americanas, todas, están todavía en el proceso de sublimación, que no han alcanzado su apogeo, su punto más alto de desarrollo. De modo que no intento menospreciar la novela, pero creo que si mi camino fuera el de la novela, ya la hubiera escrito.

HÁBLENOS UN POCO DE SUS PERSONAJES FEMENINOS, PRIMERO EN SUS CUENTOS REGIONALES Y LUEGO EN SUS CUENTOS DE FANTASÍA.

Pues en mis cuentos regionales y costumbristas los personajes que resaltan son hombre, porque recuerda que yo estoy describiendo el momento en mi vida en que yo me esforzaba por hacerme hombre, y vivía en el mundo del ganadero, del vaquero, que es un mundo muy macho, y los hombres con quienes yo tenía contacto eran muy machos, hasta la médula. Yo, jovencito y con la ilusión de hacerme hombre, pues los tenía a ellos de modelos, y esa realidad masculina casi absorbía mi atención. Fui creciendo y el mundo se me va haciendo más amplio. Ya adolescente, y después, empiezan a aparecer más mujeres en mis escritos. Mi abuela que fumaba puros es una mujer que yo describo con todo cariño y ternura. Fue una mujer fuerte, firme, brava, pero al mismo tiempo tierna y compasiva. Es una mujer real, y yo no inventé ese personaje. Yo pinto al personaje tal y como yo lo recuerdo, y como pasa con el campo, es muy probable que el personaje también resulte un tanto idealizado. En mis cuentos más recientes, donde estoy haciendo cuentos de fantasía, allí los personajes sí son inventados, y aparece otro tipo de mujer, ya no la mujer campesina, ya no los hombres campesinos como anteriormente, sino más bien tipos más modernos, acaso más sofisticados. Y como aquí el personaje es una creación, allí sí me esmero por darle carácter y personalidad al personaje. Y las dimensiones que estos personajes alcanzan, pues eso queda por ver. Yo no puedo saber en este momento si esos personajes están logrados o no. Yo quisiera que lo estuvieran. Pero antes yo copiaba aspectos de la realidad, en estos nuevos cuentos estoy inventando esa realidad y tratando de hacerla creíble.

¿Y EN LA POESÍA?

Allí verás a otra mujer. En la poesía encontrarás una mujer espiritual, una mujer que es casi toda alma. Y desde luego idealizada. Elevo a la mujer a un plano ideal, con toda reverencia, con todo respeto. Son versos de amor, a veces, y muy pocas veces, con elementos eróticos. Es un amor más bien platónico.

¿ENTONCES EL TEMA PRINCIPAL DE LA POESÍA ES EL AMOR?

Sí. De eso se trata. Son versos de amor.

¿CÓMO VE UD. LA CRÍTICA QUE SE HA ESCRITO HASTA HORA SOBRE SU OBRA?

Bueno, los críticos siempre son buenos si están a favor de ti; son malos si no lo están. Y por lo general, yo he tenido buena crítica y no debo quejarme. Aún cuando han señalado fallas en mis escritos, al verlo honradamente, en muchas ocasiones tengo que aceptar que ellos tienen razón. El escritor no escribe para los críticos. El escritor escribe para su pueblo y si se pone a pensar en los críticos, no va a escribir nada. Pero no hay que menospreciar, ni despreciar al crítico. El crítico tiene una función. Ha habido escritores en la literatura que han pasado sin ser apercibidos hasta que un crítico los descubre y los revela al mundo entero. De modo que yo hablo con respeto, y algún cariño, no mucho, de los críticos. Dependiendo del crítico, como dije antes; si le gusta lo mío, a mí me gusta el crítico.

SE HA DICHO QUE SABINE ULIBARRÍ NO ES UN AUTOR VERDADERAMENTE CHICANO PORQUE NO TIENE, O NO TRATA, CIERTOS ASPECTOS QUE SE CONSIDERAN DE LA LITERATURA CHICANA.

Y yo estoy de acuerdo con los críticos que dicen eso. Yo no soy autor chicano. Lo que quiero, y espero lograrlo, es ser escritor, sin adjetivo. El movimiento chicano fue un movimiento social y político, y yo no estoy haciendo ni sociología ni política. Lo que quiero hacer es contar cuentos, hacer versos. Y tantos de los escritores chicanos, o algunos, tienen una agenda política, están comprometidos en alguna acción social. Yo no. No en mi literatura. Pero como tú sabes, en mis conferencias y en mis artículos, yo me pongo tan bravo como cualquiera de los chicanos profesionales. Pero yo no he hecho profesión del chicanismo, y no voy a hacerlo nunca. El tono de mi literatura no es bélico. No hay retos. No hay quejas. No hay portestas. Todas eso está bien; no me opongo, y alguien debe hacerlo, pero no creo que a mí me toque hacerlo en mis cuentos y en mis versos. Además que mi historia, mi vida, acaso sean bastante distintas de las de algunos de los escritores chicanos con agenda política. Yo no pasé por la experiencia del barrio; nunca viví en el barrio, de modo que yo no conozco esa vida. Además yo no pasé por la injusticia que muchos de los chicanos han sufrido en otras partes, más fuera de Nuevo México que en Nuevo México.

En Tierra Amarilla, donde yo me crié, nosotros no éramos la minoría; nosotros éramos la mayoría. De modo que yo no tengo mentalidad de minoría. Si es que tengo alguna, tengo mentalidad de mayoría. Así es que eso de hacer literatura de minoría, no me corresponde. Además, yo escribo en español, y si no español clásico, es un español respetable. Trato de utilizar el español de Nuevo México lo mejor que puedo. Donde hay necesidad de palabras no conocidas en Nuevo México, entonces introduzco palabras clásicas. Pero por lo general, tanto mi vocabulario como mi gramática son el vocabulario, la gramática, la lengua de Nuevo México. Y tengo allí un compromiso: demostrar e ilustrar que el español de Nuevo México, cuando se habla, es buen español. Puede resultar arcaico aquí y allí, y puede tener diferencias de léxico aquí y allí, pero en lo esencial el español de Nuevo México es tan buen español como el de México, o el de la Argentina, o el de España. Y mis escritos, espero demuestren eso. Yo no mezclo el inglés y el español, y no digo esto con intención de criticar a nadie. Hay algunos escritores, Alurista por ejemplo, que mezclan el español y el inglés para producir una literatura de categoría. Y son pocos. Alurista es el mejor ejemplo, que ha sabido manipular los méritos de las dos lenguas y combinarlas para producir un efecto poético de gran valor. De modo que el no mezclar las lenguas me separa también del grupo de escritores chicanos por lo menos en alguna medida.

Y la crítica, con frecuencia, tiende a echarnos a todos en el mismo saco, y no pertenecemos allí. No somos estereotipo. Los escritores chicanos de Texas hablan de una realidad que es la suya, y lo hacen a su manera. Los escritores chicanos de Arizona y de California hacen la misma cosa. Y los chicanos de Texas, de Arizona y de California no son como los de Nuevo México. Y hay razones históricas, y hay razones políticas, y hay razones sociales porque eso existe. La historia que tuvo lugar en Texas, por ejamplo, no tuvo lugar en Nuevo México de la misma manera. Y en Nuevo México los hispanos somos la mayoría, y los números te dan categoría. Para nosotros no ha sido necesario crear partidos políticos para elegir a nuestra propia gente, porque ha sido eligida a puestos políticos importantes a través de los partidos establecidos. Y hay que resistir el estereotipo, porque nosotros criticamos a los angloamericanos porque nos estereotipan, pero si nosotros mismos comenzamos a estereotiparnos, que para ser escritores hay que escribir de cierta manera, a eso sí me resisto. Yo voy a escribir a mi manera, y los otros escriben y deben escribir a su manera. Cada quien por su propio camino.

¿Puede decirnos algo más sobre sus ensayos?

Mis ensayos son escritos más bien como conferencias para determinados públicos y determinadas ocasiones. Yo me pasé once años dando conferencias sobre cultura como consultante del Departamento de Agricultura a su personal administrativo, un grupo muy difícil y convencido de su manera de ser. Allí es donde hay que convertir y convencer, no a nosotros mismos como frecuentemente se hace. Porque muchos de esos prejuicios los han tenido tanto tiempo que ni se dan cuenta, les parece algo normal, y en muchas ocasiones me decían: "Yo no había visto esto desde ese punto de vista." Tanto éxito tuvieron estas conferencias que mi equipo y yo (un indio, un negro y una mujer) fuimos convidados por otras agencias del gobierno federal, y hasta por las fuerzas armadas, para hacer estas presentaciones.

¿Qué podemos esperar de Sabine Ulibarrí en el futuro?

Bueno, como ya tú sabes, estoy explorando nuevos caminos. Entre otras cosas, he publicado un libro de cuentos infantiles, algo que no había hecho antes. Y recientemente se publicaron *El gobernador Glu Glu y El Cóndor*, que son cuentos de fantasía, de invención. Y yo no sé hasta dónde me lleve este camino, pero una cosa te aseguro: que voy a volver a mis cuentos antiguous, los tradicionales, los regionales, costumbristas. Una colección que me estoy fraguando en estos momentos es un libro con un título algo así como *Las mujeres que yo he conocido.* Ya les he dado a conocer a mi abuela. Pues así quisiera dar a conocer a mi esposa, a mis hermanas, a alguna novia que he conocido, alguna compañera o colega. Porque tú sabes, María, que todo el mundo habla de la mujer mexicana, todo el mundo habla de la mujer argentina, habla de la mujer española, pero nadie habla de la mujer nuevomexicana. Y la mujer neuvomexicana tiene características todas suyas, y quisiera yo retratar a esa mujer que yo admiro y estimo tanto. Claro que en esto, como en otras cosas, muchas de las historias más interesantes no se pueden contar nunca, porque corres el peligro de lastimar o de ofender a alguien, y hay una cortesía que rige en estos casos. Que yo pudiera contar cuentos de aventuras, incidentes o accidentes de mi vida, donde si los publicara, lastimaría a alguien, y eso no quiero hacerlo.

Sabine Ulibarrí es escritor, pero también es educador y lo has sido por muchos años. ¿Qué cree que ha aportado Ud. a la educación de aquéllos a quienes a instruido?

Mira, María. Como te pasa a ti y nos pasa a todos los que llevamos un nombre hispano, es que somos modelos para los jóvenes. Ésa es una de mis funciones y ha sido una de mis funciones en la universidad. De que un chico salido de la aldea, como salí yo, esos chicos que salen de una atmósfera, de un ambiente totalmente hispánico, llegan a la universidad y se encuentran aquí en un ambiente, en una sociedad totalmente ajenos a la vida que ellos conocían. Se sienten aquí un poco aislados, un poco abandonados, un poco confundidos. Pero si esos chicos tienen modelos dentro de la universidad, dentro de ese campo ajeno, se pueden decir muy bien: "Pues si Ulibarrí pudo, yo también puedo."

Entre mis quehaceres a trevés de los años, yo voy por las escuelas secundarias y primarias hablándoles a los chicos, tratando de animarlos, de orientarlos hacia la educación, porque la educación es la única salvación para nuestro pueblo. Cuando entran en mis clases, quiero convertirlos, contagiarlos, contaminarlos con mi propio entusiasmo, mi propio amor, mi propia dedicación a la lengua y a la cultura de España, de Latinoamérica en general, de México en particular, y de lo nuestro, para qe sientan ellos un orgullo de ser lo que son, de venir de donde vienen, y de ir adonde van. Es ésa la función que tenemos todos los hispanos que funcionamos en la universidad o en las escuelas públicas. Es una responsabilidad y una obligación. Mi vida siempre fue la educación; el escribir es más bien una afición.

Quiero decirte una cosa más. Se ha escrito demasiado de los nuevomexicanos. Llega aquí un tipo a dos saltos de Chicago, camino a California, y cuando llega a la frontera de Nuevo México, empieza a escrbir la historia de Nuevo México en un sobre. Cuando llega a Arizona ya tiene un libro donde nos ha analizado. Muchos de esos estudios son buenos, y son muy útiles, pero todos esos estudios nos están viendo por fuera. Esta generación de escritores está haciendo la historia sentimental de los nuevomexicanos, escribiendo esa historia que llevamos bajo la piel. Cómo somos, quiénes somos, cómo funcionamos allá adentro, allí detrás del ombligo, donde está lo secreto, lo privado, lo limpio, lo puro. Ésa es la función de los escritores chicanos, y muchos de ellos lo han conseguido y creo que lo están consiguiendo cuando ya superaron esa furia con que se inició el movimiento chicano y la literatura chicana, cuando se estaba haciendo literatura de protesta. Pues yo creo que la literatura chicana va madurando, se va haciendo cada vez más profunda, se va haciendo más sofisticada, más universal; la literatura chicana ahora está hablando una lengua universal. Cuando estaba limitada a las necesidades inmediatas, a una zona limitada, no tenía trascendencia. Ahora, cuando ha superado ese momento, y ese momento fue necesario, hay que hacer una fogata más grande para hacer brasas para rescoldar la carne ¿no? Y esa llamarada fue importante. Pero ya el brasero está bien caliente y ahora es cuando se está haciendo el pan, y la literatura chicana se está reconociendo en los círculos nacionales e internacionales.

FIN

INTERVIEW WITH SABINE REYES ULIBARRÍ

María I. Duke dos Santos

You were born and raised in New Mexico, and you have always lived here. When and from where did your ancestors come to New Mexico?

Well, I don't know exactly. I have in my possession a document, a diary written by a captain, Juan de Ulibarrí, in 1706. The governor at Santa Fe sent him to Kansas on a mission to rescue thirty-five Tegua families held prisoner and enslaved by the Apaches. He did just that and wrote a diary of his experiences. I don't know if he is my ancestor because I have no proof, but later, in the nineteenth century, there was another Juan de Ulibarrí, also a captain, who served under New Mexico Governor Armijo, and he is the ancestor we know. My family comes from a small town called Abiquiú. It was then a frontier town that protected Rio Grande inhabitants from Apache and Ute incursions. From there my family went to a hamlet called Las Nutrias, nine miles south of Tierra Amarilla. They bought 14,000 acres along Las Nutrias River, including the mountain to the east of Tierra Amarilla, and there they established their haciendas. The family raised livestock—cows, sheep, horses—and the sierra was used for summer pastures. When I was a child, my father sold horses to the army of the United States. The buyers would come from El Paso and the horses were chosen at a big rodeo.

DID YOU LIVE AT THE RANCH ALL YEAR?

We lived at the ranch all year until we moved to Tierra Amarilla, where my father bought a house. I was born in Santa Fe because my mother went there to give birth, but we lived in Las Nutrias.

DID YOU ALWAYS RETURN TO THE RANCH?

Yes, the ranch was there and my grandmother remained there to live. My father continued to administer the cattle ranch from Tierra Amarilla, so there was much traveling between Las Nutrias and Tierra Amarilla.

WHAT IS THE ORIGIN OF THE NAME SABINE?

My father's name was Sabiniano Reyes Ulibarrí. Reyes because he was born on January 6—it is a name, not a last name. When the Texas cowboys arrived in New Mexico, they couldn't pronounce "Sabiniano," so they named him "Sabine," apparently after the name of a river in Texas. It became his nickname, and when I was born, it became my first name.

DID YOU ATTEND THE UNIVERSITY AFTER GOING TO SCHOOL IN TIERRA AMARILLA?

Yes. Since I was a child my father's dream was that I would become a lawyer; my family spoke about it, and I thought it was a great idea, so going to the university was not a sudden decision. I think it was established when I was born.

HOW DID YOU BECOME A COLLEGE PROFESSOR?

When I was in my last year of high school my father died. I was fifteen years old. My mother moved to Santa Fe and built a house there. My father wanted me to go to Georgetown, but there was no way I could go to Washington D.C., leaving my widowed mother with three young children, so I went to the University of New Mexico. Just before that, my cousins returned from the East after graduating from college and loaned me several books. Like other Latin Americans, they had turned to philosophy. So, while I was still in high school, I was reading all these books, including *The Origin of the Species*, and this had a profound effect on me. Consider the time, the circumstances, my immaturity, well, those revelations sent me into orbit, and I had difficulties with the nuns at school because I was expressing radical ideas that to them were heresies. My cousins then obtained a fellowship for me at an eastern university, and I was ready to leave when my father was still alive. When the nuns realized this, they immediately obtained another fellowship for me at Notre Dame. This was a great stimulus for me, a boy fascinated with sports; to go to Notre Dame, famous for its football team, was like going to heaven. Then the nuns explained that I also had to work in the dining room. Fine, I thought. But when I was told tat I would have to pay an additional $800. I don't remember whether per semester or per year; well, who could afford $800 during the depression? And I said, "I am sorry Sister, but being a Catholic is too expensive and I don't have any money." So that also influenced my decision to stay.

DID YOU CONTINUE YOUR STUDIES?

Well, there I was, a boy full of ambition. I had decided to graduate in three years, not four, so I went directly from high school to summer school, then fall and spring, and again summer school. Then my mother died. I was sixteen years old and had three younger brothers, so I had to leave school and provide for them. My uncles and grandparents had already decided to split us up between them, but I did not agree with that and I said, "You will not take anyone because they will stay with me." So at sixteen I had that responsibility, and everyone was waiting to tell me "I told you so."

I obtained an emergency certificate, and I went to teach in the public schools. I taught at Ranchitos, a small village where there was no school, between Riverside and San Juan and close to Santa Fe. The superintendent of schools of Rio Arriba County was my first cousin, as was the school supervisor, and my uncle was the head of education, so a school was opened and I went to teach there. I was seventeen years old at the time and some of my students were my age. I taught there one year, and one year in San Juan.

SABINE R. ULIBARRÍ AS A SOLDIER DURING
WORLD WAR II.

Later I went to El Rito, to what was then called the Spanish American Normal School. I taught there two years, and during that time my sister married. I still felt a responsibility to my father to go to Georgetown, so when she married and could take charge of the younger brothers, I went to Washington. But I was unable to register at Georgetown because it was too expensive, so I went to George Washington University while I worked nights for the government as an interpreter. I was there three months because the war was going on in 1942, and although I thought that I did not have to go, I forgot I had to live with myself, and it began to bother me. I worked in a building with five hundred people, twelve of whom were men who were either over sixty years old or physically impaired. I became ashamed. I called my sweetheart, Connie, and asked her to marry me. I came from Washington, and I got married and enlisted the same week.

How old were you then?

I was twenty-two at the time because I had taught four years in the public schools.

So you enlisted and went to the front?

Yes. And I asked for active duty at the front, but my request was not easily granted since everywhere I went, when they saw my credentials they wanted me to work in an office.

How long were you on active duty?

Three years. I flew thirty-five combat missions over Germany. When I returned I had earned a lot of points; you were given a certain number of points for combat flights and for serving overseas, so I was one of the first veterans. I received the Air Medal four times and the Distinguished Flying Cross.

And then you returned to the University of New Mexico?

Yes. I finished my B.A. and immediately obtained a teaching assistantship. Soon after obtaining my master's degree I received an appointment to teach at the university. Do you know that I have never filed an application for a job? I started as an instructor, a position that has almost disappeared today, and then I obtained a three year leave of absence to go to UCLA for my doctorate. I returned to New Mexico to teach and to work on my dissertation.

You have been teaching here ever since?

I received a teaching appointment in 1950, and I have been here ever since, with the exception of those three years. I went through all the ranks: from instructor to assistant professor, associate professor, and full professor. I became a full professor about twenty-five years ago. In July 1990 I retired, and now I teach only one course per semester.

What other activities have you pursued while being a college professor?

I directed programs for the university in Quito, Ecuador. I took two groups of students there for NDEA . I directed a full-year institute in Spanish, the only one in the country then, because there was one in Spanish an one in Russian. That lasted three years. I was also director of the second-level summer institute abroad; the first-level summer institute was held here. I was therefore director of two institutes at the same time. I obtained a sabbatical when I went to Spain. Then I went to Quito to establish the Center for Andean Studies for advanced and graduate students, which lasted eleven years. I was its first director.

How long were you in Spain?

Let me see. Four summers and then an entire year, twelve months.

Considering all your activities, when do you have time to write?

I taught two courses a year for a long time, and this is a full load since it is the policy of this university to reduce the teaching load for those of us who write.

Have you had any difficulties publishing your work?

No. My first book to be published was *Al cielo se sube a pie*, a book of verse. I had written many poems but never had them published because I felt that it would be like baring my soul to the public. In poetry you reveal things, intimate confessions, and sometimes you are afraid of being misinterpreted, of lowering your defenses. A friend of mine said, "Look, I am going to Mexico; let me take some of your poems to be published." And I said, "There are the files, choose those you want." And he chose fifty and took them to Mexico where they were published. The book was not widely distributed, but it made me known. Critics started to comment on my poetry, and when I went to Ecuador and La Casa de la Cultura published *Tierra Amarilla*, I became better known. From then on, I have had no problems being published.

What advice would you give a person who would like to embark on a writing career?

The first thing to do would be to read, read, and read. To learn to write one must first learn to read, because there you will find your inspiration, models of style, of lexicon, of points of view, of attitudes, themes, if you like. Then the future writer needs to have the desire to write, the need to write. To write for the sake of writing does not lead anywhere. The right way is to write with a goal in mind, with a purpose. If you can tell a story, pay a compliment, then you can write poetry or short stories. And then you have to be daring, plunge into it and go forward.

One of the most difficult things for a young writer, and it was for me also, is how to begin. And you can't search for a literary beginning; the one who consciously wants to produce literature can't write short stories, or poems or novels. The good short story writer is the one who has a story to tell and does it. And it could be that it turns out to be a literary work, but if I am so conceited to say that I am going to write literature, this is a laugh. You may not know how to begin even when you have a definite idea of what you want to say. With a little experience one realizes that the beginning is really very easy, gratis. The entrance is anywhere, through the front door, the back door, or even the window. If one doesn't know exactly how to begin, describe the setting, then introduce the character, then the action.

DID YOU HAVE AN EARLY INTEREST IN LITERATURE?

I was born and raised on a rather isolated ranch until I was eight years old. The closest neighbors lived two or three miles away, so I grew up alone. My days were spent in the fields with my dogs, and these circumstances opened the way to thinking and dreaming. Recreation consisted of fantasizing and evenings spent listening to my father as he read works of literature. I thus became acquainted with the *Quijote* at an early age, as well as the *Lazarillo de Tormes*, the old romances, the *Count of Monte Cristo*, Edgar Allan Poe. And I tell you, María, that this was a lot more valuable than what there is on television today. After he read us a chapter, I would go to bed with mind and heart full of fantasy and illusion, and the following day I would wonder and speculate about what would come in the next chapter, impatiently waiting for it. I was thus introduced to prose.

I was also brought up within the oral tradition of recounting stories. But my father was also a first rate *declamador*, so I was memorizing poems since I was a child, almot since I learned to talk, and then my father would encourage me to recite poetry, and I was doing it very well since I was six years old. And do you know, María, I still remember those poems I learned as a child, but I have already forgotten those I learned last week; maybe this could be a message to parents and teachers, that they should encourage kids to learn poetry, because it is a lifelong gift.

When I was eight years old, we moved from the ranch to Tierra Amarilla, the county seat, so my brothers and I could attend school. I had the good fortune, which I did not appreciate at the time, to study with the Franciscan nuns, who brought to Tierra Amarilla from the Midwest all those ideas and American values that are so ingrained in that part of the country, so I learned much from them. The school principal had a doctorate and spoke seven languages. All my secondary school teachers had a master's degree, something not common at the time in New Mexico. Neither in Albuquerque, nor in Santa Fe, nor in Roswell or Las Cruces could you find teachers as well trained as the ones I had. However, a conflict ensued between them and me over discipline, and it was not until later that I wanted to thank them for what they did for me. They introduced me to American literature, and I had a secondary school Spanish teacher that I consider the best Spanish grammar teacher I ever had, and all this was in Tierra Amarilla. There all the currents came together, oriented toward literature, so that I was writing poetry since I was very young. The short stories came much later. Poetry came first.

YOUR EDUCATION BEFORE THE AGE OF EIGHT WAS AT HOME?

Yes. My parents met in Las Vegas, New Mexico, at a teachers (normal) school, although neither one of them became a teacher because they married and my father had to take charge of the ranch after his father died. But both taught me all they knew, so when I arrived in Tierra Amarilla to start school, I was already reading books, not only short stories, in both Spanish and English.

WHICH WOULD YOU SAY ARE THE MAIN INFLUENCES ON YOUR WORK?

Well, first came my father's influence, because he was so dedicated to reading. So through my parents, since early in my childhood, I was already acquainted with world literature, Spanish as well as Latin American, English, North American, plus French and others in translation. That is the primary influence, and maybe my dedication to poetry, which also came from my father. So when I reached secondary school I was already composing verses and writing essays, and when I came to the university I graduated with a double major, one in Spanish and one in English. At UCLA my doctoral specialties were four: first, Peninsular literature; second, Latin American literature; third, Portuguese literature; fourth, French literature. So my doctorate is dedicated entirely to literature.

WHAT OTHER INFLUENCES DO YOU CONSIDER IMPORTANT?

My readings. From a very early age I was fond of Gustavo Adolfo Bécquer, Edgar Allan Poe, and the picaresque novel. Many who have read my works comment that there is a picaresque element in my stories. Also the Spanish mystics and Sor Juana Inés de la Cruz.

JUAN RAMÓN JIMÉNEZ HAS ALSO BEEN MENTIONED AS A STRONG INFLUENCE.

Certainly. My contact with Juan Ramón is either entirely accidental or totally determined. One of the two. All my readings told me that Juan Ramón was considered the spiritual father to all the twentieth-century poets in the Spanish language. I read Juan Ramón and he did not tell me anything. But I proceeded to study him carefully, because to know and understand modern literature, one had to know the father. As I continued to read, the works of Juan Ramón began to open up like a beautiful flower, and then I appreciated him and admired him enthusiastically.

THE INCLUSION OF CATHOLIC RELIGIOUS ELEMENTS IS APPARENT AS ONE READS YOUR WORKS. WERE YOUR PARENTS VERY DEVOUT?

My grandmother was devout and religious. My mother and my father were Catholic, but to them Catholicism was a silken cloak, not a *cilice* (a shirt made of coarse goat hair, formerly worn by monks and others doing penance.); that is, they were easygoing, not fanatics in any way, even though fanaticism existed there. However, they had gone away to the university; therefore, they were emancipated, so to speak. Homer said in one of his poems, "I am part of everything that I have known." And what comes through in my writings are all of the social, sentimental, intellectual, and family experiences. In one way or another, it all filters through to what I write.

Did you grow up speaking Spanish?

Yes. And the Spanish spoken in New Mexico at that time was superior to what it is today. It has crumbled and become old, but at that time it was a vital instrument. My grandmother did not speak English and the chores at the ranch were all conducted in Spanish, although my parents were both bilingual.

It has been said that the language you use in you writings is a classical form of Spanish, correct in a classical way.

That may be true, although that doesn't come only from my studies but also from my relationships—the kind of society in which I lived, the fact that Tierra Amarilla was the county seat, that the courthouse was the social gathering center and many of those who worked there were my relatives or knew me. As a child I played at the courthouse, I played cops and robbers at the real jailhouse, where we would lock each other up. I remember on one occasion my playmates left me there all night and did not tell anyone, so no one could find me. Well, most of those people spoke very good Spanish. Then, I was dedicated to my Spanish studies since I was in secondary school in Tierra Amarilla.

Did you have bilingual instruction at the secondary level, or was it all in English?

It was in English. Only the Spanish-language class was in Spanish. The nuns did not speak Spanish. I did, however, continue to devour books in Spanish.

When you write, do you favor one language? Or is it as easy for you to write in English as in Spanish?

I write my short stories and my poems in Spanish, always. Everything that I have written for publication, in the area of literature, is in Spanish. I translate it later. Other things, like lectures, I can write in either English or Spanish, since I learned both languages simultaneously.

BUT SOMETHING IN YOUR SOUL IS MORE SPANISH THAN ENGLISH?

It was said about Mariano José de Larra that he received a classical education in France, so he had a classical style but his heart was that of a romantic. I believe that my heart is very Spanish. My orientation is toward Hispanicism. We are all Hispanics, whether we are Puerto Rican, Cuban, Spanish, or Mexican—that is the beauty of the Hispanic world.

WOULD YOU SAY THAT NATURE, RANCH LIFE, AND THE COUNTRYSIDE OF NEW MEXICO ARE IMPORTANT ASPECTS IN YOUR WRITINGS?

And solitude. Because I spent so much time alone during my early years. And my father would take me out of school a month early because it was then that everyone returned from the winter stations, and I would spend those months in the sierra. I have read that some critics say that there is a certain mysticism in my writings; if there is, and I am not sure that there is, it has not been learned. It was something that existed in the air, in that solitude, in nature and in fantasy. I am not alone in this love of the earth; it is something felt by all the people there.

DID YOU TAKE PART IN THE CHORES AT THE RANCH?

Yes, since I was a child. It was an obsession with my father that I should learn to be a man, so I was assigned chores since I was little.

MANY OF YOUR STORIES HAVE A RURAL BACKGROUND.

Well, the culture of New Mexico is a rural one since New Mexico was rural until World War II. Look, in 1940, the Albuquerque census registered 38,000 inhabitants, a small city. Now we have a million, and all of that since the war. But something strange occurred. When the native New Mexican comes to the city from the farm, where does he end up? In the barrio. And he brings to the barrio rural customs and traditions, so it is as if he never left the countryside. The extended family, the rural way of life, are all in the barrio. And they live there, isolated from the rest of the community, a community within another larger one. So there is something rural and country in our culture, even in the city.

WHAT INSPIRES YOU IN THE DEVELOPMENT OF THE CHARACTERS FOR YOUR STORIES?

I don't think I have any particular inspiration in the development of my characters because they are real, and what I try to do is to sketch a character as I knew him or her; so I am not creating characters, I am bringing characters from my past to my stories. I have a problem in Tierra Amarilla in that someone says, "You forgot, Ulibarrí. It was not here, it was there; and it was not him but that other one." And I reply, "Look, I am writing stories, not history, and every writer starts from a basis of reality. The material is based on facts, real facts, and he shuffles these facts until he gets a good hand, and that is what is written." The facts are the same. What has perhaps changed is the relationship of one to the other, the combinations. So I am not creating characters. In my more recent stories, which are based on fantasy, there I need to create characters, but in those rural and *costumbrista* stories, well, they come from my past, they are people I knew.

WAS THERE A COWBOY LIKE EL NEGRO AGUILAR?

Yes. Although he did not die the way I described in the story. I invented that. I am only copying from memory, including the particular way in which each character speaks. I don't know if you have read "Brujerías o tonterías," where I talk to a witch of Ensenada who speaks in a peculiar way. Well, I try to reproduce the way she used the language, not the way I would use it.

IS "LOS PENITENTES" THE MOST TRUE-TO-HISTORY STORY THAT YOU HAVE WRITTEN?

Yes. That is not really a story, it is more like a narration. But there is also the story about a penitent who did work for my father. I did not know the activities and adventures of this *penitente*. So much of the activities of the brotherhood were a mystery to us. We went to see on Holy Thursday and on Good Friday when they would flagellate themselves, but that was like going to see a spectacle, a football game. The brotherhood held so many secrets, even from us. Only the brothers knew what went on in their residences and private services.

WAS YOUR GRANDMOTHER THE SAME WONDERFUL WOMAN OF YOUR STORY?

Exactly as I remember her. You may have realized that the drawing, the sketch they did of her, doesn't match my description. I said, "She was straight, tall, slender," or something like that, and in the sketch she looks short, overweight, and heavyset.

DO YOU THINK THERE IS A CERTAIN IDEALIZATION OF THE COUNTRYSIDE IN YOUR STORIES?

Jorge Manrique says that any time past is better. And it's possible that there is some idealization. But it was not something I tried to do. I am looking at that world through memories, and remembrances soften, ennoble, and enrich the experience. Through the eyes of our memories everything seems more beautiful, more ideal. And maybe without realizing it, I may be doing that myself. I live with the Tierra Amarilla of my childhood and my youth, and the world smiles and is sweet when one is young. That childhood and that youth were truly happy in every sense of the word, and the world seen through laughter and joy is a much more attractive world. So it is quite possible that I did idealize it without trying to or thinking about it. That was never my intention.

I UNDERSTAND THAT YOU ARE NOW WRITING A NEW TYPE OF STORY BASED ON FANTASY, ON THE IMAGINATION. IS THIS A NEW DIRECTION FOR YOU?

Yes. This in no way means that I have abandoned the rural and *costumbrista* stories; that is the path I will eventually return to. Writers like to try new avenues, and I don't really know where this one will take me, but wherever it takes me, I will always return to the land. Something curious that I did not realize until later is that these new stories are longer than the previous ones. I asked myself why, and finally I found the reason. In the rural stories I don't have to invent or justify reality; it's there. But in these other stories I have to invent reality, make it believable, and that's why they are longer.

One of the collections is, but it's not published yet. It has been in Ecuador looking for a publisher. It is a collection of legends from Quito, which is full of legends, some of them full of mischief and happy, others sinister and terrible. I was mainly interested in the happy ones, and at first I thought only of collecting and publishing them, something like the Peruvian legends. So I collected them, but I was not satisfied because I felt they left a void, several voids, too many unresolved issues. There is a Quito legend that deals with "the house of the bull," and in this house hangs the head of a bull. It was said that the legend came from colonial times. It deals with an adolescent girl who woke up screaming from a terrible nightmare. She told her parents a bull had come into her room and tried to kill her. Her parents tried to calm her down, and her mother had to stay with her all night so she could sleep. Some time later there was a bullfight in the main square, as it was done those days. Barricades were set up and people could watch the spectacle from their balconies and windows. It was a day filled with joy and music and laughter. Everyone in Quito was there, including the girl and her parents. Suddenly a bull appeared. He refused to charge the bullfighters but kept looking around, as if searching for someone. The girl, petrified with fear, suddenly screamed "That's the bull!" and fainted. She was taken home, and meanwhile the bull managed to jump over the barricades, went straight to the girl's house, and killed her. That's the end of the legend. But do you see how much is left in the dark? It doesn't explain why, for what reason, why the girl. Well, I take this legend and invent a story about why, and the ending. And I did this with all the legends in the collection. In a legend there is no need to explain anything, the mystery is enough, but a story requires a beginning, a middle, and an ending.

Is there a South American theme in your book entitled *El Cóndor y otros cuentos*?

It really has that title because I could not think of another one. The longest story in it is entitled "El Cóndor," so the editor and I agreed that the title should be *El Cóndor y otros cuentos*.

Is it a story about the Indians in Ecuador?

Yes, but the rest of the stories have nothing to do with Latin America. They are fictional stories. I get ideas and I enjoy myself as I write them.

Then "El Cóndor" is also entirely fictional?

No. I was profoundly affected by the plight of the Indians. The first time I arrived in Quito I read a full-page advertisement in the newspaper about the sale of a ranch. There was a list of the assets, including so many hectares of pastures, crops, heads of cattle, pigs, horses, and at the end it said "two hundred Indians." This is true. And this moves and shocks one and makes one want to weep, that the Indians were being sold like cattle. So even in these stories of fantasy there are elements of truth.

Have you ever thought of writing something based on your experiences during World War II?

What a coincidence that you should ask me that, because that's what I am now doing. Only after more than forty-five years have I been able to return to my memories of the war. God is merciful because he made us in such a way that as time passes we tend to forget the unpleasant aspects of our past and only remember what's beautiful. Thank God this is possible, because if we remembered all of the suffering, the pain, the frustrations and the anger, and all the nightmares of our lives, life would be unbearable. So these memories of the war have been in a trunk in the back of my mind, and they have not bothered me. I have lived a happy and contented life since then. But now that I am opening that trunk, can you see how those memories have moved me again?

Oh, yes! I already have three written and others in mind. When I think about a story to write, I have the idea going around and around in my mind. It may be a character looking for an author, like Pirandello. One day the idea gels, and then I start to write; and when I do, I write it all at once. Maybe I will take the whole night to do it. I may be writing until dawn, but that does not mean it just took me six or twelve hours to do it, because I had the idea in my head for a long time, and when I sit down to write I already know where I am going. What I don't know is how I am going to arrive there. My destination is fixed, but I have to open up the way. Other writers, as we sometimes see in the movies, sit and type a page, they don't like it and toss it in the basket or on the floor, and at the end of the scene the floor is littered with paper. Maybe that's what I do, but in my mind; there I am, adding, eliminating, and revising, and I do it in a state between consciousness and unconsciousness. I am not a professional writer. I write when I am inspired. A professional writer has a schedule, and he sits at the table and he honestly works a set number of hours, day after day. What has happened to me sometimes is that once I start to write and I become enthused, I can go from one story to the next, because one story seems to beckon another one; but I don't have a definite schedule.

EVEN YOUR PROSE IS POETIC. HOW DO YOU INCORPORATE SOUND AND CADENCE INTO YOUR PROSE?

I think I told you that I began to write poetry before prose and that I continue to compose poems even if I don't always write them. To me, poetry is like a stream. It just comes to me. Poetry is natural to me, and language with all its nuances and musicality has always intrigued me. I enjoy playing with words, it's a sport. I write orally; that is, I listen to myself write, so that the phonetic aspects and the musical values of the language are very attractive to me. So I listen to what I am going to write, and if I like it I write it. If it doesn't sound right, I don't. I not only want to communicate information but I also want to reach the senses and emotions, and sounds have a way of saying things that words don't. Look, words like *murmullo, susurro,* and *suspiro* have onomatopoeic value because they not only refer to actions but also to sounds. So there is a lot of onomatopoeia in what I write, a lot of alliteration and internal rhythm. Phrases are often short, with a deliberate punctuation to produce rhythm and a certain cadence. It sounds right to my ear so I write it. In my conversations I am always playing with words, combining words in a certain way to produce sound effects. I have published two books of verse, but it has been a long time since I have published poetry, although I am always thinking verse, and I feel it and write in once in a while. I have everywhere files of poems that have never been published. Perhaps because to write poetry in Spanish in the United States is to write without destination, without readers. Who is going to read you? Even in Spanish-speaking countries poets have a limited readership. Who reads poetry? So my avenue of expression has become the short story. Thus I communicate.

HAVE YOU EVER THOUGHT OF WRITING NOVELS?

On several occasions I have thought of writing a novel, but I didn't try it and I probably never will. Writing a novel requires a certain discipline and patience that I don't have. The short story is my way of expression. And though the novel requires more discipline, a lot more patience and tolerance, it also gives you more freedom. A novel provides you with more time and space to move, to develop your characters. If you make a mistake in the second chapter, you have seventeen more chapters to correct it. In a short story, if you make a mistake in the second page, you have ruined the story. Therefore, there is a different kind of discipline. The short story requires closer attention; it means setting your sights on the nucleus of it and keeping it there, because if you don't, you are lost. In a novel you can stray, but as you continue on your way you can return to your path. The short story requires fast and efficient work or you can't do it. And the short story is what I do best; the novel is for others. This does not mean that I don't appreciate the value of the novel, because to me, the novel is the most complete, the most profound and complicated literary form. But poetry was born earlier, and in primitive societies it was singing. First there was music, a drum maybe, a rhythm, a cadence; suddenly someone feels the urge to sing, and so we have singing accompanied by music, and this is poetry. Later comes dancing. The rhythm and cadence produce in the listener a certain sensation, and thus results dancing. All of this is during primitive times. And still at this time, during the dance someone sings, one day someone else decides to answer this first chant, and he in turn receives a reply, and thus the drama is born. And in this same period the story is born, because the tribal elders would tell stories to educate their youth in the traditions, legends, history, and values of the tribe. But look at when the novel appears. The first novel in history is the *Quijote*, the first in time and the first in importance. And when did the *Quijote* appear? When Spanish culture had attained its highest point of development, when decadence was beginning to set in, when the Spanish empire was beginning to crumble. And if you don't believe me, think about the fact that the great American novel has not been written yet. It has not been written in Latin America or in Anglo America. It seems that this great American novel is going to come from Latin America. In these days, the best novels in the world are being produced in Latin America, not in North America or in Europe. And this seems to indicate that those American cultures, all of them, are still in the process of sublimation, that they have not reached their pinnacle, their highest point of development. So, I don't mean to think less of the novel, but if that were my way, I would have already written it.

TELL US ABOUT THE FEMININE CHARACTERS IN YOUR RURAL STORIES AS WELL AS IN YOUR FICTIONAL STORIES.

In my stories about the countryside the characters that stand out are men. Remember that I was writing about a time in my life in which I was trying to become a man, and I lived in the world of the cattle rancher and the cowboy, a very masculine world, and those with whom I had contact were *muy macho*. I was a youth but with the hope of becoming a man, so I had them as role models, and this masculine reality absorbed my attention. As I grew older, my world expanded, and as an adolescent and later, more women begin to appear in my writings. My grandmother who smoked cigars is a woman I describe with love and tenderness. She was a strong woman but at the same time, compassionate and tender. She is a real woman. She was not invented. I drew her as I remember her, but as it happened with the countryside, she could be somewhat idealized. In my more recent fictional stories, where the characters are a product of my imagination, there is no longer the country woman or the country man but a more contemporary, maybe more sophisticated type of character. And since they are fictional, I try to develop their personalities as best I can. I don't know how successful I am in achieving this, although I would like to be. Previously I would copy aspects of reality. In these recent stories I invent reality and try to make it believable.

WHAT ABOUT IN YOUR POETRY?

There you will see another type of woman. In my poetry you will find a spiritual woman, a woman who is almost all soul. And, of course, idealized. I elevate woman to an ideal plane, with reverence, with respect. These are love poems and sometimes, very few times, with erotic elements. It is a platonic kind of love.

THEN THE MAIN THEME OF YOUR POEMS IS LOVE?

Yes. That's what they are about. They are love poems.

HOW DO YOU VIEW THE CRITICISM THAT HAS BEEN WRITTEN SO FAR ABOUT YOUR WORK?

Well, critics are always good when they are in your favor; they are bad if they are not. In general, I have received good criticism and I can't complain. Even when flaws were pointed out in my writings, in looking at it fairly, I must admit that in several instances they were right. A writer doesn't write for the critics. A writer writes for the people, his or her people, and if one starts thinking about the critics, nothing will be written. But one can't underestimate or not appreciate the critics. A critic has an important function. There have been writers who have remained unknown until a critic discovers them and brings them to the attention of the whole world. So I speak with respect, and maybe some affection, not too much, about the critics. It depends on the critic, as I said before; if he likes what I write, I like the critic.

I agree with those critics who say that. I am not a Chicano author. What I aspire to be, and I hope I will succeed, is a writer, without adjective. The Chicano movement was a social and political movement, and I am not delving into sociology or politics. What I want to do is tell stories, write poems. And so many Chicano authors, or at least some, have a political agenda; they are involved in some social concern. I am not. Not in my literature. But as you know, in my lectures and in my articles I can become as angry as any of the professional Chicanos. But I have not made a career of being a Chicano, and I never will. The tone of my literature is not bellicose. There are no protests, no complaints. All of that is fine. I am not against it and someone has to do it, but I don't think I should do it in my stories and in my poetry. Besides, my history, my life, has perhaps been different from that of those writers with a political agenda. I never had the experience of the barrio. I never lived in the barrio. Furthermore, I never experienced the injustices that many Chicanos had to endure in other places, more outside of New Mexico than in New Mexico.

In Tierra Amarilla, where I was raised, we were not a minority; we were the majority. So I don't have a minority mentality; if anything, I have a majority mentality. So it's not my place to write minority literature. I also write in Spanish, maybe not a classic kind of Spanish but an acceptable Spanish. I try to use the Spanish of New Mexico the best way I can. Where there is a need to use a less-known word, then I may introduce a more classical one, but in general, my vocabulary as well as my grammar are those of New Mexico. And I have there a duty to show and illustrate the fact that the Spanish of New Mexico, when spoken, is the best kind of

Spanish. It may be archaic here and there, and it may have lexical differences here and there, but in general, New Mexican Spanish is as good as that of Mexico, or Argentina, or Spain. And my writings, I hope, will demonstrate that. I don't mix English and Spanish, and I don't say this to criticize anyone. There are some writers, Alurista for example, who mix English and Spanish and produce a high-class literature. But they are few. Alurista is the best example. He knows how to manipulate the merits of both languages and combine them to produce poetic effects of great value. So that not mixing the languages also separates me in some way from the group of Chicano authors.

Critics often tend to put us all together in the same group, but we don't belong there. We are not stereotypes. Chicano authors from Texas speak their own reality, and they do it in their own way. The authors from California and Arizona do the same thing. And the Chicanos from Texas, Arizona, and California are not like the ones from New Mexico. And there are historical, political, and social reasons for this to exist. The history that took place in Texas, for example, did not take place in New Mexico in the same manner. In New Mexico, we Hispanics are the majority, and numbers give you prestige. For us it was not necessary to create political parties in order to elect our own people, because they were elected through the established political parties. And we have to resist the stereotypes, because we criticize the Anglo-Americans for stereotyping us, but if we start doing it to ourselves, that to be a writer one has to write in a certain manner, that I do resist. I am going to write in my own manner, and others should write in their own manner. Each in his own way.

CAN YOU TELL US SOMETHING MORE ABOUT YOUR ESSAYS?

My essays are written more like lectures for special audiences and special occasions. I spent eleven years giving lectures on culture as a consultant for the Department of Agriculture for their administrative personnel, a difficult group, very set in their ways. Those are the ones we have to convince and convert, not our own selves like we often do. Because so many of those prejudices have existed for so long that people don't even realize they have them, it seems something normal to them. On manyoccasions they would tell me, "I had not seen this from that particular point of view." Those lectures were so successful that my team and I (an Indian, an African American, and a woman from the local area) were invited by other agencies of the federal government, and even by the armed forces, to present these lectures.

WHAT CAN WE EXPECT OF SABINE ULIBARRÍ IN THE FUTURE?

Well, as you know, I am exploring new avenues. Among other things, I have published a book of children's stories, something I had not done before. Recently *El gobernador Glu Glu* and *El Cóndor*, collections of fictional stories, were published. And I don't know where this road will lead, but I assure you of one thing, I will return to my old traditional stories, the rural and *costumbrista* ones. A possible collection that I am now thinking about is one called something like *The Women I Have Known*. You already know my grandmother. I would also like for you to know my wife, my sisters, maybe a girl I knew, or a colleague. Because you know, María, that everyone talks about the Mexican woman, the Argentine woman, the Spanish woman, but not about the New Mexican woman. And the New Mexican woman has definite personal characteristics. I would like to picture this woman I appreciate and admire so much. Of course, in doing this, as in other things, many of the more interesting stories can never be told, because you run the risk of offending or hurting someone. There is a basic courtesy that has to be observed. If I were to write about some incidents, or accidents, in my life, I might offend someone, and that I don't want to do.

SABINE ULIBARRÍ IS NOT ONLY A WRITER BUT ALSO AN EDUCATOR, AND FOR MANY YEARS. WHAT DO YOU THINK YOU HAVE CONTRIBUTED TO THE EDUCATION OF THOSE YOU HAVE TAUGHT?

Look, María, as it happens to you and all of us who are Hispanic, we are role models for our youth. This is one of my functions, and it has been so at the university. A young person coming from a small town, like I did, from a totally Hispanic environment, arrives at the university and finds himself or herself in an environment and a society totally different from what he or she knew. But if those young people have role models within that new society, they can tell themselves, "If Ulibarrí could do it, so can I."

As part of my chores through the years, I have gone to elementary and secondary schools talking to the kids, trying to encourage them and orient them toward education, because education is the only way to save our people. When they come into my classes, I want to convert them, to make them participate in my own enthusiasm, my own love, my own dedication to the Spanish language and the culture of Spain and Latin America in general, of Mexico in particular, and of our own heritage, so that they will be proud to be who they are, proud of their origins and of where they are headed. That is the function of all of us who work at the university or in the school system. It is our responsibility and our obligation. My life was always dedicated to education; writing is more like something I am fond of and enjoy.

I would like to tell you one more thing. So much has been written about New Mexico. Someone arrives here from Chicago, on his way to California, and when he arrives at the New Mexico border, he starts to write the history of New Mexico on an envelope. When he reaches Arizona, he already has a book in which he has analyzed us; some of those works are good and useful, but all of them are seeing us from the outside. This generation of authors is writing the sentimental history of the New Mexicans, writing the story that we have under our skin. How we are, who we are, how we function deep inside ourselves where the good and the pure side of us is. This is the task of the Chicano authors, and many of them have accomplished it, and I believe they are continuing to do it when they go beyond the anger with which the Chicano movement was initiated, when the literature of the day was that of protest. I believe that Chicano literature is coming of age, becoming more profound, more universal. Chicano literature is now speaking a more universal language. When it was confined to immediate needs, to limited horizons, it lacked transcendence. Now that it has overcome that moment—and that moment was necessary because you have to light a big fire to heat the coals and cook the meat, right? And that flame was important—now the hearth is hot and the bread is cooking and Chicano literature is being recognized in national and international circles.

MEMORY, FOLKLORE, READER'S RESPONSE, AND COMMUNITY CONSTRUCTION IN *MI ABUELA FUMABA PUROS/ MY GRANDMA SMOKED CIGARS*

María Herrera-Sobek

This literature [resistance literature], like the resistance and national liberation movements which it reflects and in which it can be said to participate, not only demands recognition of its independent status and existence as literary production, but as such also presents a serious challenge to the codes and canons of both the theory and the practice of literature and its criticism as these have been developed in the West
—Barbara Harlow (1987)

Américo Paredes, the internationally renowned folklore scholar, has posited a theoretical construct for the analysis and comprehension of Mexican-American literature. This theoretical construct views much of Chicano literature as arising from a specific sociohistorical political situation: The clash of cultures between the Catholic Latino native populations of the American Southwest and the Protestant English-speaking Anglo-Saxon colonizers who invaded and acquired through the Mexican-American War (1946–48) Mexico's northernmost territories (see Paredes 1958; Saldívar 1990: 3–42). Many of the oral and literary tests extant during that period and subsequent eras can be viewed within the parameters of resistance literature. That is to say, the defeated populations bereft of publishing houses and denied access to mainstream publications developed through oral literature, small printing presses, and other genres of popular culture (e.g., the *teatro de carpa*) a corpus of literary productions whose underlying theme was a critique of the political and social oppression of the Mexican-American population living in the Southwest. Thus many of the *corridos* (ballads), folk songs, folktales, essays, novels, and poems and much of the folk humor critique the social structure, institutions, and laws in the United States and the economic disparity between Mexican Americans and the Anglo-Saxon population, among other issues. Such ballads as "Gregorio Cortez," "Joaquín Murrieta," and "Jacinto Treviño" arose out of the cultural clash between Anglo-Americans and Mexican Americans in the second half of the nineteenth century and the early twentieth century. Similarly, within the folklore genre of the jest or humorous narrative, the Anglo-American is frequently the butt of a large number of jokes (see Paredes 1968; Reyna 1980). The figure of the trickster, important in oral tradition, underscores the position of the subaltern, conquered society. It is a figure that, lacking the power and influence of hegemonic society, relies on his or her wit, intelligence, and cunning to outwit and outperform the members of the ruling class.

It is with the above parameters in mind that I examine Sabine Ulibarrí's collection of short narratives published under the title *Mi abuela fumaba puros/My Grandma Smoked Cigars* (1977). In this study I focus on Ulibarrí's short stories and posit that they are part of the resistance literature that arose during the Chicano movement in the 1960s and 1970s. It is my position that Ulibarrí's discursive strategies are aimed at structuring a series of narratives that display (in his view) a harmonious and peaceful lifestyle existing before Anglo hegemony came into full force in New Mexico. Furthermore, I posit that the response will be different for the "informed reader" (i.e., those with the knowledge of and sensitive to Mexican/Chicano culture) and for the "uninformed reader" (i.e., those lacking this cultural background). On reading his account of a rural lifestyle in which respect for an established hierarchical, patriarchal order and hard work was the order of the day and contrasting it with the historical accounts describing the brash and disruptive actions of Anglo settlers, particularly during the early colonization period (1848 to the early 1900s), the idyllic Mexican American manner of life is depicted as far superior. Ulibarrí need not spell out in detail the destructive onslaught of Anglo colonization; he only has to narrate "the way we were" for his audience, particularly his Chicano audience, to contrast the Anglo hegemonic structures that discriminated against Mexican Americans with the egalitarian Hispanic/Mexican past, a past where Mexican Americans were the majority and were in charge of their own destiny.

Although Ulibarrí is frequently not considered a Chicano militant and has stated that "he is different from many Chicano writers in that he was raised in a majority Hispanic culture and does not have an axe to grind in creating the world of Tierra Amarilla," nevertheless, as Charles M. Tatum has stated in *Chicano Literature: A Reference Guide*, this does not mean he is not socially committed (Martínez and Lomelí 1985: 389). Indeed, I contend that Ulibarrí's stories can be read as part of the militant Chicano literary movement arising in 1965 with the appearance of the Teatro Campesino. The Teatro Campesino was established under the direction of Luis Valdez for the expressed purpose of providing farmworkers with a forum to air their grievances during the drive to establish a labor union in the agricultural fields of California. Thus contemporary Chicano literature arose out of a revolutionary movement that was fighting to secure economic, social, and political justice for *mexicanos*. It has been a resistance literature par excellence that has developed out of a specific political need at a specific historical juncture in time: the turbulent 1960s with the black civil rights movement at its height, the Vietnam War raging in the Far East, the women's movement, and gay and lesbian liberation groups mobilizing to obtain equal rights in American society.

Ulibarrí's political project can be viewed as that of reconstructing a collective memory, of recuperating and restoring a past that defines the present for the collectivity, for the community. He does this through the process of remembering and recapturing the preterit through writing. By reconstructing and reconstituting a past through his personal historical experience, he provides the Hispanic/Chicano community with a linkage to their own history, for in a politically repressed minority community the experience of one is the experience of the many. Ulibarrí, through his personal reminiscences, proffers a history of his people obliterated and silenced by hegemonic society. It is instructive to remember Walter J. Ong's statement vis-à-vis functionally oral cultures and the past.

> Persons whose world view has been formed by high literacy need to remind themselves that in functionally oral cultures the past is not felt as an itemized terrain, peppered with veritable and disputed "facts" or bits of information. It is the domain of the domain of the ancestors, a resonant source for renewing awareness of present existence, which itself is not an itemized terrain either. (1982: 98)

The New Mexican author's first political statement is that of language. For although he is perfectly bilingual, he consciously chooses to write in Spanish. Barbara Harlow underscores the paramount importance of such a choice.

> The very choice of the language in which to compose is itself a political statement on the part of the writer. . . . The debate on language is crucial to a discussion of resistance literature, involving as it does questions of writer and background as well as issues of readership and audience. (1987: XVIII)

To write in Spanish in the United States is a political act, because after the Mexican-American War of 1848 when the Southwest became part of the United States, the suppression and eradication of the Spanish language has been of primary importance in Anglo-American society's drive to assimilate the Spanish-speaking population. And although the Treaty of Guadalupe Hidalgo, signed in 1848 by the U.S. government at the conclusion of the Mexican-American War, guaranteed certain political rights with respect to retention of language, religion, and culture, these guarantees—with the exception of religion—were systematially ignored. Not only has there been a sustained attempt at obliterating the Spanish language from the Mexican-American population (e.g., through punishment of children for speaking Spanish in the schools, laws prohibiting the teaching of Spanish, the English as Official U.S. Language drive [dubbed the English Only drive]) but its marginalization from mainstream society guaranteed the marginalization of poets, novelists, and authors in general who would have preferred the Spanish tongue or could only write in that language. Ulibarrí's choice was, therefore, a political choice of the utmost importance. The renowned Spanish author Angel González underscores this point in his introduction to the collection of poetry, *Al cielo se sube a pie* (1966).

> Ulibarrí presents, above all, an effort—perhaps final?—of an ancient culture that tries to affirm itself and to survive in a hostile environment; a culture oppressed by the weight of a different and irrepressible civilization. Ulibarrí is a direct heir—through tradition—of the language carried to New Mexico by the first Spanish colonizers. He sees today how the language of his childhood and his people is being reduced in his own land to the precarious condition of being a university course, exiled—one could say stripped away—from the people who not very long ago continued to speak it spontaneously. (1966: 7; MY TRANSLATION)

To save the Spanish language in the United States is not an easy task, as González points out.

> It is possible that his [Ulibarrí's] effort will save no one and will condemn his own literature. For to write in a language that is becoming only a memory, surrounded by a people who speak another language, is a difficult as well as a dangerous experience. Ulibarrí is cognizant of this fact, but he nevertheless consciously assumes the risks and difficulties involved because for him it is a matter of personal commitment, not a trivial pursuit: it is a necessity, not just a passing fancy. (IBID., 8; MY TRANSLATION)

In addition, for Ulibarrí's project of recuperation—of the retrieval of memory for an increasingly amnesiac community—it was imperative that he use Spanish, for it was the language of a "glorious" past. It was the language, one must not forget, of the Spanish conqueror who ruthlessly subjugated the Indian populations living in the Southwest. Ulibarrí glosses over this and would have us believe the Spanish and the Indians lived a harmonious existence. He instead underscores the cultured, literary tradition of Spanish letters in the Southwest and points out its continued cultivation.

Ulibarrí is therefore recuperating, to a certain extent, a romanticized past—a "fantasy heritage," as some Chicano scholars have labeled it. However, in spite of this mythicizing process, the project of recuperation was extremely important for the Mexican-American people during the early stages of the Chicano movement, for they were in the process of ethnic bonding and community construction, of "imagining" a new community, applying Benedict Anderson's (1991) phrase. Nevertheless, for this political project to succeed it was imperative for Chicanos to try to recuperate their past since history had been denied to them. Frantz Fanon warns us that the obliteration of the history of the conquered populations has always been a primary goal of the colonizer. Fanon underlines the significance of this strategy in his book, *The Wretched of the Earth*.

> Colonialism is not satisfied merely with holding a people in its grip and emptying the native's head of all form and content. By a kind of perverted logic, it turns to the past of the oppressed people, and distorts, disfigures and destroys it. This work of devaluing pre-colonial history takes on a dialectical significance today. (1978: 210)

Similarly, the political activist Amilcar Cabral reiterates the importance of history in any national liberation movement. "The national liberation of a people is the regaining of the historical personality of that people, it is their return to history through the destruction of the imperialist domination to which they have been subjected" (Harlow 1987: 30). Ulibarrí s "history" of his community embedded within the short stories is not the "official" history of a people but the personal experience narratives that explode on the face of institutionalized documented history and render a more intimate picture of the lives of the people. It is what Harlow calls narratives of resistance, which demand of the reader a historical referencing "and the burden of historical knowledge such referencing enjoins" (ibid., 80). Tatum elaborates on this important aspect of Ulibarrí's prose writings.

> Ulibarrí's prose can best be characterized as a kind of intrahistory, a chronicling and recording of the values, sentiments, relationships, and texture of the daily lives of his friends and family, the Hispanic inhabitants of his beloved Tierra Amarilla. The writer himself has commented that with his short stories he has tried to document the history of the Hispanics of northern New Mexico, the history not yet recorded by the scholars who have written otherwise excellent studies of the region. Ulibarrí believes that these historians do not understand at a deep level the Hispanic heritage that predates by hundreds of years the arrival of the Anglo soldier and businessman in the mid-nineteenth century. He recognizes that the Hispanic world that he knew as a child is fast disappearing under the attack of the aggressive Anglo culture. His stories, then, constitute an attempt to document the *historia sentimental*, the essence of that culture, before it completely disappears. (1985: 388)

Ulibarrí is correct. For presenting the history of a people in charge of their own destiny, working their lands in harmony with their neighbors and the seasons, a people knowledgeable in the ways of nature and at peace with their God, contradicts the negative imagery propagated by the Anglo-American ruling classes, such as those found in many history books. The Chicano historian Rodolfo Acuña has detailed many of these negative conceptualizations of the Mexican people in his book, *Occupied America*. Acuña cites the racist words of California legislator G.B. Tingley, who unabashedly projects an extremely pejorative view of Mexicans and Latinos.

> Devoid of intelligence, sufficient to appreciate the true principles of free government, vicious, indolent, and dishonest, to an extent rendering them obnoxious to our citizens; with habits of life low and degraded; an intellect but one degree above the beast in the field and not susceptible of elevation; all

these things combined render such classes of human beings a curse to any enlightened community. (1988: 113–114)

Acuña further points to a report prepared by Dr. L. Garis of Vanderbilt University for Rep. John Box of Texas (who was lobbying against Mexican immigration) in the 1930s as an example of this type of xenophobic, racist mentality pervading the United States during that period. Garis quoted one of his informants, whom he declared was fairly representative of the Anglo population and their views toward Mexicans.

> "Their [the Mexicans] minds run to nothing higher than animal functions—eat, sleep, and sexual debauchery. In every huddle of Mexican shacks one meets the same idleness, hordes of hungry dogs, and filthy children with faces plastered with flies, disease, lice, human filth, stench, promiscuous fornication, bastardy, lounging, apathetic peons and lazy squaws, beans and dried chili, liquor, general squalor, and envy and hatred of the gringo. These people sleep by day and prowl by night like coyotes, stealing anything they can get their hands on, no matter how useless to them it may be. Nothing left outside is safe unless padlocked or chained down. Yet there are Americans clamoring for more of this human swine to be brought over from Mexico." (IBID., 201)

The anthology *Mi abuela fumaba puros* engages in a dialogue with the official Anglo-American histories of the Southwest; it is the counterhistory of the subaltern, of a conquered population as Rosaura Sánchez and Beatrice Pita phrase it (1992: 5). The New Mexican author, like his predecessor from the late nineteenth century, María Amparo Ruiz de Burton, focuses

> On the demise of a heroic society (the aristocratic/feudal Californios) [;] it differs [from nineteenth-century historical romances] in that it is not written from the perspective of the conquerors with the usual portrayal of a backward people constrained by an outmoded feudal order and unable to cope in the modern post-feudal state. On the contrary, the novel [*The Squatter and the Don*], written from the perspective of the conquered, questions whether the new order indeed brought

progress to the region, and if so, at what cost, in view of the crassness and immorality of much of the invading population, whether squatters or monopolists, its corrupt political leaders and their legislation, and its reprehensible treatment of the conquered. (IBID., 6)

In a similar manner, Ulibarrí's narrative constructs stand in contestatory opposition to Anglo-American historical narratives of the nineteenth and early twentieth century.

I view Ulibarrí's project as veering toward the construction of an ideal community with which the collectivity, that is Chicanos, can identify. (Anglo readers can enjoy the representation of nonstereotypical Mexican Americans.) Keeping in mind Jans Robert Jauss's theories of receptivity where he views a literary work as "an orchestration that strikes ever new resonances among its readers" (1982: 21) and in which the author "predisposes [the] audience to a very special kind of reception by announcements, overt and covert signals, familiar characteristics, or implicit allusions' (23), Ulibarrí employs a series of semiotic codes that are embedded within the text for the reader to decode. These codes consist of folklore motifs, character types, customs and traditions, folk beliefs, and so forth. Through these semiotic codes, the Chicano reader will recognize himself or herself in a new modality and the Anglo reader will gain a new knowledge of a people she or he has often seen represented in a dehumanized caricature.

I find current reader's response theories particularly useful in the analysis of the relationship between Ulibarrí's strategies in embedding his semiotic codes and the reader's task of decoding them and the subsequent responses to these codes. In his *Reception Theory: A Critical Introduction*, Robert C. Holub informs us that

> the function of art. . . is to dehabitualize our perception, to make the object come alive again. The role of the recipient is thus of primary importance; in a certain sense it is the perceiver who determines the artistic quality of the work. For an object can be created as prosaic and perceived as poetic, or conversely, created as poetic and perceived as prosaic. (1985: 17)

Holub was basing his comments on the Russian literary theorist Viktor Shklovskii who has posited,

> This shows that the artistry attributed to the poetry of a given object is the result of our perception; artistic objects, in the narrow sense, are those that are created with special devices whose purpose is that these objects, with the greatest possible certainty, be perceived as artistic. (IBID.)

Holub also based his analysis on Roman Ingarden (1973) who was later to underscore, as Holub states, "intentional or heteronomous" nature of a literary work (i.e., one that is neither deterministic nor autonomous but strictly "dependent on an act of consciousness"). (Ibid., 24) That is to say, in order for the words on a text to come alive, it is necessary that a conscious entity read them. Therefore, according to Ingarden, reader interaction and cognition is absolutely necessary for the literary work to have meaning (1973: 305) He views this process of reader-text interaction as "concretization" of the artwork and used this concept as Holub states "designate the result of actualizing the potentialities, objectifying the seme-units, and concretizing the indeterminacies in a given text" (ibid., 26). Jauss agrees, adding that the reader does not approach the literary work with a blank mind but engages it with what he denominates a "horizon of expectations", which in turn Holub defines as "an intersubjective system or structure of expectations, a 'system of references' or a mind-set that a hypothetical individual might bring to any text" (Holub 59). Jauss further posited the vector of personal experience as an important component in the apprehension of a work during the reading process.

Similarly, Wolfgang Iser focused on the interconnection between reader and text. His principal interest centered on the act of reading as process. Iser based some of his principal theoretical concepts on Ingarden's notion of the aesthetic art object being constituted as an "act of cognition" on the part of the reader, as cited earlier. Iser reiterates the Ingarden notion of the text as being actualized or concretized by the reading subject. However, he insists that "effects and responses are properties neither of the text nor of the reader; the text represents a potential effect that is real-ized in the reading proper" (Iser 1980: ix). To this end, he postu-lates the concept of the "implied reader"—which he defines as "incorporat[ing] both the prestructing of the potential meaning by the text, and the reader's actualization of this potential through the reading process: (ibid., xii). Iser further elaborates that

> the poles of text and reader, together with the interaction that occurs between them, form the ground plan on which a theory of literary communication may be built. . . . It is presumed that the literary work is a form of communication, for it impinges upon the world, upon prevailing social structures, and upon existing literature. Such encroachments consist in the reorganization of those thought systems and social systems invoked by the repertoire of the text; this reorganization reveals the communicatory purpose, and its course is laid down in a wide range of specific instructions. (IBID. IX)

All of the above reader's response theoreticians postulate the interconnection between producer, audience, and text. In empha-sizing this conceptualization of artwork, Holub states, "The art-work becomes an *objet ambigu,* to use Paul Valéry's term, whose construction and cognition depend on the receiver or observer as well as the producer" (1985: 76). And Iser perceives the reader-text interaction as a dialectic process.

> Aesthetic response is therefore to be analyzed in terms of a dialectic relationship between text, reader, and their interaction. It is called aesthetic response because, although it is brought about by the text, it brings into play the imaginative and perceptive faculties of the reader, in order to make him adjust and even differentiate his own focus. (1980: x)

The above reader's response theoretical constructs are impor-tant in our hermeneutical analysis of the incorporation of memory and folklore in Ulibarrí's texts. There will be two kinds of readers who will be reading Ulibarrí's vignettes: those who have a back-ground in Mexican-American folklore and culture and those who do not have such a background. If we adhere to the concepts underlying the reader's response theories cited above, we can postulate that those with a knowledge of Mexican-American culture will have a different "horizon of expectations" than those who do not. Thus the literary work will function differently for the two sets of readers. Both may enjoy the work equally and both may find it aesthetically pleasing (or there is the distinct possibility that they may not find pleasure in the work). However, it is my contention that those with a greater knowledge of folklore and Mexican/Chicano culture (most particularly if they learned this during their childhood from their parents, other relatives, or neighbors) will experience a reader's response different from those without folklore or Mexican cultural experiences. In this sense the culturally aware Mexican-American reader more closely fulfills Stanley Fish's concept of the "informed reader."

> The informed reader is someone who 1.) is a competent
> speaker of the language out of which the text is built up. 2.) is
> in full possession of "semantic knowledge that a mature . . .
> listener brings to this task of comprehension." This includes
> the knowledge (that is, the experience, both as a producer and
> comprehender) of lexical sets, collocation probabilities, idioms,
> professional and other dialects, etc. 3.) has *literary*
> competence. . . . The reader, of whose responses I speak, then,
> is this informed reader, neither an abstraction, nor an actual
> living reader, but a hybrid—a real reader (me) who does
> everything within his power to make himself informed. (1970:
> 145: SEE ALSO ISER 1980: 31)

This is because a reader with a Mexican-American cultural background will experience self-recognition and will identify with the characters and situations in the text. While the reader lacking a folkloristic background may derive great pleasure from the text for other reasons, for example, the novelty of the experience, seeing a more "exotic" culture than their own, learning a new culture, the response nevertheless will be different. The most plausible outcome of positive self-recognition (as opposed to negative self-recognition, which would elicit a "resisting reader" as Judith Fetterly has elaborated in her book, *The Resisting Reader*) in

Ulibarrí's text is a pleasurable experience. I believe that for Mexican Americans, this self-recognition and self-identification aids in the construction of community, in the "imagining" of community as cited earlier (see Anderson 1991). (Even in those cases in which the literature presented evokes painful experiences, self-recognition and self-identification produce group solidarity and sense of community, ethnic bonding in the reader.) For in seeing the folk experiences depicted in Ulibarrí's text, Chicanos/as will recognize their own experiences, their own selves. In the following pages I will examine some of these folk characters and folk motifs that Ulibarrí has included in his short stories which serve as cultural markers or cultural codes (Iser refers to them as readers' guides) that are designed to involve the Chicano reader in a Mexican-American consciousness of community and of self.

LA LLORONA

The legend of La Llorona (the Weeping Woman) is one of the most widely known folk narratives among Mexicans and Chicanos. Most recently, Clarissa Pinkola Estés includes in her best-selling book, *Women Who Run with the Wolves*, a chapter entitled "Clear Water: Nourishing the Creative Life" in which she discusses and updates the La Llorona legend. Pinkola Estés first cites the various versions of the Weeping Woman legend she had heard as a child:

> [La Llorona appearing] as the female protagonist in a union-busting war in the north woods . . . La Llorona dealing with an antagonist involved in the forced repatriation of Mexicans from the United States in the 1950s . . . La Llorona from the old Spanish Land Grants farmers, who said she was involved in the land grant wars in New Mexico. (1992: 301)

The most recent La Llorona tales heard by Pinkola Estés are truly startling: "La Llorona wanders and wails through a trailer park at night. [La Llorona] as 'a prostitute with AIDS' . . . plies her trade down at the town River in Austin" (ibid., 301). And here is the final contemporary version supplied by Pinkola Estés as told to her by a ten-year-old informant who insisted La Llorona had not killed her children:

La Llorona went with a rich *hidalgo* who had factories on the river. But something went wrong. During her pregnancy La Llorona drank from the river. Her babies, twin boys, were born blind and with webbed fingers, for the *hidalgo* had poisoned the river with the waste from his factories.

The *hidalgo* told La Llorona he didn't want her or her babies. He married a rich woman who wanted the things the factory manufactured. La Llorona threw the babies into the river because they would have such a hard life. Then she fell down dead from grief. She went to heaven but Saint Peter told her she could not come into heaven until she found the souls of her sons. Now La Llorona looks and looks through the polluted river for her children, but she can hardly see, for the water is so dirty and dark. Now her ghost drags the river bottom with her long fingers. Now she wanders the riverbanks calling for her children all the time. (IBID., 302–3)

There are two strands to the legend of La Llorona: one deriving from the Mexica Colhua (Aztec) tradition and one from the European and colonial Mexican period. The Weeping Woman legend associted with the Aztecs narrates the wailing of a woman dressed in white and running in the middle of the night through the streets of the ancient Aztec capital of Tenochtlitán. Her wails predict the loss of the Aztec empire, the loss of her children through the destruction of the conquest that was to come (se Anderson and Dibble 1950; Book I: 3–5). The second strand derived from European folk legends describes how a *mestiza* falls in love with a Spaniard and has children by him. The Spaniard does not marry her but instead marries a Spanish woman. The spurned *mestiza*, in a fit of revenge at her lover's betrayal and inconstancy, murders their children. Cognizant of her deed, she goes insane and is doomed to wail in the night "¡Ayyyy mis hijos!" (Ohhhh, my children!), forever looking for her lost children (see Arizpe 1963: 7–12).

Ulibarrí provides us with a new version of La Llorona. In his chapter "Witcheries or Tomfooleries?" the New Mexican author writes,

Another mysterious figure that appears from time to time in the villages of the north to give people something to talk about is La Llorona. She is a traditional and folkloric personage.

I don't know the real history of this unreal woman. I only
know that she is a nebulous figure that appears at night and
wails like a lost soul. Naturally everyone is afraid of her because
she brings with her all the terror that lies beyond the grave.

When Ulibarrí's narrator hears La Llorona's wail, it becomes a
supernatural experience involving a wide spectrum of emotions:

I breathed and palpitated to the rhythm of the melodic spirals
and arabesques that rose and fell, that sometimes pierced the
heavens, sometimes the earth. Now with joy, now with
delirium, now with grief.
    The lament was a chant. Studied, disciplined, orchestrated.
The measures were punctuated with fleecy sobs and metallic
tears. The rhythm, rhapsodic and hysterical, kept pure with
the guitar of the diaphragm. Every note a spasm. Every pause a
wound. Trills in the throat that were gasps of agony. (IBID., 51)

As it turned out, the wails were emanating from a poor, mentally retarded woman named Atanacia, who was crying out because the narrator's dogs were attacking her. Atanacia was the
abused wife of a man who constantly left her alone as he enjoyed
himself at bars and with other women. Atanacia, through the figure of La Llorona, sought to scare her husband into staying at home
with her. This "feminist" version in which the normally passive
woman becomes an active agent confirms José Limón's thesis that
La Llorona can be perceived first as

a positive, contestative symbol for the women of Greater
Mexico and second as a critical symbolic reproduction of a
socially unfulfilled utopian longing within Mexican folk
masses who tell her story. She speaks to the social and
psychological needs of both Greater Mexican sectors, needs left
unmet by the hegemonic, hierarchical, masculinized, and
increasing capitalistic social order imposed on the Mexican
folk masses since their beginning. (1986: 60)

More specifically, Limón posits that "to this extent [the in-
fanticidal act committed by La Llorona], it is here that the legend poses a more fundamental oppositional threat to men

because by her act she symbolically destroys the familial basis for patriarchy" (ibid., 76).

Limón, nevertheless, sees the above as "too simple a reading," which tends to follow too mechanistically Friedrich Engels's conceptualization of the bourgeois family. He therefore amplifies:

> We must remember the most often neglected motif in this legend, namely that she also continues to search for her children near a body of water which, if I may take Freud as my authority in this feminist analysis is, in folklore, intimately associated with birth. As such, I submit that La Llorona offers us a fascinating paradox: the symbolic destruction of the nuclear family at one state, and the later possible restoration of their maternal bonds from the waters of rebirth as a second state. One must conclude that waters will also heal her patriarchally induced insanity. (IBID., 76)

As can be surmised, the La Llorona legend is an open-ended narrative with numerous possibilities of interpretation. It is a narrative well known to Mexican/Chicano children. A great number of Chicano/a artists such as Rudolfo Anaya, Alejandro Morales, Alurista, Sandra Cisneros, and Mónica Palacios have been inspired by her creative power and have weaved the La Llorona narrative within their oeuvres. It is a powerful icon within the Mexican/Chicano culture that through the Weeping Woman's wail speaks for the weak and disenfranchised in Mexico and the United States. As Limón phrases it,

> Symbolically, this motif seems to suggest that the utopian renewal of a recovered Mexico with her children pointedly excludes the reappearance of a masculinized hierarchical, treacherous class authority. Power as patriarchy must be destroyed if a new social order is to re-emerge and survive in Greater Mexico, one that, in the most powerful kind of feminism, speaks not only of women but through the power of women for *all* of the socially weak. (IBID., 88)

In Ulibarrí's presentation of La Llorona, the possibility of liberation for Atanacia is truncated. However, because of the open-endedness of the Weeping Woman legend (and of the narrative), the possibilities remain endless. The reader acquainted with this open-endedness responds with hope and optimism for the future of the weak and repressed. Thus the Weeping Woman narrative aids in the construction of community through identification with a cultural icon that offers the possibility of redemption to her orphaned and lost children. Chicanos have come to identify themselves as sons and daughters of La Llorona and thus to see themselves as brothers and sisters.

In addition to the Weeping Woman legend, Ulibarrí recounts encounters with the devil. This experience entails the devil playing tricks on him while he is descending from the mountains with a pack of animals on a rainy day.

> They say animals can see the devil, or feel his presence, when we cannot.
> My horse was trembling from head to foot. He snorted. He squirmed. And squirmed again. Wanting to soothe him I stroked his neck. A living flame of light would sprout from my hand. I felt electrical stabs over my entire body. My two dogs, so very brave before, were now cowards. . . . According to tradition, the devil was riding along with me and amusing himself at my expense. The animals knew it. (Ulibarrí 1977: 39)

Other examples of folk beliefs include the narrator's experience with the "witch" Matilde, the supposed black magic (*mal puesto*) done on his invalid uncle (who probably had poliomyelitis, according to the narrator), the belief that witches assume the form of owls, and the charismatic *sanador*, or folk healer.

An interesting folk tradition described by Ulibarrí is that of the Penitentes. The author holds a very positive view of this Catholic religious brotherhood. He sees them as a "disciplined organism" that aided in maintaining the religious tradition of Catholic Spain in the isolated villages of New Mexico. They filled the "administrative, religious and cultural vacuum." They provided government for the community and maintained public order; they "served to establish communication, harmony and union among the diverse and scattered villages" (Ibid., 159). The Penitentes were in charge of educating the faithful and thus promoting standard Spanish through religious instruction. They are best known for the torture they inflicted on themselves during Lent (see Chávez 1986). The narrator views them as strong, upright, religious men who should be admired instead of maltreated.

FOLK CHARACTERS

With a few masterful strokes, Ulibarrí delineates folk characters of mythic proportions. This is in keeping with the type of world the author wants to represent—a world in which the Mexican American is strong, intelligent, and in charge of his or her own life but is simultaneously leading a simple, upright life. Such is the figure of the grandmother who smokes cigars, Grandmother Turriaga, the protagonist of the narrative by that same title. Grandmother Turriaga was a woman whose life and manner of being radically departs from the stereotypical imagery of women rendered in the literature written by Anglo journalists, writers, and travelers passing through or settling in the Southwest during the second half of the nineteenth century and the early twentieth century (see Paredes 1977; Robinson 1977; Mirandé and Enríquez 1979; Pettit 1980; and De León 1983). Ulibarrí depicts life in New Mexico at the turn of the century. This was a period when Anglo-American settlers had not completely appropriated New Mexico; they considered it less attractive than California or Texas. Its mountains and arid deserts together with the substantial number of Native Americans and Mexican Americans living there deterred the new colonizers from rapidly taking over the region. Thus Hispanics in that state were able to retain their lands for a longer period of time. The Turriaga family is a ranching family with cattle, sheep, and large tracts of land. They were more or less similar to the *hacendado* families (those owning large landed estates) in Mexico, where the *patrón* (employer) rules with paternal kindness in the best of cases. Ulibarrí provides us with a hint of the relationship between *patrón* and ranch hand in his comments on the smoking (or nonsmoking) of cigars.

My grandfather smoked cigars. The cigar was the symbol and the badge of the feudal lord, the *patrón*. When on occasion he would give a cigar to the foreman or to one of the hands on impulse or as a reward for a task well done, the transfiguration of those fellows was something to see. To suck on that tobacco was to drink from the fountain of power. The cigar gave you class. (1977: 19)

The narrator's grandmother, as the title indicates, smoked cigars and thus metonymically was part of the power structure of that world.

She was strong. As strong as only she could be. Through the years, in so many situations, small and big tragedies, accidents and problems, I never saw her bend or fold. Fundamentally, she was serious and formal. . . .

The ranch was big business. The family was large and problematic. She ran her empire with a sure and firm hand. Never was there any doubt about where her affairs were going nor who held the reins. (IBID., 19)

The woman described as "straight, tall and slender" is rendered in mythic proportions. She is a tower of strength, far from the negative stereotypes of the passive, dirty, promiscuous women Yankee travelers described to their readership on the East Coast. Through the recounting of his family life, Ulibarrí reconstructs a period of history from the perspective of the colonized. His vignettes seek to erase the distortions and misrepresentations of his people. Life before Anglo incursions was paradisiacal; New Mexico was a land of milk and honey.

When my parents married they built their home next to the old family house. I grew up on the windy hill in the center of the valley of Las Nutrias, with pine trees on all the horizons, with the stream full of beaver, trout and suckers, the sagebrush full of rabbits and coyotes, stock everywhere, squirrels and owls in the bars. (IBID., 21)

Equally arresting is the figure of Uncle Cirilio, the sheriff of Río Arriba County. Sheriff Cirilio was big, fat, and strong, and the entire valley respected and feared him. He carried the law in his face and his muscular strength; his presence was sufficient to bring peace and quiet into any situation. Again, Cirilio subverts the commonplace stereotypical imagery of the criminal Mexican. Cirilio is the law, and valley people are law-abiding citizens.

Racial harmony is proffered through the folk figure of El Negro Aguilar, a black cowboy who is represented as being bigger than life. El Negro Aguilar is skillful at cowboy tasks: roping, branding, castrating bulls, stretching barbwire for fences, cutting pine trees for the mill, making adobes. "He was the master of all the arts" (ibid., 73). The fact that he was black is overlooked in the valley, where the color of the skin was of small importance. According to Ulibarrí,

> I don't think anyone ever noticed it. I know I didn't. We have never had, nor do we now have, that terrible obsession the Anglo-Saxon has over the color of the skin. With us it would be absurd. In any one of our families we have the whole gamut of human pigmentation, from the lily white to the darkly brown, from the bluest eyes and blondest hair, to the blackest eyes and hair. (IBID., 73)

Ulibarrí posits a harmonious world. A world of law and order, discipline, love, and respect. A world in which all are hardworking citizens happy with their status in life: the cattleman, the sheepherder, the ranch hand, the sheriff, the housewife all know their place in society and live in peace and tranquility with each other. It is an ideal, paradisiacal world that Ulibarrí remembers and seeks to convey to his readers.

CONCLUSION

Iser's reader's response theories are based on the premise that reading is a communicative act. Applying J.L. Austin and John Searle's postulates in regard to the illocutionary act that in their speech act theory involves a performative act (this illocutionary act by its force is designed to elicit a response from the listener), Iser underscores the importance of the reading subject in the production of meaning. Meaning, Iser stresses, arises from the situational context of the reader and the reading of the text (see Iser

1980; Holub 1985: 86). In Iser's seminal study, *The Act of Reading*, he elucidates.

> The language of literature resembles the mode of the illocutionary act, but has a different function. As we have seen, the success of a linguistic action depends on the resolution of indeterminacies by means of conventions, procedures, and guarantees of sincerity. These form the frame of reference within which the speech act can be resolved into a context of action. Literary texts also require a resolution of indeterminacies but, by definition, for fiction there can be no such given frames of reference. On the contrary, the reader must first discover for himself the code underlying the text, and this is tantamount to bringing out the meaning. (1980: 60)

It is my position that it is precisely through the underlying codes structured by means of folkloric entities and customs that the Mexican-American reader, with his or her rich heritage of cultural traditions, many based on this same oral tradition and folklore extant in the text, is able to easily identify with the world represented in the short stories. This identification with the "others" in the text enables the Chicano/a reader to begin to form a sense of community. Thus the identification of an imaginary community such as Aztlán begins to form with the reading of such texts as Ulibarrí's. The reader begins to recognize others in the text who are very much like him or her. The Texas Mexican, the *Coloradense*, the Californio, the New Mexican, and the *Arisoniano* all share in small or great amounts part of these Mexican and Mexican-American oral traditions. Ulibarrí is cognizant of these when he states,

> My memory recalled things never seen, never heard. My intelligence recognized segments of the unknown. My body, my blood and my nerves harmonized with echoes and resonances of a past beyond my own. (1977: 53–55)

Later in the same story Ulibarrí questions,

> Is it that there is a heritage, an intrahistory, that has nothing to do with biology or with intelligence, that flows unknown

from generation to generation? Something that one carries in his blood? (IBID., 55)

The New Mexican author is positing here a hypothetical Jungian collective unconscious. Jung's theory of archetypes defines archetypes as part of the structure of our unconscious which are stimulated to manifest themselves during certain periods of mental activity such as the creative process. Many of these archetypal images, according to Jung, are the same for all humans and are stimulated to appear within certain historical contexts.

I am not positing here a Jungian collective unconscious. What I do contend in this study is that the folk genres and folk motifs described by Ulibarrí form part of the Mexican-American cultural experience (and to necessarily part of the collective unconscious) and thus serve as unifying elements in our construction of community or in the process of what I call ethnic bonding.

Ulibarrí is aware of his role as a "historian" for his people—of chronicling reconstituting, and bringing back to life a past that he cherished and perceived as positive. In his last vignette, "The Penitentes," he explicitly states,

> In my old age I look back on what was the life and history of
> Tierra Amarilla. Across so many memories, so much sympathy
> and a little antipathy here and there, there appears in the eyes
> of my affection a living mosaic, lovely in every way, pleasant
> in every way. In it there are beloved figures, deeply felt
> incidents and accidents, remembered contours. . . . A human
> landscape, animated and lively. The palpitating and dramatic
> representation of what one day was, today is, and tomorrow
> ought to be. (IBID., 157)

Ulibarrí's personal memories and personal history are what Iser denominates as "familiar territory." Holub amplifies what it is in this familiar territory where "text and reader meet to initiate communication" (Holub 1985: 86–87). However, Ulibarrí has organized this "familiar territory" in an unfamiliar context—the written word, a literary production. Thus fulfilling Iser's dictum that literature should be structured such that the reader "is forced to produce the meaning of the text under *unfamiliar* conditions, rather than under his own conditions (analogizing), that he can bring to light a layer of his personality that he had previously been unable to formulate in his conscious mind" (1980: 50). For the Mexican-American writer there is a double task in recuperating a lost oral, literary, and cultural heritage. This lost Hispanic/Mexican heritage that had been denigrated by hegemonic Anglo society must be reframed in a different context. The written literary text affords this venue, for through writing, which is a privileged mode of expression in Western society, a cultural heritage is recuperated and reevaluated. Writers such as Ulibarrí perform this function as literary scribes who recapture a long-forgotten past for the enjoyment and edification of people. In this respect the author is constructing a larger community, for through the pleasure of the text, borrowing a Barthian phrase, the human spirit soars to greater heights and is offered the possibility of communicating with the Other.

WORKS CITED

Acuña, Rodolfo. *Occupied America: A History of Chicanos*. New York: Harper Collins, 1988.

Alurista. "must be the season of the witch." *Fiesta in Aztlán: An Anthology of Chicano Poetry*. Santa Barbara: Capra Press, 1981. P. 83.

Anaya, Rudolfo. *Bless Me, Ultima*. Berkeley: Tonatiuh–Quinto Sol, 1972.

———. *The Season of La Llorona*. One-act play produced by El Teatro de la Compañía de Albuquerque, October 14, 1979.

———. *Heart of Aztlán*. Berkeley: Justa, 1976.

———. *The Legend of La Llorona*. Berkeley: Tonatiuh–Quinto Sol, 1984.

Anderson, Arthur and Charles Dibble. *Florentine Codex (General History of the Things of New Spain)* by Fray Bernardino Sahagún. Santa Fe, 1950.

Anderson, Benedict. *Imagined Communities: Reflections on the Origin and Spread of Nationalism*. New York: Verso, 1991.

Arizpe, Artemio de Valle. "La Llorona." In *Leyendas y sucedidos del México colonial*. México, D.F.: El Libro Español, 1963. Pp. 7–12.

Barakat, Robert A. "Aztec Motifs in La Llorona." *Southern Folklore Quarterly*, 29(1965):288–96.

Burton, María Amparo Ruiz de. *The Squatter and the Don*. Houston: Arte Público Press, 1992.

Chávez, Fray Angélico. *My Penitente Land: The Soul Story of Spanish New Mexico*. Santa Fe, New Mex.: William Gannon, 1986.

Cisneros, Sandra. *Woman Hollering Creek and Other Stories*. New York: Random House, 1991.

De Aragón, Ray John. *The Legend of La Llorona*. Las Vegas, New Mex.: Pan American Publishing Co. 1980.

De León, Arnoldo. *Greasers: Anglo Attitudes toward Mexicans in Texas, 1821–1900*. Austin: University of Texas Press, 1983.

Estés, Clarissa Pinkola. *Women Who Run with the Wolves: Myths and Stories of the Wild Woman Archetype*. New York: Ballantine Books, 1992.

Fanon, Frantz. *The Wretched of the Earth*. New York: Grove Press, 1978.

Fetterly, Judith. *The Resisting Reader: A Feminist Approach to American Fiction*. Bloomington: Indiana University Press, 1981.

Fish, Stanley. "Literature in the Reader: Affective Stylistics." *New Literary History*, 2(1970):123–60.

Harlow, Barbara. *Resistance Literature*. New York: Methuen, 1987.

Hernández, Guillermo E. *Chicano Satire: A Study in Literary Culture*. Austin: University of Texas Press, 1991.

Holub, Robert C. *Reception Theory: A Critical Introduction*. New York: Methuen, 1985.

Horcasitas, Fernando, and Douglas Butterworth. "La Llorona." *Tlalocan: Revista de Fuentes para el Conocimiento de las Culturas Indígenas de México*, 4(1963):204–24.

Ingarden, Roman. *The Literary Work of Art*. Evanston: Northwestern University Press, 1973.

Iser, Wolfgang. *The Act of Reading: A Theory of Aesthetic Response*. Baltimore: Johns Hopkins University Press, 1980.

Jauss, Hans Robert. *Toward an Aesthetic of Reception*. trans. Timothy Bahti. Minneapolis: University of Minnesota Press, 1982.

Kearney, Michael. "La Llorona as a Social Symbol." *Western Folklore*, 27(1968):199–206.

Kirtley, Bacil F. "La Llorona and Related Themes." *Western Folklore*, 19(1960):155–68.

Kraul, Edward García, and Judith Beatty, eds. *The Weeping Woman: Encounters with La Llorona*. Santa Fe, New Mex.: Word Process, 1988.

Leddy, Betty. "La Llorona in Southern Arizona. *Western Folklore*, 7(1948):272–77.

Limón, José. "La Llorona, The Third Legend of Cultural Symbols, Women and the Political Unconscious." In *Renato Rosaldo Lecture Series* Monograph. Vol. 2, 1986:59–93.

Lyon, Fern. "Review of *Mi abuela fumaba puros. New Mexico Magazine*, 56(1978):2–33.

Martínez, Julio A, and Francisco Lomelí. *Chicano Literature: A Reference Guide*. Westport, Conn.: Greenwood Press, 1985.

Miller, Elaine. *Mexican Folk Narrative from the Los Angeles Area*. Austin: University of Texas Press, 1973.

Mirandé, Alfredo, and Evangelina Enríquez. *La Chicana: The Mexican American Woman*. Chicago: University of Chicago Press, 1979.

Morales, Alejandro. *Caras viejas y vino nuevo*. México: Editorial Joaquín Mortiz, 1975.

Ong, Walter J. *Orality and Literacy: The Technologizing of the Word*. New York: Methuen, 1982.

Palacios, Mónica. "La Llorona Loca: The Other Side." In *The Chicana Lesbians: The Girls Our Mothers Warned Us About*. Berkeley: Third Woman Press, 1991.

Paredes, Américo. *With His Pistol in His Hand: A Border Ballad and Its Hero.* Austin: University of Texas Press, 1958.

———. "Folk Medicine and the Intercultural Jest." In *Spanish-speaking People in the United States*, Proceedings of the 1968 Annual Meeting of the American Ethnological Society. Seattle: n.p., Spring 1968. Pp. 104–19.

———. "Mexican Legendry and the Rise of the Mestizo." In *American folk Legend: A Symposium*, 97–107. ed. Wayland D. Hand, Berkeley and Los Angeles: University of California Press, 1971.

Paredes, Raymund. "The Origins of Anti-Mexican Sentiment in the United States." *New Scholar*, 6(1977):139–66.

Pettit, Arthur G. *Images of the Mexican American in Fiction and Film.* College Station, Texas: Texas A&M University Press, 1980.

Rámirez, Arturo. "Review of *Mi abuela fumaba puros. Caracol.* 4, no. 6(1978):7.

Reyna, José R. *Raza Humor: Chicano Joke Tradition in Texas.* San Antonio: Penca Books, 1980.

Robinson, Cecil. *Mexico and the Hispanic Southwest in American Literature.* Tucson: University of Arizona Press, 1977.

Saldívar, Ramón. *Chicano Narrative: The Dialectics of Difference.* Madison: University of Wisconsin Press, 1990.

Sánchez, Rosaura and Beatrice Pita. "Introduction to *The Squatter and the Don.* Houston: Arte Público Press, 1992. Pp. 5–51.

Tatum, Charles M. Review of *Mi abuela fumaba puros. World Literature Today*, 52(1978):440.

Tatum, Charles M. "Sabine Ulibarrí." In *Chicano Literature: A Reference Guide.* Edited by Julio A. Martínez and Francisco A. Lomelí. Westport, CT: Greenwood Press, 1985. Pp. 384–95.

Ulibarrí, Sabine R. *Tierra Amarilla: Cuenos de Nuevo México.* Quito: Editorial Casa de la Cultura Ecuatoriana, 1964.

———. *Al cielo se sube a pie.* Madrid: Alfaguara, 1966.

———. *Amor y Ecuador.* Madrid: Ediciones José Porrúa Turanzas, 1966.

———. *Mi abuela fumaba puros/My Grandma Smoked Cigars.* Berkeley: Quinto Sol Publications, 1977.

———. *Governor Glu Glu and Other Stories/El gobernador Glu Glu y otros cuentos.* Tempe: Bilingual Press/Editorial Bilingüe, 1988.

THROUGH THE EYE OF THE CONDOR
The Limitless Horizons of Literary Space

Bruce-Novoa

In 1966, Sabine Ulibarrí published his second volume of poetry, *Amor y Ecuador*, in part the product of his experiences in that Latin American country as the head of a U.S. government-sponsored language institute in 1963–64. Later, in 1969, when the University of New Mexico founded its Andean Center in Quito, he returned to Ecuador to direct the new program. His affection for the country has drawn him back repeatedly over the years, both to the actual geographic site and to his memory of it as a literary re-creation within his writing. In 1989, he returned again in the form of a short story, "El Cóndor," which also became the title piece of the collection in which it appeared. As Reynaldo Ruiz (1989: 264) observes, Ecuador has influenced Ulibarrí in a variety of ways. In this essay, more than the influence Ecuador has exercised on Ulibarrí, I explore his return to it as the symbolic setting for the pursuit of an obsession with an ever-elusive *causa sui* project: to harmonize his ideal of personal transcendence with the perception of reality as a system of social and physical limitations.

PROJECT

A convincing case can be made for a persistent underlying dual focus in Ulibarrí's work: (a) a recognition of the human condition of alienation that separates people into individuals destined to death or

83

separates groups into factions, which is held in constant tension with (b) a desire to break out of alienation by melding into a higher spiritual harmony with transcendent life forces. It is the classic contest between the concrete and the ideal, between body and soul, Thanatos and Eros. This conflictive duality most often assumes the shape of a structural opposition, which in turn produces the implicit goal of balancing his concerns in a total perspective within which both sides would be expressed yet accommodated so as not to mutually exclude each other and flow in a relationship of problem and resolution. We can, then, identify this goal as Ulibarrí's *causa sui* project.

If we contextualize Ulibarrí within the prevailing philosophical trends that formed and informed him, his orientation and the project make sense. The product of his time and training, he personifies what we used to call existential anxiety—but shaped in the particular Iberian tradition of Miguel de Unamuno, Antonio Machado, and Juan Ramón Jiménez, itself heavily influenced by Kierkegaard. These were the authors of his doctoral studies in the mid-1950s, the post–World War II years when existential literary interpretation was at its zenith. These were the days of discussion of humankind's fatal inability to escape its circumstances and hence the need to come to grips consciously with the dynamics of the specific condition of existence in an always contingent reality; and while accepting the absurd necessity of being bound to a situation not of one's making, to rise above contingency through a perhaps futile but nevertheless noble integrity of purpose and action aimed at asserting human dignity in the face of the meaningless void of existence. There was a conflict between a commitment to social conditions firmly rooted in the acceptance of alienation and otherness and a desire for transcendence through some ideal sharing of the human condition as a project in and of itself. Literature was read as the playing out of these philosophical questions. These were the concepts culled form Camus, Sartre, Kierkegaard, Unamuno, and Ortega y Gasset.

WRITINGS

Ulibarrí's first book of poetry, *Al cielo se sube a pie* (Heaven Is Reached on Foot; 1966) has been characterized as a struggle between the "awareness of his identity and standing in life, and his incessant drive to reach and merge with the essence of love, beauty, and life" (Ruiz 1989: 263). The title itself encapsulates the conflict between transterrestrial desire of ideal transcendence and limited and limiting terrestrial means for its realization available to the author. Significantly, the dilemma is stated as one between the ethereal heaven, a space of disembodies souls, and a human appendage synecdochical for the physical body. The task is to find the alluded-to path that would link the physical and spiritual realms. Implicitly it also emphasizes the desire to unify the two realms by allowing the body to exceed its usual confines and cross over into the soul's exclusive domain, thus transcending the separation; in other words, to deny death its due. From the start, thus, Ulibarrí was concerned with breaking the boundaries of what Kierkegaard called Philistinism, life retained within a prescribed set of social regulations that ensure against too much freedom and dangerous flights of intense experience that might upset the precarious balance considered rational and normal (Kierkegaard 1954: 174–75).

When he wrote *Al cielo*, however, Ulibarrí seemed to accept the existential fate of being incapable of creating anything significantly beyond a statement of the problem. While writing was the chosen means of expressing his insight into the human condition, the text, with its space and reality, is not perceived as an alternative to that condition. Writing was still anchored in the same dilemma of reality, seen as a documentation of the inexorability of time, distance, and rational logic, the traditional foes of desire and the ideal.

Tierra Amarilla: Cuentos de Nuevo México ([1964] 1971) might be seen to have swung widely toward the reality pole of the worldly circumstances, with stories set in Ulibarrí's native region. Yet there filters through his constant desire to transcend limiting definitions of the self. The author explores different alternatives to prescriptive social circumstances, from actually running away from social harassment in "Forge without Fire" to the perhaps momentary, yet profoundly significant, feeling of self and communal affirmation experienced by an adolescent boy when he successfully performs a rite of passage by capturing and breaking a wild horse in "My Wonder Horse." Perhaps for the analysis at hand the most interesting piece is "Man without a Name" in which Ulibarrí begins to explore the possibility of literary creation as a reality itself, one in and through which an alternative identity can be forged.

It signals the intuition of a response to the existential insistence on the acceptance of the reality of a given situation as the initial and necessary step in exercising the freedom to choose another line of development. Writing is postulated as another type of existence, a space where things can be created and re-created according to the logic of language and, particularly significant, of desire. This implies that things do not have to be as they are given in society but can be restructured according to the creative will. While this discovery occupied only a fraction of *Tierra Amarilla*, Ulibarrí returned to it later in his career.

Amor y Ecuador (Love and Ecuador) featured the same tension between the opposing camps in Ulibarrí's world vision, the title itself accurately identifying the two sections of the collection, though inverting the order in which they appear. While his fascination with Ecuador inspired in him the sympathetic rendering of its landscape and inhabitants in terms of experiencing a profound revelation, the second section on love might seem an afterthought, an escape to another space more trivial and superficial, attached to "Ecuador" only by the coincidence of sharing the same binding. The sections seem of equal weight in the text, almost balanced: "Amor" contains twenty-six poems on the same number of pages, while "Ecuador" has two less poems but distributed over thirty-one pages. They could be treated as two separate texts, but knowing as we do the thematic duality of Ulibarrí's writing, we understand that once again he is juxtaposing a focus on social and physical circumstance and the quest for union through an encounter with the ideal order, love. If something binds the two sections, it is the motif of Ulibarrí's poetic persona searching for a revelatory experience that, once glimpsed, disappointingly leads to a sense of failure: the persona cannot successfully bond with the desired objects, and so the epiphanic moment of union experienced in Ecuador slips away, leading the persona in pursuit of a more traditionally represented loved one in "Amor," although with the same results. Far from the second being a mere escape, however, it is the logical, even desperate, refuge sought by the persona inspired and then frustrated by the ephemeral revelation of significance and purpose.

In "Ecuador," the book's opening section, the persona introduces himself in a moment of Kierkegaardian liberation: he anticipates an adventure awaiting him on a journey taking him beyond his accustomed identity. He feels exalted, leaving behind his past and traveling toward undefined possibilities of change, a dynamic expressed in terms of moving between the familiar poles of his thought: reality and the suppressed—dreamed—ideal. "Me siento ligero, / libra . . . Abajo mis penas, / mis dudas y miedos. / Arriba mis sueños" (I, "Destinación Quito," 13). He looks forward to a new, unknown experience, while simultaneously escaping his existential circumstance: "Allá me espera / un misterio. / Atrás dejo / una historia" (II, "Panagra," 14). Significantly, through the use of "mystery" and "history," Ulibarrí opposes here poetry and prose: the concentrated power of the poetic image, which supersedes the limits of time and space, the place itself beyond the realm of logical relationships of temporal and spatial causality, versus the dissipated and extended—read alienated—dispersion of narrative based on sequential relationships strung out over time and space in logical cause-and-effect patterns. Ulibarrí thus stages the adventure into liberation in terms of the same oppositional forces of social reality and ideal we have already discussed.

When that anticipated mystery allows itself to be glimpsed, Ulibarrí renders it in a divine, mythical form: "oí el resplandor de Dios," which is linked immediately to the Native American, "Vi la sombra de su voz / indígena en la alta cumbre" (VII, "Quito," 20). Ulibarrí constructs here a link between a transcendent element—stylistically supported by the synesthetic fusion of the visual and auditory senses—and society in an intuition of unity hiding in the Ecuadorean experience. This point is essential: the epiphany is not given in the same terms of mystery versus history but of the mystery of history, or the historical mystery. We could call it the historical tradition of indigenous myth. Ulibarrí's persona is privileged with a vision of the transcending connectedness of what history as he has lived it tends to disperse, fragment, and place beyond human reach. But as we might expect, the glimpse of harmony again proves ephemeral, closing back on itself. The longing to hold the epiphany, however, endures far beyond the encounter, spilling over into the next poem. And in a move that prefigures that of the difference between sections, the persona recasts the adventure in the form of another motif, the flirtatious promise of an amorous encounter:

> En un recinto de Quito
> le sorprendí una sonrisa
> a la rosa de los mitos.
>   En un instante se esquiva
> por la rendija sumisa
> de la tarde y de la brisa.
>   Es circunscrito el ratito,
> tan quebradizo e impreciso,
> como un guiño del destino.
>   Día y noche vivo y muero
> en perpetuo devaneo
> y ansias de volver a verlo.
>   (IX, 21)

This linkage of the two major thematic lines is crucial, for although on first impression *Amor y Ecuador* maintains the separation, we find Ulibarrí constructing bridges through imagery and a pattern of taking refuge in carnal love when the ideal of a more spiritual desire evades him. Significantly, the bridging project arises from stylistic and formal devices, as opposed to what we could call observations of social reality. That is to say, the persona's observations and commentaries on Ecuadorean society do not discover linkages but the opposite. In Poem X, "En Ecuador," the persona claims that everything in the country humanizes him—that is, it has a unifying effect on him—yet his enumeration of the facets that impress him includes no conjunctions of linkage, no blending grammatical structures. The features are separated into those of the lower and upper social classes: the servants and the friends; the poor, the Indians, and arrogant aristocracy. The persona recognizes that in Ecuadorean society binary opposites are strictly divided, yet in him they blend. The writing persona is the space of confluence.

In the very center of the "Ecuador" section, Poem XII, "Indosincrasia," and XIII, "Indio de Otavalo" (25–26), the Native American appears, depicted in generally sympathetic terms, although with a pathetic emphasis in the first poem that then shifts to romantic idealization in the second. They first emerge as slaves marching through time, an image clearly conveyed by the following key characterizations: "larga cadena humana," "bestia de la carga blanca," "paria," "siervo." In the last stanza of XII, the persona addresses the Indian directly as a brother and exhorts him to raise his humble eyes and look at him, to find their common suffering, to speak, and, finally, to leap out of the ditch of his captive existence. The poem can be cited as a proof of Ulibarrí's pro-indigenous sympathies, but more significant is its failure to achieve a response from the Indian characters. They remain distant, hermetic objects of observation, ignoring the persona's call. In other words, we are privy once again to the persona's now-familiar desire for communication, followed by the recognition of its failure, eliciting nothing but silence.

Poem XIII aims to remedy the situation through an idealized depiction. In place of the humble, lowly Indian, we have a strongly erect one in verses one and three: "Eres vértebra vertical. . . . Recta y tersa espina dorsal." The reason for the change is ascribed in verses two and four: "amor propio de pie. . . . Estructura de fe." Self-love and faith elevate the Indian from a beast of burden to human—"hombre y no res"—an admirable transformation. But the persona is not satisfied with the human level and seeks a more transcendent ideal state. The "penas morenas" from Poem XII not only take on a more brilliant and valued tone when they turn to "bronce" in Poem XIII but the allusion to skin color turns into "Sólido metal," just as the cloth poncho solidifies into armor. Ulibarrí, perhaps unconsciously, turns the Indian into a statue, an ideal type cast more to exemplify a concept of life than to live.

And in spite of the laudable effort, in the last stanza there seems to be an acknowledgment that, even so, the Indian remains aloof, distant from the idealizing project:

> Para tu raza, ejemplar,
> para América honor,
> para el mundo admiración:
> para ti, nada más.
>   (XIII, 26)

In the poems that follow, this central crystallization of focus on the Indian as the soul of Ecuador dissipates progressively, turning into a mist that obfuscates, stains, fools, clears away, and freezes the face of the soul that desires and loves (XIV, "Vaho," 27–28). Eventually it disappears into more familiar images of desire, women. The Indians will not reappear in the collection; they remain a nostalgic memory of the persona's frustrated effort at bonding with them in a fraternal bid to break out of a tradition of oppression.

The shift of focus to women, however, also steers him back yet again to the Ecuadorean societal division along class lines. In Poem XVII, "Azucena" (33–35), the longest poem in the collection, the character is the persona's housemaid. The twelve stanzas are divided in half, the first six dedicated to depicting Azucena's free-spirited image. All lightness and gaiety, she is perpetually in movement, characterized through such appropriate words as "fuentes de malicias," "ristra de risas y chispas," "risa . . . bailarina," "salta y brinca," "tintín y duende," "canto alegre." Her depiction balances precariously on the edge of the infantile until it finally slides dangerously into the blatantly cute and girlish ("siempre mona, siempre niña"). Ulibarrí does, however, avoid complete chauvinistic stereotyping by infusing the image with a minimum of ambiguity, hinting at the possibility that her facade masks a full, balanced life of a woman, yet it is this fullness that escapes the poet's direct observation because it lies hidden behind appearances dictated by social codes.

The second six stanzas open with the persona intervening in

Azucena's space. Her reaction is to act "infantil y seria," that is, to assume the image prescribed by her class status, which ironically coincides with the poem's imagery in the first six stanzas. In line with Ulibarrí's thematics, at this point the persona desires an encounter with Azucena, the sexual woman, which can be read as the reason for his intervention in the scene. However, confronted by the master of the house, Azucena can only interpret his approach within the codes of signification open to her, and none of them allow fraternization across class lines except in terms that would shame, humiliate, and ruin her morally and perhaps physically. She wisely retreats to the protection of her stereotypical position and escapes beyond the person's grasp. Ulibarrí's reaction to this frustrated advance is revealing. Once again, when his attempts to communicate meet with silence and distance, the persona idealizes the Ecuadorean other, but this time the product is not an admirable statue of bronze. Azucena is female, and the communication desired is gender encoded; the idealization follows suit. He imagines what kind of freer woman she could have been, had she been given the benefits of either U.S. or upper-class Spanish mores, and laments the missed opportunity. Modernity could have allowed her to become the sexually more liberal woman who might have accepted the persona's advances. In the end, since Azucena remains an enigmatic other, the persona depicts her as mired in unrealized potential and untapped sexuality, which in actuality are projections of his own desire. Ulibarrí specifically attributes blame to Azucena and her lack of will. Like the Indian before her, Azucena refuses to leap out of the ditch of her traditional subservience and meet the liberated and would-be liberating foreigner on his own level and on his own terms. The poet can wander away in free movement, lamenting missed opportunities; but Azucena, mired in her colonized mentality, according to him, is portrayed as remaining behind to cry alone in self-delusion. Ulibarrí's last resort is to use her as a mannequin to be costumed by his verses. Once again, when transcendence fails at the level of action, the persona responds with idealized transformation of the object of desire. Yet the result remains the same: nostalgia for lost transcendence.

Lest we leave this point with Ulibarrí seeming the negative, lustful patriarch, we should remember that the persona could have resorted to the traditional Latin American code of class privilege and simply forced himself on Azucena. Ulibarrí also reveals here his desire to find a satisfactory alternative to both his alienation and the history of class violence and exploitation. The transcendence he seeks is not merely personal but social in that it must not be achieved at the expense of the oppressed. His liberation must coincide with theirs. He needs to find the code through which to communicate and bridge the gulf of alienation.

The second section of the collection, "Amor," drifts farther away from the site of frustrated revelation opened by "Ecuador," in search of an alternative in love. Linkage between the two sections is set, however, in the first poem.

> Llevo azucenas en la vena
> abierta, flores en la herida.
> negras y alegres por la noche
> son tristes y verdes de día.
>   Canción que sale de la llaga,
> perfume que surge profundo.
> Lesión que contagia al mundo
> de aromas, matices y voces.
>   (xxv, 47)

The persona is driven by an unspecified impulse, yet one clearly linked to passion by the imagery reminiscent of nineteenth-century sentiments, from the romantics to the symbolists, spiced with a heavy dose of joy in sweet degradation à la the decadent poets for good measure. Passion is like a sickness, an open wound emanating a sweet scent of perfume, driving the persona to debauchery at night and nostalgia during the day. The entire world is enveloped in his mood, which readers recognize as yet another metaphor for his desire to harmonize his dual themes. Conspicuously, he calls the passion "azucenas," referring back to the poem about his Ecuadorean maid and leading us to read the entire second section as an extension of the first, a search for the insight and sensation of the epiphanic transcendence that escaped him in "Ecuador."

The following excerpts are examples of the sentiments expressed in the "Amor" section.

> No te engañen, astro hermoso,
> las cenizas de mi sangre
> ni las luces de mis ojos.
> Son destellos de la tarde,
> y vislumbres y ecos de oro,
> que expiran de amor y males.
> (XXVI, 48)

> Un día estuviste
> en mi vida
> y quise quererte.
> Imposible.
> Un día te fuiste,
> y sin querer te quise.
> (XXVI, 49)

> Pensamiento encendido,
> ilusiones en llama.
> Sentmientos en brillo,
> corazones en ascuas.
> (XLIV, "Sol de retorno," 66)

Love assumes the sign of the impossible yet desired goal. Fulfillment is thwarted by a lack of communication or mere absence and distance.

In the end, the last poem of the collection, L, "Negra mujer" (72), the woman remains as immaterial and impossible to hold as before, associated with "niebla," "amor de emboscada," "tinieblas," "Negra Luz," "brisa nocturna del alba." The search for a harmonious blending of his thematic concerns remains equally unattainable, its pursuit documented and left suspended in the text. Ecuador has been identified as a possible site for realization, but the opportunity slips once again beyond reach into the alienation of the human condition.

EL CÓNDOR

After two collections of short fiction dedicated to his regional culture of New Mexico (*Mi abuela fumaba puros/My Grandma*

Smoked Cigars y otros cuentos de Tierra Amarilla and *Primeros encuentros/First Encounters)*, Ulibarrí returned to the Ecuadorean site to renew his efforts. The difference in the manner of his return, however, is significant. "El Cóndor: appears in a collection of eleven narratives written in a style we can loosely call magical realism.[1] Here Ulibarrí continually mixes fantastic, even supernatural elements with realistic ones, blurring the usual boundary of separation without, however, allowing the fantastic to completely take over. The blend is maintained, resulting in the treatment of the extraordinary as if it were normal. This approach is the characteristic technique of magical realistic writing. That Ulibarrí's use of the technique is not always as smoothly handled as we might want is not the point here;[2] what is more important is the more pertinent observation that this style responds exactly to the conflictive duality inscribed in his writing from the beginning. In magical realism the author found an approach that not only allowed but insisted on the fusing of the real and the extraordinary, the other, the fantastic, the magical—in short, the ideal. And in this context, "El Cóndor" is placed in the position of last and culminating piece in the collection, its location reflecting its function of goal to which the author has progressively worked over time and space.

In "El Cóndor," Ulibarrí creates a barely disguised fictional doppelgänger, Professor Ernesto Garibay. They share a historical identity, even in the origin of their fascination with Ecuador and the topics at hand.

> It had all started in 1963 when Ernesto had taken a summer institute to Ecuador. He returned to Ecuador for several summers and later returned to establish the Center for Andean Studies.
>
> From the very first moment the sierras and jungles, the wide beaches, the high skies, the overwhelming light, the fierce sun, the sensual breezes and rains of that feverish and fertile world enchanted and intoxicated the literature professor from the University of New Mexico.
>
> But what touched him more than anything else was the

friendly and hospitable people of the heartline of the world. Ernesto had never known so much goodness and generosity in human relationships. So much respect. Civilized, in every way. Ernesto soon felt at home. He began calling Ecuador his second homeland. He wrote around then:

Everything humanizes me here:
the bizarre ways of courtesy,
the poetic minuet of words,
the rituals of the people. (181)

Readers will recognize the translated stanza from Poem X, "En Ecuador," from Amor y Ecuador. It is only the first of nine stanzas of Ulibarrí's poetry cited in the story as though having been written by Ernest O. Garibay in reaction to his experience in Ecuador. The verses function as excerpts from a lyric diary kept by the protagonist. Like f contemporary musician constructing a recording from borrowed elements of previous recordings, Ulibarrí samples stanzas from his own poems and by attributing them to his protagonist fuses himself and the character to produce a hybrid of fiction and reality. Furthermore, this practice takes "historical reality" and "fiction," categories usually juxtaposed as opposites, and melds them in one general category of raw material for the writer—or better stated, for the writers, both the exterior and the interior one. As raw material, this data loses its determinant character; time and historical progression become malleable, susceptible to manipulation by the author. This allows desire to rule over necessity and chronology, imposing its design on the logic and the rules of material reality.

Ulibarrí's purpose can be surmised if we focus on the recasting of his poetic material. Recalling the above reading of Amor y Ecuador, we saw how the order of the poems traces the development of the thematics, leading from approach, anticipation, humanization, discovery of Indians, epiphany, dissipation, loss, and regretful withdrawal to final pursuit of the ideal in another space and along another thematic line. The humanization, the discovery of Indians, and the epiphany follow one upon the other in the story as well, but the lyric stanzas cited are taken out of order—quite literally out of context since they now stand as isolated units free of the original surrounding verses—shuffled, and recast to alter their significance. Ulibarrí does to the poetry what he has discovered can be done to life when one liberates it by taking it to literature: it can be remolded to the shape best suited for the purposes of the textual project. So-called reality is at best just one more possibility among others in literary space.

A comparison of the sequence in which the nine stanzas appear in the two texts is revealing. On the left in the chart below are the page numbers from *Amor y Ecuador*; to the right, the stanza numbers in the new sequence and the page on which each appears in "El Cóndor" (page numbers from the Spanish version). Connecting lines have been added with the dual purpose of assisting the reader in tracing the restructuring of the linear sequence in the poetry book into the new order in the story and to graphically suggest the woven pattern of relationship created by the Ulibarrí's act of rearranging what could be taken as a set historical pattern from the previous text.

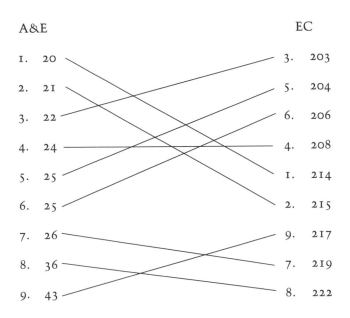

A&E

		EC	
1.	20	3.	203
2.	21	5.	204
3.	22	6.	206
4.	24	4.	208
5.	25	1.	214
6.	25	2.	215
7.	26	9.	217
8.	36	7.	219
9.	43	8.	222

By changing the order and context in which the fragments appear, Ulibarrí redefines their meaning within a new tale of fulfillment. We can take this liberation of the elements from their historical context as a metaphor of what the author intends to do with the societal elements of Ecuadorean history. He means to disrupt the flow of time, to bring certain elements locked in the past back to the present and allow them to evolve into a different future. This is possible because he no longer respect the logic of rational thought within the space of writing. In literature, where anything is possible, the author can reshuffle his own life or the past of a nation as easily as a deck of cards.

Especially notable is his attribution of the bronze statue image of the Ecuadorean Indian (XIII, "Indio de Otavalo," *Amor y Ecuador*) to the story's protagonist, Garibay, to fuse the New Mexican outsider and Ecuadorean insder figures in a shared image that transforms both characters. This coincides with the metamorphosis, in typical magical realism fashion, of the U.S.-born Latino professor into a reincarnation of an Inca emperor-god, a physical change that coincides with yet another, that of Garibay's lover when her "nalgas de oro" (golden buttocks) become bronze as well.

The amorous subplot might seem superfluous, even chauvinistically so, but in the context of our discussion it clearly is not. Ulibarrí's first excursion to Ecuador was marked with frustrated sexual desire, which itself already constituted a sublimation of the original failed desire to communicate with the Indian. So in the story Ulibarrí is careful to link the sexual motif with the social, because his goal is to transcend all these old, discrete signs of alienation. The couple's love, both sexual and emotional, deepens as they carry out their plot to save the indigenous population from the oppression of the ruling class and simultaneously raise the social consciousness of the Ecuadorean people as a whole. The result is the salvation of the entire nation, coinciding with the sublime realization of the couple's love.

In the end, instead of the frustrated departure that sends the persona in search of love relations that fail as well, the protagonist achieves transcendence in sexual love and social action, while the author manages to fuse his thematic concerns in one overarching image. The realization of a fusion in opposing forces, reality and the ideal, is facilitated by magical realism. The virtues of the style allow the author to disregard the limits that had previously frustrated his will. Once he discovers and accepts the otherness of literary space, its unlimited possibilities, he is free to guide the text to the desired goal.

CONCLUSION

One should not overlook the problems raised by the story. Ulibarrí's narrator incarnates, not just a great avenger of the common people, but an elite patriarch whose paternalistic attitudes border on sinister populism. The depiction of the indigenous population as children who come to pay homage to their father and protector, El Cóndor, should provoke readers to question the author's colonizing ideology, albeit ameliorated by the sincere desire to serve the best interests of the people. That Ulibarrí sees the Ecuadorean Indian as too burdened by a tradition of dehumanizing servitude is perhaps more revealing of his deep-seated Usonianism than of the Indians' real character. But I have enunciated these concerns elsewhere (Bruce-Novoa 1990).

What concerns me here is that the story, when viewed in the context of Ulibarrí's creative project, marks a successful resolution of what he had until then deemed irreconcilable forces. That possibility comes from the discovery of literary space as free from the demands of reality. Once the requirements of contingency are left behind, the writer liberates himself to take advantage of that space of free play. Readers can and have submitted the text to a historical and cultural critique, but that takes little or nothing away from the fact that "El Cóndor" is a sublime moment of transcendence for the author.

Finally, and ironically, the author's discovery of the proper channel for the realization of his personal transcendence leads him to what many consider the archetypical style of Latin American writing. That is to say, Ulibarrí finds his answer, finds himself, when he lets slip the rational- and material-based form of though—linked not only to midcentury existentialism but to both a U.S. and a socialist realist insistence on circumscribing the human realm of action—in favor of a freer-flowing, open perception of magical realism. And magical realism, I venture to add, is a style in which the characteristics of literary space itself are just more visible than usual—not an exception but the rule made manifest. In "El Cóndor," Ulibarrí, like his character, is first seduced by and then reincarnated as the Latin American tradition.

NOTES

1. The history of the term and the heated debate it never ceases to provoke among critics is easily found in any of the numerous bibliogrphies on the subject. Perhaps the best source from which to begin is Chanady's 1985 study.

2. I have addressed the technical and ideological problems Ulibarrí encounters in the writing of these old stores in "Magical Regionalism," *American Book Review* 11, no. 6 (January–February 1990): 14.

WORKS CITED

Bruce-Novoa, "Magical Regionalism." *American Book Review* 11, no. 5 (January–February 1990): 14.

Chanady, Amaryll Beatrice. *Magical Realism and the Fantastic: Resolved versus Unresolved Antimony.* New York: Garland, 1985.

Duke dos Santos, María. "La tradición hispano-católica en la obra de Ulibarrí," Paper delivered at the V Congreso Internacional, Culturas Hispanas de los Estados Unidos: El Poder Hispano, Madrid, July 9, 1992.

Kierkegaard, Søren. *The Sickness Unto Death.* New York: Anchor Books, 1954.

Ruiz, Reynaldo. "Sabine R. Ulibarrí." In *Dictionary of Literary Biography. Vol. 82, Chicano Writers, First Series.* Edited by Francisco A. Lomelí and Carl R. Shirley. Detroit: Bruccoli Clark Layman Book, 1989. Pp. 260–67.

Ulibarrí, Sabine. *Al cielo se sube de pie.* Madrid: Alfaguara, 1966.

———. *Amor y Ecuador.* Madrid: Ediciones José Porrúa Turanzas, 1966.

———. *El Cóndor and Other Stories.* Houston: Arte Público Press, 1989.

———. *Mi abuela fumaba puros/My Grandma Smoked Cigars.* Berkeley: Quinto Sol, 1977.

———. *Primeros encuentros/First Encounters.* Ypsilanti: Bilingual Press/Editorial Bilingüe, 1982.

———. *Tierra Amarilla: Stories of New Mexico/Cuentos de nuevo Mexico.* Bilingual edition. Translated by Thelma Campbell Nason. Albuquerque: University of new Mexico Press, 1971. Originally published, Quito: Editorial Casa de la Cultura Ecuatoriana, 1964.

THE MYSTERIOUS MUSE

IMAGES OF A FEMALE PRESENCE IN THE POETRY OF
SABINE ULIBARRÍ

PATRICIA DE LA FUENTE

Ulibarrí's first collection of poems, *Al cielo se sube a pie*, published in Madrid in 1966, has been called "fifty poems in search of heaven" by a critic in the *New Mexico Quarterly* who also claims that the poet "borrowed from woman's environment of arts and toils" to create his descriptions (Ferrer 1962–63). While this is perhaps true, it might be argued that the poet not only borrows from such feminine sources to enrich the imagery of his poems but also incorporates, in his poetic search to integrate what another critic has called his "intimate dreams and exterior reality" (Bosch 1963), the muse-like essence of a feminine presence. Such a presence reverberates throughout the collection, sometimes explicitly but more often than not implicitly: an image of a vision glimpsed, a truth half-perceived, a dream almost grasped. As a poetic device, the ambiguous treatment of this presence creates a sense of both erotic and spiritual urgency and provides the poetic tension and energy that gives both depth and dimension to Ulibarrí's poetry.

The recurring imagery of this female presence often appears to suggest the conflictive juxtaposition of the spiritual and material urges in the narrator's nature. One of the clearest examples occurs in Poem *IX*, *"Mujer imagen,"* in which the poet addresses the mysterious muse-like presence that haunts so many of his poems as "the flower and fruit in fertile longing" ("flor y fruto en ansia fértil," 18) and sets up an ambiguous dichotomy that suggests two distinct levels of reality: the earthbound world of the narrator and another, perhaps more rarified existence of the female presence addressed in the poem.

This dichotomy appears to reflect the different textures of these two states of existence. On the sterile, earthbound level, the female addressed cannot survive.

> En paseos y salones,
> en iglesias y avenidas,
> vagas, sufres y pereces,
> hierba y polvo en ansia estéril.
>   (18)

In the fertile world of the imagination and dreams, the female presence is in her element and can flourish and flower.

> En recuerdos e ilusiones,
> en visiones y, en sueños,
> vives y eres y perduras,
> flor y fruto en ansia fértil.

In the following stanza, the narrator suggests that the limitations of the woman's earthly existence may be transformed through his act of poetic creation.

> En ti, por ti, no eres nada;
> ansia terrestre en suelo agreste,
> En mí, por mí, lo eres todo,
> en aire nuevo ansia celeste.
>   (18)

While on a superficial level this poem may be read as a lover's lament and the contrasts set up between "you" and "me," "nothing" and "everything," "earth" and "heaven" might appear to reflect the unattainability of a real woman, on another level, there is no real woman in the poem at all. There is, however, the illusory presence of a woman, a female image, "imagen de mujer, mujer imagen" (19), invented by the narrator every day and created by him every night. She is the feminine ideal who, we are told, lives in illusions, in visions, in dreams, but who cannot exist "en paseos y salones, en iglesias y avenidas" (18); that is, in the real world. Emanating from the poet's own "ansia fértil," the fertile longing of his imagination, she is the symbol of his creative energy, his inspiration, a personification of his Muse, that traditionally elusive feminine figure.

The relationship between the narrator and the female presence that inspires him is alive and vigorous in *"Mujer imagen,"* and this same sense of spiritual and physical fulfillment, or at least the possibility of it, is evident in other poems as well. Poem XXV, for example, is structured along similar lines, using the dichotomy of opposite forces or characteristics: the female presence possessing all the spiritual, nonrestricting qualities, while the narrator claims the material, earth-binding ones. The actual contrasts in this poem include the following:

> *Eres alma . . . hecha llama*
> *Yo soy sangre . . . hecho carne.*
>
> *tú andas siempre perdida*
> *Yo sí conozco el camino*
>
> *Soy el ancla*
> *Tú, el éter*
> (35)

The narrator again seems to suggest that if these opposing forces—the spiritual and material, the inspirational female presence and the male poet—can be reconciled, the result would be what the narrator terms the "luz única" or fusion of these forces in the created work of art.

> *Ven a habitarme la vena*
> *y a encender los ojos.*
> *Ven a hallarte la huella*
> *y la senda de oro.*

Lleno de ti, de mí llena,
en mí, por ti, subir hemos
a luz única
en pies míos.
  (36)

In a poetic extension of the original imagery cited above, the narrator invites the female presence to enter his veins, "Ven a habitarme la vena," and to find the path of gold, "la senda de oro." Thus united and full of each other, her spirituality will take on the substance of his flesh, and his knowledge of the right road will give direction to her spirituality. Together they will combine the divine light of inspiration and the earthbound physicality of the poet, suggested by the feet image.

Critics have identified one of Ulibarrí's more evident temperamental traits as "una pasión espontánea e indestructible que adhiriéndose primariamente a las cosas terrenas y al amor carnal, no se agota ni debilita en nada en el inmenso salto hasta la esencialización depuradora" ["a spontaneous and indestructible passion that, associating itself primarily with earthly things and carnal love, does not exhaust itself or weaken in the least in the immense leap towards purifying spirituality."] (Bosch 1963). While the validity of the claim that Ulibarrí's *priorities* lie with earthly concerns and carnal love is open to debate, there is no denying the presence of a certain current of eroticism and sensuality in this collection of poems. However, the critic's reference to the poet's impulse to take that immense leap towards a level of distilled or essential perfection accurately describes the philosophical basis for the dialogues between the narrator and the female presence in so many of the poems.

The short poem, *XXVI, "Amor vertical,"* (37), presents an interesting glimpse of the philosophical conflict between the real and the ideal, the physical and the spiritual; between so-called carnal love and the spirituality or imaginative experiences associated with the act of creation. Ostensibly a love poem to a real woman, *"Amor vertical"* suggests the inability of this carnal experience to compete with the female presence of the imagination.

Quiero verte sin olores:
busco imagen y no sustento.
De aire son mis amores;
mis cosechas transparento.

Casta y moral tan esquiva
eres sólo carne y beso.
Vinieras a mi fantasía,
te haría yo, alma y verso.
  (37)

The dissatisfaction of the narrator with his material experiences is evident in his desire for a woman without the distracting reality of normal human odors—"quiero verte sin olores"—and in his rejection of a woman who is *only* flesh and kisses—"eres sólo carne y beso." In the final two lines of the poem, the narrator expands his search for image over material sustenance, "busco imagen y no sustento," by imagining the real woman transformed into the female presence of his fantasies. Only there does she become accessible to his imaginative experiences; only there can she become one with him in soul and verse, in "alma y verso."

A more extended treatment of the same idea occurs in Poem *XXIV*, in which the narrator begs the mortal woman to cast off her materiality as if it were "hábitos falsos" (34) in order to attain a form of freedom on a different level of experiences.

Quítate ese cutis y esas carnes,
que te quiero ver los huesos . . .

Esos muslos y esos senos
que a la muerte te están llevando,
libérate, mi amor, de ellos,
cuelga los hábitos falsos.

Libre, desnuda y osada,
sube azul, sube a mi nube
  (34)

The mortal woman is again challenged to throw off her trappings of mortality—her flesh, her human odors—and assume an ethereal form so she can inhabit the imaginative world of the narrator, up on his cloud as he calls it, and both share and stimulate the idealistic experiences of his fantasy.

> ¡Qué amores castos los nuestros,
> sin olores, sin calores,
> y sin besos deshonestos
> entre maitines y albores!
> (34)

In this case, the ambiguity of the role assigned to the female presence is suggested by the double level of experience implied in the poem. On the one hand, the narrator creates an erotic seduction scene to entrap the mortal woman he wishes to seduce. On the other, the irrationality of his demands suggests a strong desire to escape from the encumbrances of a mortal relationship, the inevitable "cutis," "carnes," "muslos," and "senos," those restrictive and deceptive "hábitos falsos," and aspire to the more perfect, platonic experience of a "chaste love" "sin olores, sin calores, / y sin besos deshonestos" (34). Both possible worlds exist within the poem: the sensuous relationship with the mortal woman, which inevitably leads to death, and the imaginative experience with the ideal woman, that "mujer imagen" who can provide the inspiration for the creative activity through which the poet, and the woman, may live forever.

At times, however, the poet-narrator's allegiance to his muse and his dedication to the esoteric levels of existence they share are threatened by the real world in the form of the real flesh-and-blood woman he has tried to relegate to forgetfulness.

> A veces sueño
> con la mujer idea
> y subo a los cielos
> con mi Dulcinea.
>
> Mas en el olvido arde
> la mujer de sangre . .
> (xvii, 26)

At other times, the narrator seems to doubt the possibility of a creative consummation between himself as poet and the elusive female presence, whose very identity and existence he questions in Poem *XVIII*, *"Tu-Tu."*

> *¿Cómo definir tus veras,*
> *y cómo saber siquiera*
> *si eres ansia o eres carne,*
> *si eres, o no eres, quimera?*
> (27)

There is both disillusionment and disorientation in the narrator's voice as he questions the validity of his inspiration and wonders if his pursuit of the ideal is only a chimera. At other times, there is a sense of total disconnection from the source of his inspiration.

> *En la memoria lo mío,*
> *mortal, fecundo y maduro.*
> *Lo tuyo, en el olvido,*
> *eterno estéril capullo.*
> (XIV, "RECUERDO," 23)

The poet's stylistic use of parallels is again evident in the juxtaposition of "mío-tuyo," "memoria-olvido," "mortal-eterno," "fecundo-estéril," and "maduro-capullo." This time, however, the focus is on the inability of the female presence to sustain the illusion of the poet. By calling himself "fecundo y maduro" the narrator implies that his productivity is self-generated, perhaps a product of his own maturity, while the female presence is distanced from his memory as the unproductive yet eternal, sterile bud, unopened and hence unfulfilled and unfulfilling.

Therefore, not all appearances of the female presence in Ulibarrí's poems are positive experiences for the narrator. In many cases the poet seems to have lost touch entirely with the level of experience inhabited by his "mujer imagen." These poems are filled with images of tombs, darkness, tears, immobility, grayness, death, mourning, coldness, hardness, failures, silence, vain hopes, sterility, and above all, an immense sense of loss. In *II*, *"Soy,"* the narrator talks of his "vida gris interna" (10); *III, "Crepúsculo,"* ends with the image of "angustia eterna" (11). In *V, "Fuego fatuo,"* there is a feeling of having taken the wrong path in life in leaving his family behind to follow the enticing female presence, "iluso salí tras la estrella: (13), who turned out to be a "perversa burladora / engañadora y maliciosa" (13), always just beyond the narrator's frenzied grasp. The narrator's ultimate disillusionment with the inspirational relationship he had previously enjoyed with the female presence of his imagination is expressed in two distinct images. One is serious and considers the end of this relationship as the final curtain.

> *Telón caído, función cumplida,*
> *candado sellado y sin llave.*
>
> *La ventana no tiene dama*
> *virgen, divina y joven.*
> *Latido inútil, esperanza vana,*
> *ansia perenne en lenta noche.*
>   (XIII, 22)

Here the creative longing remains, but the environment is no longer conducive to creation. The show is over, the key is lost, there is no longer the presence of the idealized female—young, divine, and virgin—to inspire the poet's imagination. The adjectives "slow," "useless," and "vain" all add to the futility of the attempt to keep the relationship alive.

The other image adopts an unusually humorous tone and suggests a playful acceptance of an ideal marred by the encroaching "pies de polvo" from the real world.

> *A pedestal de mármol te elevara*
> *si no pesaras tanto,*
> *si yo pudiera mirarte la cara*
> *y olvidar tus espantos.*
>   (XXX, "SIN PIES," 43)

It is almost as though the mortal and the ideal woman have converged into a hybrid creature, a goddess with feet of clay:

Diosa, estilada en tus pies de barro
que a la tierra te ligan
  (43)

An interesting switch has occurred in the narrator's relationship with the female presence in this poem. Rather than beg the mortal woman to shed her materiality to become closer to the inspirational ideal, the narrator now brings the ideal woman down to the material level. Not only does she have "pies de barro" and "pies de polvo, piedra y pasto" but she is now heavy and irrevocably tied to the earth through her feet of clay. She is still the goddess, but definitely a fallen goddess, too heavy and imperfect to rise to those ethereal heights of imagination she inhabits in other poems. No longer the "Señora, sincera y alta" (62), who floats in the rarified air of the narrator's imagination, she has become the prosaic goddess, with a soul still beautiful, but a goddess whose feet are now on the ground, not on the marble pedestal.

WORKS CITED

Bosch, Rafael. "*Al cielo se sube a pie* de Sabine R. Ulibarrí." *Hispania* 46 (September 1963).

Ferrer, Olga Prjevalinsky. "*Al cielo se sube a pie* by Sabine R. Ulibarrí." *New Mexico Quarterly* 33 (Autumn-Winter 1963–63).

Ulibarrí, Sabine R. *Al cielo se sube a pie*. Madrid: Alfaguara, 1966.

PER ASPRA AD ASTRA
THE POETRY OF SABINE ULIBARRÍ

SANTIAGO DAYDÍ-TOLSON

The poetry of Sabine Ulibarrí, collected in two brief volumes, deserves critical attention because of its subtle relationships with the whole body of his work. Well known for his sentimental and humorous narratives of life in a traditional New Mexico Hispanic community, Ulibarrí represents among Chicano writers the nostalgic view of a disappearing world that he relates, with obvious effects, to the experiences of an idealized childhood, an idyllic period of life in itself, also gone forever. This sentimental idealization of the past, with its undercurrents of implicit criticism of the new and nostalgic confirmation of the old, has a definite traditional component in the tacit embracing of old values and conceptions, some of which find a direct manifestation in his two books of poems, *Amor y Ecuador* and *Al cielo se sube a pie*. The nostalgic view that inspires Ulibarrí's prose is not as clearly visible in his poetry, although the feeling of being uprooted, counteracted by a strong affirmation of old conceptions and values present in most of his short stories, underlies his poems (Tatum 1985: 388).

Profoundly influenced by his traditional Hispanic upbringing, Ulibarrí chooses lyrical poetry for dealing with those few issues that present in an emotional, more directly personal way, his most intimate views on life as received from a cultural background greatly dependent on the conception of two levels of existence,

III

the natural and the spiritual. He uses a poetic language that recognizes its roots. Using metrical forms, themes, and images that try to continue within a tradition of popular Spanish verse, Ulibarrí composes all his poems within a basic pattern of oppositions that represents a transcendentalist view of life and the world. His main concern as a lyrical poet is to give form in traditional Hispanic poetic terms to the very personal and emotional experience of cultural reaffirmation. To do this, Ulibarrí follows closely and dutifully the best example of a traditionally inspired contemporary Hispanic lyrical poetry, that of Juan Ramón Jiménez, the Spanish master whose poetic techniques were the subject of Ulibarrí's systematic analysis in *El mundo poético de Juan Ramón* (1962). The affinities of Ulibarrí's poetry with Juan Ramón's are all too clear in matter of forms, images, and some basic themes.

Ulibarrí tries to reproduce Jiménez's concise, brief poems, following in many instances the parallel pattern of composition characteristic of the old popular forms of Spanish poetry. He imitates, not always successfully, the seemingly simple traditional metric forms known to him through New Mexican popular poetry and used with unsurpassed effectiveness by the Spaniard. The many irregularities in rhyme and meter in Ulibarrí's compositions generate a totally different effect, creating a personal style of metrics that is difficult to evaluate. This breaking of the patterns of the basic structure can be interpreted either as the poet's inability to compose correctly measured verses or as an intentional exemption of the rule for stylistic purposes. Although the results of this practice tend to support the first interpretation, it is also true that those intentional or unintentional lapses in technique could have been allowed by the poet to fulfill an expressive function. The rhythmic tension produced by the technique would help to convey a feeling of indecisiveness in a poetry that combines idealized images of transcendental spirituality with a strong inclination to embrace concrete reality in direct terms. The perfect meter, the exact rhyme, the irreplaceable image could be seen as inappropriate in a poetry that looks for a contrast between the perfection of an ideal (rooted in a lyrical tradition) and the imperfection of human nature and of everyday, concrete reality.

In Ulibarrí's poems, then, the failure to reproduce the perfect structure and, consequently, the perfect lyrical mood introduces a level of ambiguity as to the nature of the experience and as to the attitude of the poet with respect to it. This duality has its correspondence in a conventional, clearly spiritualistic dichotomy of "high" and "low" as seen in the opposites of body and soul, matter and spirit, concrete and transcendental reality. While one opposing aspect represents the idealized beauty and goodness of the spiritual values, the other accounts for the contingent, even the grotesque, of the purely physical. This negative feel for matter, which could be related to Juan Ramón's poetic aim, explains the idealization of reality in Ulibarrí's poetry. The well-known set of symbols he chooses to represent the ideal does not come only from a received traditional Hispanic literary language and world view; it also comes from the accurate observation of the region where the poet was born and raised: his cultural landscape.

The cultural issue, the recognition of his belonging to a vanishing culture being lost to the pressures of another, more powerful, cultural project is alluded to in Ulibarrí's "Fuego fatuo," (will-o'-the-wisp) from *Al cielo se sube a pie* [Heaven Is Reached on Foot] (13–14). The conflict, manifest in the personal experience of the poet who leaves his ancestral land in search of an elusive different world, takes the form of a nostalgic sense of loss made more dramatic in the contrasting geographic images of mountain and sea. The opposing realms of the high mountain, where the individual lived in direct contact with his tradition, and of the sea, an open lower space that represents infinity, symbolize in the allegorical story of the poem the two extremes of "high" and "low" characteristic of the simple dichotomy that defines the poet's understanding of existence.

The high lands of New Mexico are the actual place where the values of his idealized Hispanic roots are, and as a symbol of height they represent poetically such an ideal. The opposite world, the one for which he abandons his own land, is represented first by the proverbial unreachable star of a dream.

Soy el único de mi casta
que ha salido de la montaña.
Iluso salí tras la estrella
que en cumbre fugaz aletea

I am the only one among my people
who has left the mountain.
I left in illusory pursue of the star
that flickers briefly high above.

In his search for the star the poet reaches that other world, the new cultural realm that is represented by the lowest possible geographic level, the sea; there the star of his search disappears:

Del cerro saltó a la mar cana
y se entronó en el agua blanca.
En la playa, cansado y viejo,
magia, la vi morir a lo lejos.

From up the hill the star fell to the whitened sea
and settled itself in the white water.
On the beach, tired and old,
I saw it die, magically, far away.

An even lower level is that of the tomb, where the foolishness of the search will end, as the wanderer is unable to return to the mountain of his youth:

Y anhelo bien el blando hogar,
tan lejano del blanco mar.
Mas los caminos campesinos
se me han cerrado en el pasado.

Para mi alma ya no hay retorno
a ti y al pan fresco del horno.
Al pie de su honda sepultura
morirá también mi locura.

And I yearn for the sweet homeland
so distant from the white sea.
But the country roads
have been closed to me in the past.

For my soul there is now no return
to you and the freshly baked bread.
My madness will die also
at the deep sepulcher.

Of much interest for understanding Ulibarrí's views is the explicit recognition in this poem of a definite loss in the abandonment of the ancestral values of the poet in exchange for a purely apparent better world of the future. "High" and "low" can be seen at this point not only as symbolic representations of cultural duality but also as indications of two realities in two different times: the ideal past and the concrete present.

The clear set of traditional images used in these poems—mountain, star, roads, sea, and tomb— is repeated in different variations and in combination with related images in several other texts of both books of poems. In all instances the different images of "high" and "low" are the constant representation of a duality that serves as much to explain Ulibarrí's individual experience with respect to his cultural dichotomy as to express the old Christian division of material world and transcendental reality that underlies the poet's interpretation of his own existence. Body and soul, matter and spirit are the main components of Ulibarrí's conflictive lyrical concerns: cultural nostalgia and human love.

Amor y Ecuador, as suggested by the title, contains both central subjects in two separate, seemingly unrelated sections. In the first part of the book, a series of poems about a trip to Ecuador, the poems form almost a narrative of the poet's experience as an individual who considers his lost roots and tries to reestablish his sense of belonging. First in order are the several texts that deal with the flight from New Mexico to Ecuador; they are followed by several compositions about the poet's recognition in Ecuador of a cultural communion of both worlds: Hispanic New Mexico and the Andes.

The "story" closes in Spain, the center of Hispanic cultural identity, with an evocation of the visit to Ecuador. In all of these poems the two opposites of "high" and "low" are central to the images of personal definition in terms of world and spirituality, both of them directly related to the cultural experience of discovering the common roots. The mountains of Ecuador, that Andean "vertical country" (*patria vertical*), represent the spiritual values of the Amerindian cultures of the Andes, a clear reference to the pre-Columbian roots common to Ulibarrí's New Mexican Hispanism and the contemporary Latin American spirit.

In "Quito" (20), a very brief poem, the synesthesia confirms an almost magical view of the Amerindian world of peaks and clouds as the sacred land of God. It is a direct reference to Ulibarrí's recognition of the essentially superior spiritual values of the Latin American world:

> Yo vi el resplandor de Dios,
> indómito en el áurea nube.
> Vi la sombra de su voz
> indígena en la alta cumbre.

> I saw the brightness of God,
> powerful in the golden cloud.
> I saw the shadow of his indian voice
> in the highest summit

The recognition of a world in which the true values persist is given in the poem "En Ecuador: (22–23), where the repeated verse "Aquí todo me humaniza" (*Everything here makes me more human*) expresses the essence of Ulibarrí's search. The last stanza establishes clearly the basic elements that make that land a humanizing one:

> Este mundo me humaniza:
> hecho de macho y hembra;
> nada neutro, nada estéril,
> todo alma y todo sangre.

> This world humanizes me:
> It is made of male and female;
> nothing in it is neuter, nothing is sterile,
> everything is soul and blood.

"Soul" and "blood" (and one could say also "female" and "male") are terms that can be equated to "high" and "low" as they belong to the same set of recurrent images that recognize and sustain a division between concrete material reality and spiritual existence. Humans are complete when these two realms coincide, but Ulibarrí's poems are also implying that this ideal harmony is not easy to reach: the human spirit strives for transcendence even as it succumbs to the laws of matter.

Bodily images are the most telling representation of the material aspect of being human; with them the poet enriches the physical concreteness of his cultural landscape. Poem VII (19) is an explicit recognition of the close relationship between the two geographically similar locales and makes more evident the significance of these high places:

> *Albuquerque,*
> *beso hispano*
> *en la casta frente*
> *de un continente*
> *castellano.*
>
> *Alto Quito,*
> *pulso latino*
> *del mismo organismo,*
> *late en el templo*
> *del hombre y el tiempo.*

> *Albuquerque*
> *is a Hispanic kiss*
> *in the brow*
> *of a Spanish*
> *continent.*
>
> *High Quito*
> *is the Latin pulse*
> *of the same oganism,*
> *that pulsates in the temple*
> *of man and time.*

Geography coincides with symbolism. The well-known image of the mountain as representation of high spiritual values is reinforced by the real space of New Mexico and Ecuador, two geographic as well as cultural "high" regions to which the poet wishes to return from his symbolically "lower" standing. The Hispanic ancestry is also related to high lands when the poet travels to Spain and establishes the relationship between the two worlds, first remembering a mountain city of Ecuador from the high plateau of Madrid—"Aquí en Madrid pienso en ti / villa de Juanes ilustres" ("Ambato," 30) ["Here in Madrid I think of you / Town of illustrious Juanes"]—and then creating a symbolic image to represent the spiritual relationship between Spain and America. The grandiose vision of a rainbow uniting both lands with its celestial arch across the ocean in "Cuenca" (41) is clearly related to the different images of high spirituality accorded to the Hispanic culture:

> De una cuna de los Andes
> se alza un arco iris extraño.
> Cruza la tierra y los mares,
> posa en la frente de Iberia.

> From a cradle in the Andes
> grows a strange rainbow.
> It crosses lands and seas
> and sets in Iberia's forehead

The reference to altitude as representation of spiritual values is direct as the rainbow soars to incredible heights and gleams with lights never seen before: "Sube a altura inusitada / lanza luces nunca vistas" ["Climbs to incredible heights/and sends lights never seen before"] (9–10).

Similarly, and again using traditional images as they are commonly interpreted but taking them from a real circumstance where they reproduce concrete objects, the poet stresses the opposition between "high" and "low" as seen from the airplane in flight to Quito:

> Por caminos del aire
> y alfombras de espuma
> persigo una estrella.

> *Me siento ligero,*
> *libre y ufano*
> *tras el astro huraño.*
>
> *Abajo mis penas,*
> *mis dudas y miedos.*
> *Arriba mis sueños.*
>
> *By airways*
> *and carpets of foam*
> *I follow a star.*
>
> *I feel light,*
> *free and happy*
> *following the star in flight.*
>
> *Down there are my sorrows,*
> *my doubts and fears.*
> *My dreams are above.*

The first poems from *Amor y Ecuador* treat the subject of his flight to Ecuador in very clear terms: a series of symbols—which are inherited from old—serve the poet to express his traditional dualistic view: "star," "clouds," "mountain," "air," "earth," "feet," "road," "carpet," "dust," "up," and "down." All of these terms are related to a set of concepts corresponding to a religiously inspired Manichaean interpretation of "high" and "low" in vaguely moral valuations: God and creature, soul and body, dreams and desires, mystery and reality, ideals and facts. The poet lives in a state of uncertainty between the heights of idealism and the lows of material existence:

> *Vuelo solo siempre*
> *sobre la tierra.*
> *Ando solo siempre*
> *bajo los cielos.*
> (v, 17)
>
> *I always fly alone*
> *over the land.*
> *I always walk alone*
> *under the sky.*

"Flying" and "walking" are both representations of life as a journey from the low station of human life to the heights of spiritual existence. All images of "high" and "low" are referring to this search for transcendence and the anguish of the process. "Niebla" [Fog] (18), the last poem about the flight, compares the airplane, a mere object, with the poet's own experience as a human being lost in the fog:

> No lleuve,
> mas el ala va mojada,
> lanzada por el turbio abismo.
>
> No lloro,
> mas la pupila inundada
> proclama angustias ocultas.
>
> It is not raining
> but the wing is wet
> as it soars through the dark abyss.
>
> I do not cry,
> but my flooded eye
> proclaims a hidden anguish.

Fog symbolizes the ignorance and confusion of the individual in front of the spiritual mysteries represented by most celestial phenomena. Among these, the clouds are ambivalent images. They represent celestial as well as earthly elements that, conversely, become symbols of both spiritual and material life. "Soy" [I am] (10) defines human existence in terms of an enormous cloud that "does not fit in the sky" and therefore "rolls down to earth / and floods the ground":

> La nube entera
> no cabe en el cielo.
> Rueda a la tierra
> e inunda el suelo.
>
> Entra en los ojos
> e invade la vena.
> Abre los poros
> y se hace conciencia.

The cloud
does not fit in the sky.
It rolls down to earth
and floods the ground.

It gets into the eye
and invades the vein.
It opens the pores
and becomes conscience.

The material aspect of the cloud becomes purely symbolic when it "enters the eyes / and invades the vein." "Eyes" and "vein" carry the meaning of material, physical human existence. As it happens with other parts of the body, they take the same representation in several of Ulibarrí's poems. "Pores" and "conscience" instead convey in the opposition of material and immaterial the two values of the cloud as an image. The end of the poem, with its strong echo of Juan Ramón, establishes the final and most important dichotomy, the one that really matters; it is the conception that the rest of the symbols and representations try to signify—that of the internal life as different from and superior to the external world:

Nube mía fuera,
mi nube dentro,
vida gris interna,
y en el mundo sueño.

My cloud outside,
my cloud inside,
my grey interior life
and dreams in the world.

Several other examples from both books would show that for Ulibarrí the clouds represent spirituality and elevation from matter. In "Vértigo" (*Al cielo se sube a pie*, 21), the clouds represent love ascending in the night and later descending to the high peak of desire. The wish for a pure, nonphysical love is seen in Poem XXIV (34) when the lover asks the woman to liberate herself of her body, which "is taking her to death," and to reach for his cloud, in this case a representation, as in the previous example, of his own idealized passion:

> Libre, desnuda y osada,
> sube azul, sube a mi nube.
> Tus ansias y tus nadas
> trae a las nupcias cumbres.

> Go up in blue, go up to my cloud,
> free, naked and daring.
> Bring to the nuptial heights
> your desires and your nothingness.

Clouds can be seen also as "alfombras," [carpets] an image related to walking and the low level of the earth instead of the higher level of the sky. Through this contradictory image the cloud partakes of the material and sensual nature of the low object. Seen from above while in flight, the clouds are below, and in spite of their mostly ideal nature—as received from seeing them normally from below as elements of the sky—they can be confused and mistaken for the floor, a sensual one, for that matter. In a similar manner, other oppositions dealing with the same set of values point to an interpretation of the human destiny as a conflict between spiritual aspirations for transcendence and physical desire to be in touch with matter.

The correspondence is complete. In love, which is at the same time spiritual and physical, the individual finds the same opposing forces of "high" and "low" exerting strong influence as they pull him apart with their two conflicting aims. But conflict is always resolved through a transitional mental process by which materiality transcends itself and reaches pure spirituality. The title of one of the books is quite clear in this respect: *Al cielo se sube a pie*, Heaven Is Reached on Foot. In this book, Poem XLV (59) uses several of the terms under consideration—"cloud," "vein," "mountain," "sky"—summarizing the meaning of these terms and their interrelation within the symbolic system.

As several of Ulibarrí's poems, this text develops a brief argument that, in its mirrorlike structure, tries to express the sense of exchange between the two contrasting realms, that of body and that of spirit. The first stanza states the fact in the much-repeated symbolic terms:

> *Sube a la nube la vena,*
> *destino dudoso y lejano,*
> *a pie por monte antropoide,*
> *lento, su camino fragoso.*

> *The vein goes up to the cloud,*
> *a doubtful and distant destiny.*
> *It goes on foot through the human-like hills,*
> *slowly on the hard road.*

The third and last stanza describes the opposite movement in the same symbolic terms:

> *Viene a la vena la nube,*
> *fragante quimera del aire,*
> *por senderos ya abiertos,*
> *roja, su flamante mentira.*

> *The cloud comes to the vein,*
> *a fragrant airborne chimera.*
> *It comes through trodden walkways,*
> *its falsehood shines red.*

It is impossible to avoid interpreting these rather imprecise verses as a negation of spirituality. "Quimera" and "mentira" are clear indications that the "cloud" is, as indicated in the second stanza, only a desire in the "infinite and sterile sky":

> *Marcha frágil en alta gasa,*
> *remolino de fondo humano,*
> *hambre, contagio y sed de vida*
> *en infinito azul estéril.*

> *Delicate walk in high gauze,*
> *vortex of human depth,*
> *hunger, contagious thirst for life*
> *in the infinite and sterile blue.*

Much as the "star" that was never reached in "Fuego fatuo," the clouds are deceiving images of the ideal. For the poet such an ideal remains as only a desire, a purely psychological construction.

Another symbolic element common to his poetry is also present in this poem: the image of "walking up," which refers to the concept of life as a journey and leads to the image of the "foot," a repeated and even obsessive image in Ulibarrí's poetry. *Al cielo se sube a pie*, a book created around the images of walking, contains a series of poems about "feet"; several instances of the same image appear also in the other book. One poem, 'Transparancias," [Transparencies], is included in both collections, indicating the close relationship between the poems devoted to the feet in *Al cielo se sube a pie* (62) and those in the "Love" section in *Amor y Ecuador* (69).

A possible reason for the inclusion of the poem in both books could be its representation of woman in highly idealized terms. The ideal woman of traditional love poetry has in this poem a particular significance because of the almost explicit reference to the conflicting levels of the lofty ideal and of the lower, more material, physical love. Most significant in this example is the positioning of the woman's feet—her lowest extremities—at a higher level, where they coincide with the symbolic altitude of the clouds and the sky. The lover looks up to her, because she "hovers in the air" (v. 10): "A tus pies sube mi ensueño, / a ellos elevo los ojos" [My dream climbs to your feet / to them I raise my eyes] (vv. 1–2). The woman exists in an unwithering height ("tu altura inmarcesible" [v. 6]) like the star or the clouds.

This view of woman as an untouchable and pure being is reinforced in other poems where her feet are again seen above the low level of natural existence and its earthly desires. In "No te quiero" [I do not love you] (53), from *Amor y Ecuador*, the implication is very clear:

> Si mis amores fueran puros
> haría alto el pedestal
> que te libre, todo tuyo,
> di mi aliento feroz y fatal.

If my love were pure
i would build a high pedestal
for you to be free
from my furious and fatal breath.

Likewise, in Poem XLII (64) from the same book, the ideal of a pure love is made explicit by the same images of "high" and "low." The exact correspondence between woman and the heavenly bodies insists in the purely ideal character of love:

Vago y vivo en la estala
de la remota estrella.
Respiro el aroma de la dama
y aspiro el vapor de la luna,
mas nunca me acerco a ninguna.

I roam and live in the wake
of the far away star.
I breathe the woman's scent
and I inhale the moon's vapors,
but I never get near to any of them.

In the second stanza, the reference to physical desire is represented by "blood," another term related to "vein" and the body. The enumerations are here quire expressive:

Estrella, luna y dama,
de fuego me encienden,
de luces me ciegan,
de sangre me manchan,
de angustias me matan.

Star, moon and woman
burn me in their fire,
they blind me with light,
they smear me with blood,
they kill me with anguish.

The poem concludes stressing love's ability to make possible a transition from the physical to the spiritual:

> *Estela y vapor y aroma*
> *son la forma de mi anhelo.*
> *Por ellos subo al cielo*
> *y los pies en la tierra dejo,*
> *sano, salvo, extasiado y mío.*

> *Wake and vapor, and aroma*
> *are the shapes of my desire.*
> *Through them I climb to the sky*
> *while leaving my feet on the ground,*
> *healthy, safe, ecstatic.*

Only his feet stay down, in contact with the earth, with matter and physical love. This is the level of reality that the ideal figure of the woman has to avoid:

> *Huye, huye, bella imagen,*
> *de la tierra de mis manos,*
> *de la piedra de mis males,*
> *de los huesos de mi abrazo.*
>   (XXXII, 54)

> *Fly, beautiful image, fly away*
> *from the ground of my hands,*
> *from the rocks of my ills,*
> *from the bones of my embrace.*

Woman is seen as an "image," not unlike those images of the Virgin Mary standing high on their pedestals or among the clouds, far from those three lower elements "earth," "stone," and "bones," which together with "feet"—a clear reference to the lowest aspects of the human body—represent material love, death, and the sexual desire. Two other compositions, these from *Al cielo se sube a pie*, refer to the figure of woman as an image. "Mujer imagen" (IX, 18) and Poem X (19)—which begins with a verse that repeats the title of the previous poem, "Imagen de mujer, mujer imagen"— talk about an ideal woman created by the dreams of the lover. In one case, there is a definite contrast between the real woman who exists in everyday material life:

> *En paseos y salones,*
> *en iglesias y avenidas,*
> *vagas, sufres y pereces,*
> *hierba y polvo en ansia estéril.*

> *In parks and parlors,*
> *in churches and avenues*
> *you roam, suffer and die,*
> *you sterile desiring herb and dust.*

and the ideal woman created by the imagination of the man in love:

> *Cada día yo te invento*
> *y te salvo de la inercia;*
> *y te creo cada noche*
> *an mis ansias y desvelos.*

> *Each day I create you*
> *and I save you from inertia;*
> *and every night I create you*
> *in my desires and wakefulness.*

In the other example, there is a less clear division between both levels of existence because the woman steps on the eyelashes of his dreams: "me pisas las pestañas de los sueños" (v 3).

Not always do the feet of woman suggest elevation and distance from physical love; quite the contrary. "Azucena" [Day lily] from *Amor y Ecuador* (33–35), talks about a young Indian housemaid and the description of her includes her feet:

> *Es la criada de mi casa,*
> *siempre mona, siempre niña.*
> *Tiene pies de pluma y balsa*
> *y voz de perfume y vino.*

> *She is the maid at my house,*
> *she is always pretty, always childlike.*
> *Her feet are of feathers and balsa wood,*
> *and her voice has the perfume of wine.*

"Feather" and "balsa wood" are light elements pointing to an image of the feet barely in contact with the ground but not necessarily set high on a pedestal or aloft among the clouds. It is indicative of Ulibarrí's interest in feet that in this poem they are the only direct reference to the maid's body. A similar physical quality is attributed to the feet in the series of poems devoted to them in *Al cielo se sube a pie*. In these compositions, feet are seen as objects of desire and as representation of human mortality, a symbolic meaning often attached to them (Cirlot 1981: 111).

The consciously obsessive preoccupation with feet in Ulibarrí's poetry is clearly pointing to the importance of the image in his system of representations. Walking, standing, stepping on are all actions centered on the feet as representatives of life and low materiality. In the love poems, the insistence on feet seems almost a fixation, particularly in the series of texts that in *Al cielo se sube a pie* makes the image of feet its central motive.

"Profesor del pie" [Foot's teacher] (40–41) opens this section with an explicit and direct recognition of the poet's fascination with feet. The distinction between low earthly reality, represented by the masculine desire, and high ideal spirituality, represented by woman, is maintained and stressed in its ambiguity by the use of the foot as representative of the woman in this poem. The ambiguity stems from the representation of the foot both as elevated on a pedestal and as the sensual extremity so often related to sexuality. As seen in other examples, man stands at the basis of the pedestal on which woman stands superior and elevated: "Al pie de tu pedestal, / pedestre, me hallarás" [At the foot of your pedestal / you will find me, a pedestrian man]. The alliterative insistence on terms related to "feet" underlines the difference between the earthly nature of the male and the elevated state of woman.

In spite of all these indications of a physical, sensual view of love in Ulibarrí, or perhaps because of it, his poems contain a markedly obsessive fixation with transcending the physical. A feeling of uneasiness and even of shame and sinfulness is present in the conflict between the two opposing forces. On the one hand, the physical desire is represented obsessively by feet, a well-known sexual fetish, while on the other, there is a refusal of sensuality and a search for a spiritual freedom from matter in the upper levels of mountains and sky. A good example of this categorical difference is Poem XVII from *Al cielo se sube a pie* (26), which explains the situation in brief terms. The poet declares his sexual desires in unequivocal terms—"Hambre de hembra / traigo siempre en mis tinieblas" [I always feel the hunger / of women in my darkness] (vv. 1–2)—and then goes on to compare the two opposing attitudes he takes with respect to love. He first idealizes woman in a flight to the skies:

> *A veces sueño*
> *con la mujer idea*
> *y subo a los cielos*
> *con mi Dulcinea*

> *Sometimes I dream*
> *with the ideal woman*
> *and I go up to the sky*
> *with my Dulcinea.*

Then comes the triumph of reality, of physical love described in strong terms:

> *Mas en el olvido arde*
> *la mujer de sangre,*
> *y su llama me llama*
> *al estreno y al estruendo de sus ansias.*

> *But in forgetfulness*
> *the woman of blood burns up*
> *and her flames call me*
> *to the birth and the thundering of her desire.*

The foot can have several different symbolic meanings, as Margo Glantz has observed in "De pie sobra la literatura mexicana" [Standing on Mexican literature]. In Ulibarrí's poems it represents mainly that lower realm that George Bataille attributed to the big toe, the lowest extremity of the body, which becomes naturally the symbol of the lower instincts as opposed to the higher aspirations of the spirit: "La vie humaine comporte en fait la rage de voir qu'il s'agit d'un mouvement de va-et-vient de l'ordure à l'idéal et de l'idéal à l'ordure, rage qu'il est facile de passer sur un organe aussi *bas* qu'un pied" [Human life includes, in effect, the indignation of realizing that life is a pendular movement from lewdness to ideal, and from ideal to lewdness; an indignation that is easily transferred to an organ as *low* as a foot] Bataille (1968: 76).

This traditional, Manichaean view of human nature is well represented by Ulibarrí's poetry and constitutes a strong remnant of his traditional, nostalgic world of the past. Then woman was seen in two very definite opposite lights. She was the ideal, pure lady, enthroned in a virginal world of clouds and heavenly light, and she was also the real, concrete woman of desire, firmly set on earth on her two sexually explicit feet. This second view seems to be the inspiration for the poems at the end of both books; in both cases, the image of the woman is negative as she represents sin and death.

Walking up towards the sky—the Heavens—is a popular image, reminiscent of an oral culture, and at the same time a telling image of a worldview and an attitude. For Ulibarrí, the Christian ideal is a deeply set sentiment, with all its sentimental components directly related to a visual image of Heaven as sky and of life as earthly and low. In direct relationship to it is the unconscious understanding of love in terms of opposition: physical desire and spiritual aspiration. To reach the ideal, man has only one way, his physical being. By fixing his sensuality on the feet, the poet is not so much acting a form of fetishism as recognizing in symbolic terms the essentially low nature so well represented by that part of the body which, being the lowest extremity, is in constant contact with the soil.

WORKS CITED

Bataille, George. "Le gros orteil." *Documents*. Paris: Editions Gallimard, 1968. Pp 75–82.

Cirlot, Juan Eduardo. *A Dictionary of Symbols*. New York: Vail-Ballou Press, Inc., 2nd. ed., 1981.

Glantz, Margo. "De pie sobre la literature mexicana." *Revista de la Universidad de México* 31, (1977): 25–36.

Tatum, Charles M. "Sabine Ulibarrí". *Chicano Literature: A Reference Guide*. Edited by Julio A. Martínez and Francisco A. Lomelí. Westport, Conn. Greenwood Press, 1985. Pp 385–395.

Ulibarrí, Sabine. *Amor y Ecuador*. Madrid: Ediciones José Porrua Turanzas, 1966.

———. *Al cielo se sube a pie*. Madrid" Alfaguara, 1966.

———. *El mundo poético de Juan Ramón*. Madrid: Artes Gráficas Clavileño, 1962.

MYTH AND RECURRING TIME IN
EL CÓNDOR AND OTHER STORIES

GENE STEVEN FORREST

As at least one critic has noted,[1] Sabine Ulibarrí, aside from his role as chronicler of a specific locale and ethnic identity (the Hispanic/American communities of northern New Mexico), is foremost a poet and writer who is concerned with art and the manner in which art may depict and, at the same time, transcend reality by rendering it immortal and of universal appeal. This he has achieved to a masterful degree through an idealized and highly selective re-creation of the past that is set within the timeless and familiar framework of folklore and myth. Thus the regional "history," or *historia*, that Ulibarrí's retrospective narrators set out to record is ultimately an *intrahistoria*, the collective tradition that Miguel de Unamuno insists is inseparable from eternal human experience (1916: 51).

Memory (Mnemosyne), we are reminded, engendered the creative muses, and thus, in Ulibarrí's "remembrance of things past," childhood is re-created in the crucible of artistic sensitivity and selectivity. The Tierra Amarilla or "topos" recalled from his first collection of short fiction is, therefore, an imagined place or "utopia" that the reminiscent narrator perceives affectionately as an ideal, timeless locale. This is not to say that such a place is lacking in realism or regional authenticity; but there is a free flow from narrator to narrated past, from present to past and to future, that affirms the centrality of the narrator's imagination and that undermines the notion of chronological or "literal" time and experience. One might sum up this process of recollection—indeed, the basis for Ulibarrí's entire poetics—with the following words of the narrator of "Los penitentes": "Ya viejo echo lo mirada sobre lo que fue la vida y la historia de Tierra Amarilla. A través de tanto recuerdo, tanta simpatía y una que otra antipatía se revela ante los ojos de mi querencia un mosaico vital en todo sentido bello, en todo sentido grato." / "In my old age I look back on what was the life and history of Tierra Amarilla. Across so many memories, so much sympathy and a little antipathy here and there, there appears in the eyes of my affection a living mosaic, lovely in every way, pleasant in every way" (*Mi abuela fumaba puros*, 156–57).

A pivotal means by which Ulibarrí is able to revive and immortalize the past is by configuring his "vital mosaic" along the lines of timeless myth. This mythic pattern is manifest from the earliest of Ulibarrí's works. One of his most memorable stories from *Tierra Amarilla* (1971), "Mi caballo mago" / "My Wonder Horse," recalls the narrator's childhood search for a wild stallion who eludes capture through what are popularly perceived to be magical or supernatural powers. The fifteen-year-old's heroic "quest" for the legendary "caballo mago" retraces the irrefutable paradigm of the rites of passage from childhood to adulthood that is repeated throughout Ulibarrí's work. Implicit, as well, is the Promethean myth of human achievement and failure in pursuit of the unattainable ideal. As is so often the case in these stories, the mythical or magical dimension is heralded by the substitution of conventional time and space by recurring time or eternity: "El momento es eterno. La eternidad momentánea. Ya no está, pero siempre estará." / "The moment is eternal. Momentary eternity. It no longer is here, but it will forever be" (6–7). Here, the narrator's sudden shift from the narrative past tense into the more immediate and dramatic present and prophetic future tenses reiterates the passage from the chronological to the mythical sphere.

Another example of this same manipulation of literal time by means of myth is the delightful "Se fue por clavos" / "He Went for

Nails" from Ulibarrí's subsequent collections, *Mi abuela fumaba puros/My Grandma Smoked Cigars* (1977). Here a brief errand—the protagonist, Roberto, interrupts a carpentry project he is undertaking for his sister, Carmen, to buy some nails—is extended paradoxically into a four-year absence for which the restless Roberto offers no explanation. Although in a more humorous or parodic vein than the previous example, the mythical blueprint of the quest—specifically reminiscent of Ulysses' odyssey—transforms the domestic incident into a magical event of heroic proportions. This process is enhanced by the absence of any description of the four-year idyll in the text, and in the final dialogue between brother and sister, no hint is given, at first, that Roberto's delay in returning home has been beyond the norm: —"Carmen, aquí están los clavos / —Sin vergünza, ¿por qué te tardaste tanto? / —Hermanita, me entretuve un rato con los amigos." / "'Carmen, here are the nails' / 'Shameless one. Why did you take so long?' / 'Little sister, I got tied up a while with the boys'" (152–53). This understatement, which provides the story's humorous denouement, compresses time and serves to subvert any notion of conventional chronology.

Besides these classical myths and archetypes, the entire corpus of popular custom and lore that is passed from generation to generation denotes the changeless and uninterrupted flow of time. Just so, the people who fill the narrator's memories are, by his own confession,[2] the reincarnations of a host of fictional characters who, in turn, represent a rich literary tradition deeply rooted in the soil of the European and American continents. Ultimately, such a cultural heritage reveals a broad, collective consciousness made up of basic human instincts and desires. The young protagonist of "¿Brujerías o tonerías?" / "Witcheries or Tomfooleries?" from *Mi abuela fumaba puros*, despite his rational nature and disdain for local superstitions, is inexplicably terrified and fascinated by the lament of a retarded woman who is rumored to be La Llorona, a nocturnal spirit from beyond the grave. The lament inspires feelings of empathy and recognition in the young man which he can only attribute to an unconscious, instinctive heritage or intrahistory: "¿Es que hay una herencia, una intrahistoria, que no tiene nada que ver con la biología ni con la inteligencia, que fluye desconocida de generación en generación?" ?"Is it that there is a heritage, an intrahistory, that has nothing to do with biology or with intelligence, that flows unknown from generation to genera- tion?" (52/55). It is precisely this intrahistory and its mythic mani- festations, preceding in time and space the narrow confines of Tierra Amarilla, that provide Ulibarrí's fiction with its widespread and lasting appeal.

Without a requisite appreciation for or understanding of the in- sistent mythical or universal basis of Ulibarrí's fiction, it is diffi- cult to comprehend his latest collection of short stories. In *El Cóndor and Other Stories* (1989), magical time and space all but displace the terrain of Tierra Amarilla and its colorful array of in- habitants that had become the familiar hallmarks and, for some, the very raison d'être of the New Mexican writer's work. *El Cóndor's* extensive use of exotic, cosmopolitan setting and fan- tastic plot has moved one critic to question to what extent re- gional (i.e., Chicano) writers like Ulibarrí can "act outside the mainstream traditions of their country, the United States" (Bruce- Novoa 1990: 14). Valid formalist concerns aside, such judgments reflect an ideological bias that unjustly underestimates Ulibarrí's ongoing concern for depicting *but also* transcending "mainstream traditions" through the common denominator of myth. The analy- sis that follows, limited perforce to five of the collection's most representative stories, endeavors to show that, rather than odd or ill-conceived departures from his past works, these stories are en- tirely consistent with this distinguished writer's artisic canon.

The first story, "Amena Karanova," sets the strikingly allegori- cal or symbolic tone for the entire collection. A brief synopsis of its highly imaginative plot makes this readily apparent. When a renowned European opera singer, Amena Karanova, survives a crash landing in Albuquerque, she is so drawn to the place that she de- cides to stay, establish a home, marry a local New Mexican, and pursue elaborate and mystical preparations for an heir who may survive her and fulfill her own frustrated ambitions of ideal love and art. In precise compliance with her portentous predictions,

Amena dies in childbirth, and her son, Damián (the namesake of her first love, killed in an automobile crash), becomes a great painter who travels to Europe where he meets and weds Amina Karavelha, the current sensation of the opera world. When the painter and diva return to New Mexico for their honeymoon, the narrative cycle turns one full rotation, and Amena's destiny is complete.

Although the story suffers from an overabundance of gratuitous narrative material[3]—it is the longest of the collection's eleven stories and twice the length of Ulibarrí's average short narrative—it is a key text in tracking the evolution of Ulibarrí's fascination for the themes of regeneration and universal time and space as perceived through the familiar iconography of myth. To begin with, character names alert the reader to the story's allegorical dimension and help to chart the tale's many mythical antecedents. Amena Karanova, the disenchanted "star" of the Old World rediscovers her inner inspiration and light when she turns her face ("Kara") toward the limitless horizons and brilliant illumination of the New World ("nova"). Yet to this new discovery she brings with her the ageless inspiration and beauty of the classical world. Her features conform perfectly to the classical ideal, and her beauty is described as "escultórica y clásica" / "sculpturesque and classical" (31). This same symbiosis of diverse cultures, of Old World and New, which forms the basis of Ulibarrí's *Primeros encuentros*, is reiterated in Amena's reincarnation, Amina Karavelha, whose surname implies at once the classical vision (Kara velha / cara vieja / old face) and the "discovery" of a new continent (Karavelha / caravela / caravel).

On yet another level, Amena represents the arts, and her legacy—the written prophecy together with the creative chamber ("la almohada" / "the pillow") left for her son—perpetuates her memory, which, in turn, provides the muse for Damián's artistic fruition. In this regard, the mysterious nocturnal rite practiced exclusively by women (Amena, her companion Dátil, and Amina), recalls the ancient Greek and Roman cult to the goddess Damia (Demeter) in which a victim (the Damiun) was sacrificed for the propagation and replenishment of the earth. Moreover, Amena's role as goddess and muse prefigures her reincarnation as the "anima"—contained in the anagram "Amina"—who will guide her son through his passage to maturity as artist and man.

Few readers familiar with the Hispanic cultural tradition could overlook the haunting literary antecedents present in "Amena Karanova." They bear further evidence of the undercurrent of shared experience, or *intrahistoria*, that flows throughout Ulibarrí's fiction. Of these literary resonances, the most resounding is that of Gustavo Adolfo Bécquer whose struggle to achieve total amorous and spiritual fulfillment through art is repeated in Damián's own efforts to capture on canvas the ineffable and mysterious image of the mother/muse whom he has never seen: "Se despertó tranquilo. Se desperezó. Luego, serenamente, tomó el pincel y le hizo algo al retrato. No sé qué. Quizás un beso, quizás una sombra o un sollozo. Pero de pronto se desató la mirada—hecha luz y sombra, vida y muerte, amor y odio. . . . La obra de amor estaba terminada." / "He awoke calmly. He yawned. Then quietly, picked up the brush and did something to the portrait. Maybe it was a kiss, maybe it was a sigh or a sob. Suddenly the look came alive, full of light and shadow, life and death, love and hate. . . . The work of love was ended (44/20).

Beyond this elaborate polisemy of mythical and literary allusion, Ulibarrí reinforces the timeless mythical mode by means of abrupt shifts from the narrative past to the dramatic present tense. As in the illustrations provided at the beginning of this study, the dramatic present, beyond its conventional function of heightening reader involvement with the text, freezes the narrative in a magical or eternal time frame. This occurs during the first description of Amena's mystical religious rite: "Era como si el tiempo se hubiera detenido, como si hubiera una expectativa, como si ese ambiente estuviera listo para producir un milagro. De pronto se presenta Amena. . . . Sus pasos son lentos, pausados, como una diosa." / "It was as if time had stopped with a breathless suspense ready to produce a miracle. Suddenly Amena appeared. . . . Her steps were slow, deliberate. She walked like a goddess." (37/13–14).[4] Another such "magical" moment is that of Damián's first encounter with Amina in Madrid, which sets in motion a series of romantic events foretold in Amena's prophecy.

Employing a very similar format to that of "Amena Karanova," "Loripola" is a retreatment of the theme of the regenerative and enlightening power of art. Once again, the artistic muse or ideal conforms in proportion and detail to the statuesque, classical model, only in this instance it is literally a statue. Bequeathed through a quirk of fortune to a modest New Mexican museum, this classical Greek statue, entitled "Loripola," rapidly becomes the town's top attraction and object of veneration for its eternal, universal beauty. Among its most ardent admirers is Amadeo Lucero, who, when the statue is stolen from the museum, pursues and kills the assailants but, in turn, is mortally wounded. Amadeo's sacrifice brings the statue miraculously to life, and in a tryst that seems to be predestined, he is resuscitated by Loripola's love. The spell is broken, however, by the vengeful Lobópolo, god of the wolves, and Loripola must return to her former place in the museum. The story's enigmatic conclusion leaves the reader guessing, for both statue and young suitor display a smile of inner satisfaction, and there is even the hint that their love shows promise for continued rebirth: "Unos decían que la Loripola había vuelto cambiada. . . . Que la mirada y la sonrisa de ahora eran las de una mujer contenta con el niño que lleva dentro" / "Some said that Loripola had come back different. / . . . That the look in her eyes and the smile she brought back were those of a woman happy with the child she was carrying" (95–96/87).

The encounter of Loripola and Amadeo connotes the same creative symbiosis of disparate cultures and spheres as has been seen in "Amena Karanova." Metaphorically, this symbiosis is expressed in terms of light. Placed under a skylight in a hall dedicated in her honor, Loripola is illuminated by the intense New Mexican sun by day and by the solitary desert moon by night. She, in turn, "enlightens" and transforms the place with her classical beauty and composure: "Ella, a su vez, iluminaba el recinto con su mármol y su sonrisa vital." / "She, in turn, illuminated the enclosure with her white marble and her vital smile" (89/81). Completing the "constellation" of light is the morning or brilliant star (Venus) represented by Amadeo "Lucero" whose poetic insight and love succeed in bringing the statue to life.

In "Loripola," unlike "Amena Karanova," classical mythology is reinvoked in an ironic key, and the narrator spoofs the all too human escapades and foibles of the so-called gods of antiquity. An excellent example of this is Amante, god of love, whose womanizing and otherwise scandalous behavior bring about his expulsion from Mount Olympus and his forced sojourn in the Hispanic world where he enjoys a sympathetic following. It is thus that Amante introduces southwestern food to the heavenly sphere, where it is declared the official cuisine of the gods, and it is thanks to his passionate nature that he is moved to immortalize Loripola through a statue that he fashions with his own hands. This lucid treatment of classical mythology, far from debunking the positive appeal of the classical ideal, underscores its fundamental humanity and the basic commonality or universality of all cultural tradition, legend, and myth. In this way, Amante is a link between legends as culturally diverse in time and space as those of don Juan and Pygmalion; and if chile, frijoles, and tortillas are the "ambrosia" of the inhabitants of New Mexico, there is no reason to believe that they would be any less acceptable as nourishment fit for the gods. The union of the classical Greek statue and the New Mexican native, therefore, is made possible and all the more plausible by this shared heritage.

At first glance, "El hombre que no comía" / "The Man Who Didn't Eat" appears to be very different from "Amena Karanova" and "Loripola." A mysterious foreigner, Helmut Heinz, comes to live among the inhabitants of a small New Mexican village, Santaflor, and rapidly gains a reputation for being a brilliant scientist, inventor, and horticulturist. Helmut sets about modernizing and expanding the native agricultural and livestock industries, but his major project, which is kept a mystery from his admiring neighbors, is the creation of a man made up largely of vegetable matter. Having reproduced the outer semblance of a man, he next succeeds in infusing this organism, or *patata inteligente*, with the necessary feelings and emotions to ensure its normal interaction with other humans. The result, Elmo Delo, endears himself to the local townspeople by selflessly working on their behalf, and when a laboratory accident ends his brief but beneficial existence, he make provisions for the continuation of his "father's" brilliant work.

Under closer scrutiny, however, this tale of science fiction is analogous in many ways to the other stories in the collection. The most obvious parallel is the paradigm of the fruitful exchange between foreign cultures, specifically, those of the Hispanic communities of the Southwest and the "Anglo" or Northern European cultures. Helmut's scientific knowledge and experimentation provide the indigenous inhabitants with a protective "armor" ("Elmo," Helmut's nickname, is derived from the word *yelmo*, or helmet) against poverty and disease, and the town, for its part, supplies the natural materials and support for such experimentation to succeed. But it is in the scientist's act of "procreation," the creation of a namesake in his own image who may survive him and perpetuate his work, that the story posits the strongest thematic link to the other stories of this collection. In "El hombre que no comía," the muse of science—like those of music and painting (:Amena Karanova") and sculpture and poetry ("Loripola")—imbues men with the beneficent, creative impulse that is forever perpetuating itself. When Elmo Delo dies, Helmut's creation simply disappears into the collective consciousness or the intrahistoria from which it can reemerge reincarnated at any time: "Elmo Del había sido idea, sueño, ilusión. Ahora había regresado al reino puro, transparente y atmosférico de las ideas de donde había venido. Allí, en el aire, existe todavía. Tal vez algún día venga otro genio como Helmut y capte esa idea otra vez y la haga visible y viable." / "Elmo Delo had been an idea, a dream, an illusion. He had now returned to the pure kingdom, transparent and atmospheric, of ideas from whence he had come. Up there, in the air, he still exists. Perhaps someday another genius like Helmut will appear to capture that idea again and make it visible and viable once again" (70/62).

Implicit reference to legend and myth, once again, strengthens the story's thematic coherence. Obviously, Ulibarrí is working from the Frankenstein legend, but his inspiration most probably goes back much further to classical myth and the story of Prometheus. The Promethean quest is undeniably suggested by Helmut's sacrilegious scheme to infringe on the exclusive domain of the gods ("Helmut quería ser un Dios" / "Helmut wanted to be a god" [64/56]). His "divine" aspirations appear to be reconfirmed by the surname he gives to his creation, "Delo," which recalls Delos, the birthplace of Apollo, a god whose particular associations with the sun, animal husbandry, and agriculture have particular relevance to the story.

The remaining stories to be analyzed, "El cacique Cruzto" / "Cruzto, Indian Chief" and "El Cóndor," approach the same themes of renewal and the timeless cycle of myth, but, unlike the stories just discussed, the mythological reference is almost exclusively of American Indian rather than classical Greek or Roman origin. The first of the stories tells of a legendary Indian chief, Cruzto, who preached a doctrine that was remarkably similar to that of Christianity long before the Spanish discovery and colonization of the New World. The existence of such a legend thus facilitated the Indians' conversion to Catholicism and the assimilation of the Spaniards into the indigenous, New Mexican population. When an artist who is engaged in restoring the parish church of Cruztillo fills the head of a young girl with tales of the pre-Columbian Indian leader, she is so enraptured that, elaborating on the artist's own embellishment of the legend, she proclaims that Cruzto has appeared to her in a vision and revealed to her the site of his final resting place as well as his desire to receive proper Christian burial. Miraculously, and to the confounded disbelief of the artist, Cruzto's grave is found, and the girl's "revelations" create a mystical cult to the legendary Indian leader and the young "priestess."

Aside from providing an amusingly irreverent look at the hidden dynamics of mystical rapture and revelation, "El cacique Cruzto" makes a strong case for the formidable ingenuity and creativity of the human imagination. It is not merely coincidental that the entire chain of events leading to the "miraculous" reappearance of Cruzto and the reconsecration of the small village is initiated by an artist who is employed to repaint or "restore" the colonial church to its original brilliance. In addition to his paints and brushes, words provide the artist with the tools necessary for recoloring and reelaborating the past, and it is in this capacity as storyteller that he enters into a productive collaboration with the nine-year-old María whose receptivity and boundless imagination make her the ultimate instrument for his muse. To this end, the child draws on her town talents as an actress: "Ella gozaba su papel y sabía cultivarlo y desarrollarlo. Vivía el sueño que soñaba con todo gusto." / "She loved her role and knew just how to cultivate and embellish it. She lived the dream she dreamed to the fullest" (159/153).

Ulibarrí's allegory concerning the artistic muse would not be complete, however, without the vital ingredient of myth, for it is myth that gives the story its pivotal theme of rediscovery and renewal. While, on the one hand, the sham and commercialism that surround Cruzto's rediscovery and baptism discredit the notion of supernatural or miraculous "resurrection," on the other hand, the coincidence of Christian and Indian iconography and cult corroborate the enduring spiritual imperatives (the need for a "savior" or "messiah" and the quest for immortality) that are reborn in every generation and form the rich fabric of intrahistoria.

This same reemergence of myth—in the form of a legendary Indian savior and leader—through the vital intercession of the muses forms the essential theme of the final and title story of the collection, "El Cóndor." Reflecting to some degree the writer's own experience, "El Cóndor" follows the exploits of Ernesto Garibay, a professor from the University of New Mexico, who establishes an institute in Ecuador and gradually becomes so fascinated by the region that he devises a scheme to combat the poverty and exploitation of the native Indians for whom he feels a close affinity and, even, love. Together with his wife and a loyal cadre of secret allies, Garibay fabricates the legend of a militant Indian leader, El Cóndor, who implements social and economic reforms by means of extortion and political assassination. As Garibay's coercive campaign gradually succeeds and the general lot of the Indians improves, the phantom Indian leader is venerated by the Ecuadoreans as the reincarnation of the last Inca emperor, Atahualpa. Paralleling the dramatic metamorphosis of the social and economic order brought about by their unswerving devotion to the Indians' cause, Garabay and his wife undergo a total cultural and even racial assimilation into Andean society and are miraculously transformed into Altor and Altora, the successors of the ancient Inca dynasty: "todo ponía en manifiesto que Altor y Altora tenían conciencia entera de que eran el emperador y la emperatriz del nuevo reino de los incas. Eran amos y dueños del mundo de los Andes." / "everything showed that altor and Altora knew perfectly well that they were the emperor and the empress of the new kingdom of the Incas. They were lords and masters of the world of the Andes" (223/200).

El Cóndor's legacy is an idyllic world in which Indian pride and optimism go hand in hand with brotherhood and democracy and revolutionized productivity and efficiency in farming and manufacture guarantee the prosperity and well-being of all. Such an implausible utopian realm reveals the fundamentally allegorical or poetic nature of the narrative and belies the notion that Ulibarrí might be proposing a viable blueprint for change in Latin America. Nonetheless, as Juan Bruce-Novoa (1990: 14) has noted, the well-intentioned yet paternalistic intervention of the North American scholar in the internal problems of the Latin American republic—problems that are highly oversimplified in the story—together with the restoration of an absolute, albeit enlightened, native "monarch" raise the loathsome specters of imperialistic and elitist panaceas that have perpetuated political and economic instability in the region. Even more disturbing is the professor's campaign of extortion and assassination that, no matter how benign, evokes the bloody images of world terrorism that has been anything but successful in resolving the world's social ills. Regrettably, such inevitable associations strike stridently dissonant notes in the text and seriously diminish its effectiveness.

These compelling reservations aside—and they are not easily dismissed even by Ulibarrí's most loyal readers—Garibay's evocation and eventual re-creation of a legendary Indian savior is symptomatic of the irresistible appeal of myth and the capacity of the imagination and art to reinvoke the myths of the past. In this regard, the professor's prophetic verses provide essential clues to his gradual metamorphosis or incorporation into myth. On one occasion, for instance, Garibay likens the process to one of divine or supernatural revelation: "Yo vi el resplandor de Dios, / indómito en el áurea nube. / Vi la sombra de su voz / indígena en la alta cumbre." / "I saw the splendor of God, / invincible in the golden cloud. / I saw the shadow of his voice / on the high sierras, indigenous' (214/192). Also to be considered in this light are Garibay's other texts, the anonymous letters and apocryphal newspaper editorials attributed to El Cóndor. This creative output, pursued with an intense and tenacious devotion to the common good, brings about the magical transformation: "El compromiso total es capaz de todo. El entregarse cuerpo y alma a una causa noble puede producir milagros." / "Total involvement is capable of everything. Giving yourself body and soul to a noble cause can produce miracles" (221/199).

Returning to the illustrations presented at the beginning of this study, we may ask how different Dr. Garibay's quest to embody the legendary Indian savior, El Cóndor, is from an old man's recollections of a childhood encounter with the fleeting and indomitable "caballo mago," or from a young man's startling revelation of the inescapable irrational recesses of his own soul. In each case, the pursuit of the unknown or unattainable ideal leads to a reenactment of the timeless paradigms of myth and legend, which ultimately reflect the collective consciousness or universal psyche. Symptomatic of this universality are the many encounters and assimilations of distant cultures, settings, and time periods that, although suggested in the earlier works, are emphasized to a highly fanciful or magical extent—and with varying degrees of success— in this latest collection of short stories.

El Cóndor reconfirms Ulibarrí's abiding premise that the artistic impulse, most often synonymous with a loving devotion to the past, provides the essential link in the endless chain of human accomplishment and renewal. In this regard, nearly every one of the stories in the collection is an allegorical rendering of one or more of the classical Muses, including, foremost, those of poetry, music, painting, sculpture, and comedy. That Ulibarrí's own muse has inspired him in a variety of creative directions is attested by his critical essays, lectures, collections of poems, and, naturally, anthologies of short stories. Rather than turning his back on the past and his own ethnic "roots," as one might construe from this latest venture into the magical and exotic, therefore, Ulibarrí has remained true to the aesthetic premises and thematic constants of his earliest works. It is perhaps these enduring and universal "roots" that will ensure in the long run Ulibarrí's position among the leading Hispanic writers of the Southwest.

NOTES

1. See Sackett 1972: 516.

2. "Son amigos que nacieron en la novela picaresca de España. Otros nacieron en cuentos humorísticos en este rincón del nuevo mundo. Son personajes ficticios de largo abolengo castizo y pobladores del rico mundo del folklore nuevomexicano." / "They are friends who were born in the picaresque novel in Spain. Others were born in humorous stories in this corner of the new world. They are fictitious characters with a long, native tradition and inhabitants of the rich world of New Mexican folklore" ("Mano Fashico," in *Mi abuela fumaba puros*, 112–13).

3. I concur with Bruce-Novoa's assessment that this story is flawed by distracting, gratuitous elements, although I would take exception to his judgment that such excess stems from a superfluous blend of the New Mexican and the exotic European milieus depicted here and in other of the collection's stories. The encounter and symbiosis of disparate worlds—for which there is ample precedent in Ulibarrí's previous work, *Primeros encuentros* (1982)—is consistent with the story's themes of regeneration and the triumph of the creative imagination over spatial and temporal constraints. Were the plot and characters of "Amena Karanova" placed within an exclusively New Mexican context, would narrative details such as Amena and Dátil's suitor, Count Barnizkoff, and Damián's televised portrait of Virgie Joy be any less superfluous to the plot? Suffice it to say that as Bruce-Novoa adroitly observes, "When well blended, anything can go into the content; when awkwardly done, content matters little—the story rings false" (14).

4. This analysis is based on the Spanish text. The English translation of *El Cóndor*, unlike Ulibarrí's previous collected fiction, does not interface simultaneously with the Spanish text, nor does it give either a complete or—as in the case of this quote—an equivalent rendering of the Spanish. Lacking any editorial note to the contrary, one must assume, along with Bruce-Novoa, that the author himself is responsible for both versions of the text.

WORKS CITED

Bruce-Novoa, Juan. "Magical Regionalism." Review of *El Cóndor and Other Stories*, by Sabine Ulibarrí. *American Book Review* 11 (1990): 14.

Sackett, Theodore A. Review of *Tierra Amarilla: Stories of New Mexico/Cuentos de Nuevo México*, by Sabine Ulibarrí. *Modern Language Journal* 56 (1972): 516.

Ulibarrí, Sabine R. *El Cóndor and Other Stories*. Houston: Arte Público Press, 1989.

———. *Primeros encuentros/First Encounters*. Ypsilanti: Bilingual Press/Editorial Bilingüe, 1982.

———. *Mi abuela fumaba peros/My Grandma Smoked Cigar*. Berkeley: Quinto Sol, 1977.

Unamuno, Miguel de. *En torno al casticismo*. Vol. 1, *Ensayos*. 6 vols. Madrid: Publicaciones de la Residencia de Estudiantes, 1916.

MYTHS OF MASCULINITY IN *TIERRA AMARILLA*

Wolfgang Karrer

Tierra Amarilla: Cuentos de Nuevo México (1964; bilingual edition 1971) has been misread. In spite of its subtitle, it is neither a simple collection of short stories (Tatum 1982: 79) nor an early example, slightly dated, of the first *costumbrismo* phase of Chicano short stories (Rodríguez 1979a: 61). I propose to reread *Tierra Amarilla* as a modernist story of initiation based on a problematic concept of gender identity.[1] The book challenges traditional patriarchal conceptions of male identity in the preurban world of Aztlán.

As Dieter Herms (1990: 118) has pointed out, the discussion of whether . . . *y no se lo tragó la tierra, Estampas del valle, The House on Mango Street* or *Living Up the Street* are novels or collections of short stories is as difficult as it is futile. They are both; and as I will show, *Tierra Amarilla* belongs to a well-established genre of writings with this character. The six stories in *Tierra Amarilla* can stand for themselves, and some of them clearly owe to Chicano traditions of oral storytelling. But they are also skillfully connected to map out an identity quest that culminates and finds its ambiguous resolution in "Hombre sin nombre," the last story, hardly short and even less emerging from oral tradition.

As for the short story reading, some support can be found for the costumbrismo reading (Urioste 1986), but a closer look at the text reveals very little about local customs of the Chicano community of Tierra Amarilla, New Mexico. Except perhaps—and this is a significant exception— for the *velorio* in "Juan P.," all the local customs mentioned are simply those of Roman Catholic church-goers, or farming or pastoral people anywhere in the world. As Rolando Hinojosa (1979: 44) observed, "We may write *Perros y antiperros, Ultima, Tamazunchale, Tierra* or *Peregrinos* in specifics, but always in relation to the universal." *Tierra Amarilla* is the story of a writer growing up in a small traditional Chicano community, and all we learn about the place has to bear directly on the narrator's quest for identity. Alejandro Turriaga, the narrator, comes from one of the wealthier families in the community. He accepts unchallengingly the class divisions in the community, the Turriaga ranching interest, their vaqueros, and what the narrator calls "la plebe" (47), or the dependent poor (59), depending on the charity of the Turriagas. Like the religious rites and the social rituals—again, with one significant exception—they are rather taken for granted and well known. There is no interest in exploring their historical or social ramifications. One learns much less about New Mexico in *Tierra Amarilla* than, say, about Texas in the writings of Rivera or Hinojosa. And in two central passages (51, 83), the narrator directly challenges the crippling limitations of traditional rural culture.

The gist of the book lies elsewhere. The six stories in the book follow a thematic and roughly chronological order that maps the quest for an identity by the male first-person narrator. Alejandro is fifteen in the first story, twelve in the second, fifteen again in the third, nine in the fourth and fifth. This curiously regressive movement leads into the last story, again subdivided into six gradually regressive parts. In this last story, Alejandro Turriaga is a married man and writer of thirty. If we assume some autobiographical foundations for the stories in Ulibarrí's life, the book's time span would reach from 1928 to 1949. There are short references to Berlin and the Second World War (115, 137, 141) that confirm this time frame.

From "Mi caballo mago" through "Juan P." to "Hombre sin nombre," the narration follows the well-known conventions of the bildungsroman, or initiation story. These conventions have been intimately connected with such themes as the loss of innocence and the quest for identity, both well established also in Chicano literature (Rodríguez 1979b; Lyon 1979). In a more recent study of French novels, Susan Rubin Suleiman (1983: 63–100) has developed structural criteria to identify the underlying model and its variation. She calls it the "structure of apprenticeship" and identifies it as one of the two main types of the ideological novel. According to her, the hero in a structure of apprenticeship sets out from ignorance and passivity, undergoes various experiences that she identifies as trials of interpretation, and finally reaches some knowledge (about himself) and possibility of action. If the knowledge reached is the one the author wants the reader to accept, also, we have a positive, if not a negative, case of apprenticeship. To make this an ideological novel, it has to have an underlying dualistic value system (that the hero does or does not opt for in the end), it will contain an open or implied rule of action for the reader, and it will rely on a doctrinal intertext, known to the reader. The ideological novel often has a high degree of redundancy, as the narrator tends to repeat and reformulate the recognitial experiences made by the hero. The model can be formulated thus:

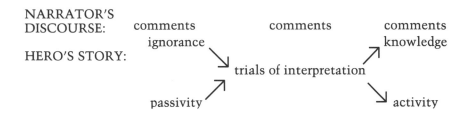

Suleiman demonstrates how the model works when applied to French *romans à thèse*. But she also succeeds in showing how many novels—sometimes almost against the will of their authors—subvert the simple dualistic value pattern when reality or history intervene in the fiction (ibid., 199–238). The quotation in which she relates "the scenario of initiation" to the apprenticeship story will lead into the heart of *Tierra Amarilla*.

This scenario consists in an individual's progress from a state of ignorance to a state of knowledge by means of a series of trials; the object of knowledge is always linked to the sacred, and the end in view is an essential transformation of the individual—a "new birth"—which will make him worthy of becoming a member of the group constituted by other initiates. The roman à thèse offers a desacralized version of this scenario: the hero attains a knowledge that transforms him, and his transformation is the prelude to action undertaken by a group: those who share the knowledge—in reality, the values— of the hero. (IBID., 77)

Tierra Amarilla is indeed a desacralized version of the initiation story, and the group as well as the action it leads to are highly ambivalent.

Alejandro Turriaga, if we assume the hero of all six stories to be the same person, starts out from ignorance or innocence—which term you choose depends on the underlying value system—and ends up with a new and terrible knowledge, born out of temporary amnesia. Whether he also moves from passivity to action is another question that I will deal with later. He undergoes six trials of interpretation that will lead to the culminating new knowledge. As the narrator and the hero are one and the same person at different stages—the double "I" of autobiographical fiction—discourse and story complement and support each other in the well-known fashion of the apprenticeship structure. There can be no doubt about the ignorance of the young hero; the narrator never loses the opportunity to underline it with a "no supe" or "no sé". The interplaying verbs of knowledge and its negation form a strong connective tissue in all six stories. Phrases like "no sé . . . sólo sé" (7), "si mi padre supo algo yo no lo supe" (25), and "sabía mucho, me parecía entonces" (39) proliferate throughout the text and establish the theme of ignorance/knowledge in its often ironic relations. The key word for Alejandro that occurs in all stories several times is "misterio" (9, 31, 43, 61, 155) or its desacralized version "secreto" (passim). Alejandro's quest is for his identity, for what he finally calls "el misterio de mi vida" (155).

His quest moves through six trials of interpretations, leading to some knowledge about himself. The first trial is that of "Mi caballo mago" (3–17). The narrator leaves no doubt what the horse stands for in Alejandro's youthful mind: "Mito del reino animal. Poema del mundo viril" (3); "Orgullo, fama y arte en carne animal. Cuadro de belleza encendida y libertad varonil" (7). Young Alejandro develops fantasies about Oriental kings and harems, imagines himself displaying the horse on Sundays to the village girls (5). "Era el orgullo del hombre adolescente. Me sentí conquistador" (13). His father congratulates him on the capture of the horse: "Esos son hombres" (15); Alejandro tries to react with the role of *muy hombre*. But the captured horse escapes, and Alejandro's father lays his arm across his son's shoulders. Alejandro feels enriched by this experience: "Ahora seguiría siendo el ideal, la ilusión y la emoción. El Mago era un absoluto. A mí me había enriquecido la vida para siempre" (17). Everything seems fine: Alejandro has learned his first lesson; his reading of male liberty seems confirmed.

The first story sets the tone and theme for what is to follow: Alejandro is to learn how to be a man, guided by his father and other role models. In the actantial scheme of A.J. Greimas, these persons are called "donors," and as Suleiman observes (80 ff.), these donors in the apprenticeship structure are almost always father-surrogates, spiritual elective fathers. Part of what Alejandro has to learn is to subdue the child in himself, especially the childish laughter that menaces to erupt after victory (15). Another part concerns that arrogance and pride so exclusively associated with the male role (7, 9).

Alejandro's second trial of interpretation comes with Padre Benito, a spiritual father, who makes his congregation laugh with his mispronunciations of the Spanish language (19–35). His exterior is grotesque. Padre Benito is the opposite of the male role model offered in the first story. Closely associated with the female world of nuns and religious women, he is more ignorant than twelve-year-old Alejandro, and he does not drink wine, which is firmly established in the male world of Tierra Amarilla. So Alejandro undergoes a parody of religious conversion to get at Padre Benito's wine. Again, the trial is tied to gender interpretations.

Ustedes no pueden saber el placer, digo delirio, digo éxtasis de una buena religiosa [las monjas] que lleva a un pecador entero y sumiso y lo pone en el regazo del Señor. Yo miraba a sus miradas rapsódicas y me estremecía, y no de placer. Hay algo furibundo y espantoso en la mujer extasiada. Cuando yo las veía se me ponían los pelos en punta, como quien dice, alzados también al cielo. Así parecía que lo interpretaban ellas. (27)

The interplay of knowledge/ignorance is neatly managed. Padre Benito stands in opposition to virile liberty and suppressed childish laughter. The submission to a feminized religion and the legacy of laughter, however repressed, are the ambivalent lessons left behind by Padre Benito (35). The anal joke about the malodorous "fundillo" of the church leads directly to trial three.

Religion and gender determine the grotesque tragedy of Juan and his two sisters. Their lives are ruined because of a female fart at a wake, where women, more strictly than men, are forced to remain in a strenuous kneeling position for long hours. Juan becomes an alcoholic, and the two unmarried sisters bury themselves for the rest of their lives in their decaying house. They cannot face the ridicule and the vulgar name "perrodas" given to them by some men in the village. Juan, who had never wondered about Juan P. and his strange sisters before, now learns about them by asking Brígido. Again, Alejandro ends up with a gender interpretation: "En cada leño veía yo la cara boba de un hombre abusivo y bruto que había condenado a tres seres humanos al infierno de esta vida" (31) and (about the wake) "La tradición, el decoro, la dignidad demandan que la mujer se mantenga rígida como una tabla, o una estatua, o una santa" (45). The themes of the earlier stories are again overturned: Juan rides a white horse, the last refuge of his male pride, and the laughter Padre Benito's fundillo aroused is now castigated as harmful. Sacrificial wine becomes drunkenness. Sex roles are reversed, and submission to tradition here becomes harmful to the community. Alejandro rebels against the customs of Tierra Amarilla by symbolically splitting logs, something his father had ordered him to do.

Alejandro's fourth trial of interpretation is perhaps the most difficult one. At least it is the only one the narrator finds no explicit moral for. "Sábelo" is a story about ignorance and how to over-come it, how Alejandro and a little friend exposed bees to the cold and thus killed them out of ignorance, and the inlaid stories of don José. The old man claims bears attack him and bees do not be-cause he had a queen bee for a mother and a young man as a father: "se volvió abeja y se casó con la reina. Y se murió, sábelo, pues los amores de las reinas son mortales" (65). All Alejandro knows is that don José never lies, but understanding the story is be-yond the nine-year-old. The fact that don José shares a "secret" with him makes him feel good: "Me sentí muy hombre" (61). Unimpressed by ridicule and traditions, don José forms a counterpiece of Juan P. His role as male storyteller repeats that of Brígido and prepares Alejandro for his art of storytelling. The real message of don José seems to be to look behind the surface story for a hidden truth.

The marriage theme is expanded in Alejandro's fifth trial of in-terpretation, his recollection of Edumenio, the blacksmith (67–83). For the nine-year-old, Edumenio embodies perfect manhood: ro-bust, tall, wide, taciturn, like a horse ("Mi caballo blanco"). Like don José, he seems to hold mythical secrets for the young boy: "Yo sentía un curioso placer secreto, me sentía partícipe de la fuerza de este hombre, digno por un momento de entrar en el mundo misterioso de los hombres" (71). But his hero succumbs, not to the fatal loves of the queens, but to village prejudice and snob-bery. Edumenio marries a woman reputed to have been a prosti-tute, and they are snubbed by everybody in the village, including Alejandro's parents. Alejandro rebels a second time and forces his mother to offer refreshments, ignoring the cause of the re-jection. The narrator heavily underlines the moral of the story with comments about boys and dirt, male silence, and contempt for girls. As a result, he admits, "Yo llegué al amor un poco tarde en mi vida" (77). His apologies and good wishes to Edumenio and Henriqueta, wherever they are, ring somehow overdone and unconvincing at the end of this story.

The accumulated interpretations of Alejandro between the age of nine and fifteen thus half-prepare the reader for what is to come in his last and most difficult trial in "Hombre sin nombre." Paradoxically, this is the first story in which Alejandro's name is given. And paradoxically, he has not become the *muy hombre* he wanted to become or he has become the *muy hombre* he does not want to be anymore. He had returned to Tierra Amarilla to write and read to them a book about his dead father only to find himself possessed by his father's voice. After an unsuccessful fight with this voice in himself, he flees back to his wife, Mima, in Albuquerque, only to find her asleep and the very image of his dead mother. He collapses, loses his memory, and only slowly repieces his identity by reading the manuscript of "Hombre sin nombre," the manuscript that Alejandro had written in Tierra Amarilla to honor his father. If the last part of this story reflects on itself, then the other five parts could be matched with the first five stories. In the first part of "Hombre sin nombre," he embodies the male values of his father ("Mi caballo blanco"); in the second, his father's voice awakes in him ("El relleno de dios"); in the third, he loses his self-determination to the voice ("Juan P."); in the fourth, he takes flight from the pursuing voice ("Sábelo"); and in the fifth, he loses his memory ("La fragua sin fuego").

Alejandro does not know what has gone wrong in his apprenticeship, and he cannot find a way out since he has no memory. His only hope is his wife, Mima. But she suffers with him and grows paler everyday (165). As it is his father who is trying to possess him, who actually did possess him through the writing about him in Tierra Amarilla, it is worthwhile to look back at the earlier stories for clues. And there are plenty. Father's voice in the sixth story ("Te defiendes como un hombre. Eres mi hijo" 111) is amply confirmed in the earlier stories: "Mi padre tenía le manía de que yo fuera hombre. Hombre de campo, robusto y fuerte, la molestaba mi predilección por los libros, especialmente por la poesía" (39). Thus the father approves of Alejandro's male fantasies about the white horse, tolerates don José at the beehives (59), but "mysteriously" avoids the wordy and feminine world of don Benito's Sunday sermons (31). Alejandro, in his trials of interpretation, deeply imbibes an ideology and mythology of masculinity that clashes with his poetic ambitions. And this ideology of strength, silence, and arrogance that implies weakness, wordiness, and humility for the other sex is at the core of Alejandro's problems, which erupt into schizoid madness in "Hombre sin nombre." *Tierra Amarilla* is not a feminist tract, but the feminist discussion and the Chicana literature of the last decades have opened our eyes to what is at the heart of Alejandro's problems: the patriarchal traditions in many Chicano communities. Padre Benito's laughter, the sufferings of Juan's nameless sisters, and the treatment of Henriqueta form an eloquent subtext to the male fantasies about indomitable horses, bear taming, and fatal queen bees. And the true poetic voice is stifled in Alejandro because of the patriarchal tradition that considers books and poetry unmanly occupations. The manuscript Alejandro has written is "arrogant" (87) like the white horse (6), and the voice that reads it is not his own but his father's. It celebrates "el ídolo, la personificación y el jefe espiritual de los Turriaga" (91). Alejandro sees his father's face in his glass of wine. They become one.

The only way to overcome his possession by the patriarchal tradition seems his wife. Mima (Mami, mi mamá me mima) represents the feminine role of life-giving support. She keeps the house, brings him the food, leads him back into his past, and finally hands him the book about his father that contains the ambiguous identity prepared for him by his father and Tierra Amarilla. She could give him a son in whom he could survive as his father did him (141). But she also seems to offer a new, shared personality development that harmoniously unites the male and female roles in a new joint personality that does away with arrogance and humility: "la mutua personalidad que compartimos" (133).

All this has obvious therapeutic overtones, and *Tierra Amarilla*, among other things, suggests a Freudian reading of parricide and the return of the repressed. Thus "Hombre sin nombre" definitely undercuts the folkloristic implications of the earlier stories. But it also retains a mythological dimension that does not only tie in with the male heroes' fantasies of the book. If "Aztlán" means "tierra blanca" in Nahuatl traditions (Blouin 1979: 179), then Tierra Amarilla is part of it. And then the land, more than the community or the village, forms the mythic substratum of the story. Alejandro voices Nahuatl philosophy and gender interpretation when he gives in to his father: "Es una estupidez que un hombre crea que un pedazo de tierra le pertenezca. . . . Mas bien posee la tierra al hombre porque ella se lo come, lo digiere, lo aniquila.— Esto lo había leído yo en alguna parte" (123). And he continues, "Lo ridículo de la situación me dio en la cara como beso de vieja atrevida y tuve que reírme" (125). The contradictions in Alejandro, his readings and his heritage, remain unresolved until the end when Alejandro plans to celebrate the publication of his book with Mima: "Esta noche celebramos el acto, ella y yo, y el que me causó toda esta desgracia. Este y yo somos inseparables, esta noche celebramos. Mañana, ¿quién sabe?" (167).

For Alejandro tomorrow may have brought the continuation of this strange ménage à trois, but for Chicano literature it brought the rise of Chicana writing and the beginning of a reevaluation of sex roles in Aztlán. *Tierra Amarilla* is not an ideological text in Suleiman's sense. Although it clearly posits a dualistic value system of male and female sex roles, it does not lead the hero through a series of interpretations to reach a clear verdict either of patriarchal traditions or of discrimination of women. It leaves its hero with an ambiguous half-knowledge about its patriarchal heritage without a clear injunction of what to do about it. The traditional intertext of male superiority is invoked several times but is fought against in the conclusion. More important still, the apprenticeship of Alejandro Turriaga leads from physical action (the capture of a horse, the deceptive religious conversion, the cleaving of logs) to one of relative inaction and passivity, almost defeat. Alejandro has not become the writer and spiritual leader for his community. His attempt to resacralize, legendarize or mythologize his father and his own history in Tierra Amarilla does not provide him with a viable system of values. Patriarchalism has become a stifling tradition. Thus *Tierra Amarilla* offers a diagnosis, no recipes.

If *Tierra Amarilla* is about gender construction rather than costumbrismo, if it is more a coherent argument about the pernicious effects of patriarchalism than a collection of short stories, there is one other dimension to *Tierra Amarilla* so far unexplored. It is a universal rather than a local dimension. The universalizing strategy has always been open to minority literature to fight its way into the official canons of teaching and criticism. And the more local the writing, the stronger the pressure to represent universal values (cf. Hinojosa 1979: 44). *Tierra Amarilla* belongs as much to the U.S. mainstream as to Chicano literature. It belongs to one of the most typical genres that modernism has developed and that has flourished especially in the United States. I am referring to the apprenticeship or initiation story fragmented into short stories with different or continuous heroes. The more conservative models seem to preserve an individual hero; the more experimental writers change the protagonist from story to story but keep the thematics or the structure of trial by interpretation going. The inventor of this model, as of so many others in modernism, seems to be James Joyce. *Dubliners* (1914) follows predominantly male heroes from childhood though adolescence to maturity in one social setting, Dublin, in one specific period of time (Schneider 1982). Joyce takes his changing heroes from ignorance ("The Sisters") to some kind of knowledge ("The Dead"), and there is little doubt that the various protagonists reflect the paralysis or stagnation of the city they come from. Individual and society reflect each other. This model was taken up and developed by Sherwood Anderson in *Winesburg, Ohio* (1919). The revolt from the village—the male protagonist George Willard experiences his hometown only to leave it in the end—becomes one of the models of American modernism. The inhabitants of Winesburgh take their turn in a series of "grotesques," people distorted by some idea or obsession in their lives.

Ernest Hemingway came next with *In Our Time* (1925) and added World War I and interchapters to the formula. The apprenticeship of Nick Adams differs from that of George Willard through the war trauma, which underlies most of Nick's experiences after the war and his interpretations of them. William Faulkner added the theme of the land and its rightful possession or lawless destruction in *Go Down Moses* (1943). The multigenerational theme reinforces the continuity of the male hero in the apprenticeship structure. An ethnic variant is Richard Wright's *Uncle Tom's Children* (1938), about the gradual awareness of repression and the action following from this awareness. Wright freely changes his protagonists, but it is clear that they represent different stages of black struggle against white supremacy (Karrer 1977). Chicanos and Chicanas have made use of these examples in *The House on Mango Street* and . . . *y no se lo tragó la tierra*.

Tierra Amarilla represents a transitional work in this series that contains many other works not mentioned here. It takes—consciously or not—the idea to reflect a community at a specific time through the development of its hero(es) from the *Dubliners*. The ignorance of the boy and the sisters at the beginning and the sad knowledge of Gabriel at the end of *Dubliners* shoes certain parallels to *Tierra Amarilla*. Alejandro's fight with his dead father has some relation with Gabriel's vision of death in the last story of *Dubliners*. And the community of Tierra Amarilla is a collection of grotesques much like Winesburg, Ohio, is for Anderson. The term "grotesque" appears several times in the text, and it is not difficult to recognize Padre Benito, Juan P., don José Viejo, and Edumenio as grotesques in the Anderson tradition. There is also the war trauma in the sense of *In Our Time*. An alternative reading of *Tierra Amarilla* could make a case of the Second World War as the cause and origin of the psychotic breakdown in "Hombre sin nombre." Alejandro draws a parallel between his paternal possession and the dark years of the war (137). He also claims to have started the book on his father, of which "Hombre sin nombre" is a part, in June when he was in Berlin (141). His nervous breakdown in Tierra Amarilla might have as much to do with war traumas as with parental obsessions leading back to his youth. There is nothing of Faulkner or Wright in *Tierra Amarilla*. Neither does Ulibarrí challenge the Anglo world and its claims on the land in the Southwest, or draw the growth of an awareness for an exploited and oppressed people as Richard Wright did in *Uncle Tom's Children*. The overcoming of Nahuatl beliefs of a devouring "tierra" and the growing feminist awareness that women had to carve out their rights in the Chicano community themselves were left to writers like Tomás Rivera and Sandra Cisneros. But *Tierra Amarilla*, as one of the first literary works in the Chicano communities, raised the problems of a patriarchal heritage for Chicano writers and Chicanas as well.

To conclude, Ulibarrí seems to have transferred his allegiances from his father to his maternal grandmother in the sequel to *Tierra Amarilla, Mi abuela fumaba puros y otros cuentos de Tierra Amarilla* (1977). The increase of humor points in the same direction. But the legacy of Tierra Amarilla remains ambivalent: grandmother smokes cigars as a ritual to honor the dead grandfather.

NOTES

1. All quotations from *Tierra Amarilla* come from the bilingual edition (1971).

WORKS CITED

Blouin, Egla Morales. "Símbolos y motivos nahuas en la literatura chicana." In *The Identification and Analysis of Chicano Literature.* ed. Francisco Jiménez, 179–91. New York: Bilingual Press, 1979.

Greimas, Algirdas Julien. *Du sens. Essais sémiotiques.* Paris: Editions du Seuil, 1970.

Herms, Dieter. *Die zeitgenossische Literatur der Chicanos (1959–1988).* Frankfurt: Vervuert, 1990.

Hinojosa, Rolando. "Literatura Chicana: Background and Present Status of a Bicultural Expression." In *The Identification and Analysis of Chicano Literature*, ed. Francisco Jiménez, 42–46. New York: Bilingual Press, 1979.

Karrer, Wolfgang. "Richard Wright: Fire and Cloud." In *The Black Short Story in the 20th Century: A Collection of Critical Essays*, ed P. Bruck, 9–110. Amsterdam: Gruner, 1977.

Lyon, Ted. "Loss of Innocence in Chicano Prose." In *The Identification and Analysis of Chicano Literature*, ed. Francisco Jiménez 254–62. New York: Bilingual Press, 1979.

Rodríguez, Juan. "El desarollo del cuento chicano: Del folklore al tenebroso mundo del yo." In *The Identification and Analysis of Chicano Literature*, ed. Francisco Jiménez, 58–57. New York: Bilingual Press, 1979*a*.

———"La búsqueda de identidad y sus motivos en la literatura chicana." In *The Identification and Analysis of Chicano Literature*, ed. Francisco Jiménez, 70–78. New York: Bilingual Press, 1979*b*.

Schneider, Ulich. *James Joyce "Dubliners."* München: Fink, 1982.

Suleiman, Susan Rubin. *Authoritarian Fictions: The Ideological Novel as a Literary Genre.* New York: Columbia University Press, 1983.

Tatum, Charles M. *Chicano Literature.* Boston: Twayne, 1982.

Urioste, Donaldo W. "Costumbrismo in Sabine R. Ulibarrí's *Tierra Amarilla: Cuentos de Nuevo Mexico."* In *Missions in Conflict: Essays on U.S. Mexican Relations and Chicano Culture*, ed. R. v. Bardeleben et al., 169–78. Tübingen: Narr, 1986.

ULIBARRÍ AS STORYTELLER
A NARRATOLOGY PERSPECTIVE

ARNULFO G. RAMÍREZ

Ulibarrí's stories are often characterized with terms like "intrahistory," "*historia sentimental*," and "*costumbrismo*" to refer to his descriptions of the daily lives of some of the residents of the northern New Mexico community of Tierra Amarilla (Martínez and Lomelí 1985: 385–95). Many of the stories included in *Tierra Amarilla* (1964) and *Mi abuela fumaba puros y otros cuentos de Tierra Amarilla* (1977) deal with individual personalities, including family members, friends, and acquaintances who impressed the writer as a young boy. In *Tierra Amarilla*, we meet "el mago," the wonder horse; Father Benito, a Franciscan friar; Juan P., the town drunk; don José Viejo, a gifted storyteller; and Edumenio, a brawny, heavyset blacksmith who seldom spoke. In *Mi abuela fumaba puros*, the writer spins tales about his matriarchal grandmother; Uncle Cirilo, the fearsome sheriff of Rio Arriba County; El Negro Aguilar, the black man whose scandalous behavior was equally matched with his skills as a horse tamer; Elacio Sandoval, the astute biology teacher who talked himself out of marrying Erlinda Benavidez; Roberto, who goes out of town one day to buy more nails and does not return for four years; and the brotherhood of the Penitentes, a religious organization of devout males that practices secret rituals.

"Brujerías o tonerías?" in the *abuela* collection introduces us to local legends and popular superstitions. We accompany characters with mysterious powers such as La Matilde de Ensenada, who was a witch as well as a matchmaker; *el sanador*, known as a healer with special knowledge of the supernatural uses of medicines and animals; and Atanacia, whom the author confused with La Llorona but was actually a mentally retarded woman in relentless pursuit of her unfaithful husband. The stories included in *El Cóndor* (1989) also take us to an enchanted world of gypsies, witches, and supernatural beings. We journey with the mysterious singer Amena Karanova and her son, Damián, a talented portrait painter; marvel at the creations of a scientist named Helmut Heinz; follow the delightful and enchanting witches, Amarti and Amarta; spend time with Feliberto Mirabal, a widower who falls in love with three different Marías; travel with Cauilo as he rides on a flying mattress; witness the return of Cruzto, an ancient Indian chief who preaches love and brotherhood; experience the special love between Gustavo and Mariliez; and join the retired professor, Ernesto Garibay, in his marvelous adventures with the Amerindians of Ecuador.

The stories noted thus far can be analyzed from any number of literary perspectives, cultural themes, or social issues. However, it is important to examine Ulibarrí's stories as narrative texts. Narratives are a basic discourse form and as such have a structure, or *fábula*, and a sequence of events, involve characters or actors/agents that perform actions, and use particular language forms or signs to tell the story (Bal 1985: 310). I have selected three stories, one from each book cited above, to illustrate Ulibarrí's verbal art as a storyteller. They are "Mi caballo mago," "Mi abuela fumaba puros," and "Amena Karanova."

THE NARRATIVE CYCLE

The event structure of "Mi caballo mago" and "Mi abuela fumaba puros" can be conceived in terms of the basic elements in William Labov's (1972) description of oral narratives;

    1. an abstract (a short summary of the story before the narrative is recounted in full);
    2. the orientation (establishes the time, the place, the characters involved, and the circumstances);

3. the complicating action (the events as they happen in the story and the actors who perform actions);
4. an evaluation (the narrator tells the point of the story, the reason for being recounted);
5. the resolution (tells what finaly happened or the outcome of the story);
6. the coda (signals the end of the story and brings the narrator and listener/reader to the present).

Within this perspective, a story has a beginning or starting point, then is developed by means of an orientation, a series of complicating actions, the resolution, and the coda. The coda, in turn, takes the reader back to the beginning. This structure can be represented graphically by a square, with each of the four components corresponding to one of its sides.

The narrative structure of "Mi caballo mago" incorporates the six components of an oral tale. The reader is introduced to the wonder horse through a brief *abstract* ("era un caballo blanco que llenó mi juventud de fantasía y poesía"). This is followed by an *orientation* to the setting that notes the special attraction the cowboys of the region had for the horse ("Alrededor de las fogatas del campo y en las resolanas del pueblo los vaqueros de estas tierras hablaban de él con entusiasmo y admiración"). The horse is depicted as a majestic figure ("paseaba su harén por el bosque de verano en regocijo imperial . . . veraneaba como rey de oriente en su jardín silvestre"). He was a legend and a source for countless stories ("Eran sin fin las historias que se contaban del caballo brujo. Unas verdad, otras invención. . . . Todas vednidas a menos. El caballo siempre se escapaba, siempre se burlaba, siempre se alzaba por encima del dominio de los hombres"). The author-narrator then introduces himself ("Yo tenía quince años. Y sin haberlo visto nunca el brujo me llenaba ya la imaginación y la esperanza"). Then the narrator starts to tell the story by relating the *complicating actions.* First, there is the visual encounter with the horse ("Luego mis ojos aciertan. ¡Allí está! ¡El caballo mago!"). Later, after many months have passed, we travel with the narrator on his horse one Sunday morning as he embarks on his quest to capture the legendary stallion ("Salí sin ir a misa. . . . Iba en busca de la blanca luz que galopaba en mis sueños"). Eventually, he succeeds in roping the horse and bringing him back to his parents' home. El mago is left loose in his fenced pasture overnight ("Decidí soltarlo en el potrero. Allí podría mago irse acostumbrando poco a poco a mi amistad y compañía"). The father is delighted with the capture and thus greets his narrator-son with a warm handshake and words of praise ("Esos son hombres") to recognize this moment as a rite of passage to manhood ("Yo hacía el papel de muy hombre").

The *resolution* of the story occurs the following morning when the narrator-protagonist discovers that the wonder horse has escaped ("No está. El mago se ha escapado"). Some hoofprints were visible along the fence and red bloodstains could be seen on the snow, as could a few white hairs on the barbed wire fence. The *evaluation* segment continues the story with the cathartic scene ("Lloraba de alegría. Estaba celebrando, por mucho que me dolía, la fuga y la libertad del mago") and the recognition that the encounter with the wonder horse was a transcendental experience ("El mago era un absoluto. A mí me había enriquecido la vida para siempre"). The final segment is the *coda* when the father and narrator-son stand speechless gazing at the hoofprints ("Nos quedamos mirando la zanja blanca con flecos de rojo que se dirigía al sol rayante"). Here, the narrative cycle seems to take us back to the beginning, to the white horse that was running free ("Era blanco. Blanco como el olvido. Era libre") at the outset of the story.

The narrative structure of "Mi abuela fumaba puros" can be described in terms of two cycles. In the first cycle, we follow the narrator as child, living, departing, and returning to his grandmother's world. In the second cycle, the narrator returns to his grandmother's home as an adult. The first cycle begins with an extensive preface to the grandfather, don Prudencio. The narrator initiates the story by telling the reader that there are many tales about his incredible grandfather ("Según entiendo, mi abuelo era un tipazo. Se cuentan muchas cosas de él. Algunas respetables, otras no tanto"). As in the tradition of the tall tale, the narrator selects a braggadocio episode to begin the story ("Una de las últimas va como sigue"). He stresses the point that his grandfather was a temperamental person ("Lo que ahora me importa es hacer constar que mi pariente fue in tipazo: pendenciero, atrevido y travieso") but acknowledges that his grandfather died mysteriously before he was born and that his marriage to his grandmother was less than idyllic ("Su vida fue una cariñosa y apasionada guerra sentimental"). The narrator eventually informs the reader that the real story is going to start ("Todo esto lo digo como preámbulo para entrar en materia: mi abuela").

In the *orientation* segment, the characteristics of the grandmother are sketched in terms of the author recalling a vivid portrait etched in his memory ("un retrato que tengo colgado en sitio de honor en la sala principal de mi memoria"). The grandmother's physical and personal attributes as well as what she symbolized as described ("Estatua animada. Alma petrificada"). The reason for the title of the story becomes apparent as the narrator tells the reader about how his grandmother came to smoke cigars to give the illusion that her husband was around and later took up smoking, an act that established a mystical form of communication with the grandfather ("Estoy convencido que en la soledad y el silencio, con el olor y el sabor del tabaco, allí en el humo, mi abuela establecía alguna mística comunicación con mi abuelo"). The *complicating actions* include the segments narrating the author's description of his experiences in the valley of Las Nutrias, near the old family home; the move to Tierra Amarilla and adjustments to the new environment; and the return to Las Nutrias, which had dramatic consequences.

The return journey to the grandmother's home is recounted in great detail and excitement. It was a winter day; the car got stuck on the snowy road; Juan Maes, the ranch foreman, came with a team of horses to pull the car; Juan Antonio, an uncle, arrived at the grandmother's home to report the news about Alejandro, the father (who shot himself accidentally while cleaning his rifle). The scene is accentuated with dialogue and emotional reactions ("Mi madre lloraba desaforadamente, en punto de ponerse histérica. Nosotros la abrazábamos, todos llorando. Mi tío con el sombrero en la mano sin saber que hacer. . . . Entonces entró mi abuela en acción. Ni una sola lágrima. La voz firme. Los ojos espadas que echaban rayos"). The grandmother's apparent fury ("Entró en una santa ira contra mi padre. Le llamó ingrato, sinvergüenza, indino (indigno), mal agradecido. . . . Una furia soberbia") against the tragic event forced everyone present to shift their attention to something else ("La abuela creó una situación dramática tan violenta que nos obligó a todos, a mi madre especialmente, a fijarnos en ella y distraernos de la otra situación hasta poder acostumbrarnos poco a poco a la tragedia"). The grandmother's heroic behavior provides the *resolution* to the story. The narrator notes in his *evaluation* that his grandmother had acted courageously before in the face of a harsh world ("Como tantas veces, la abuela había dominado la realidad difícil en que vivió"). The *coda* serves to report the special talents of the grandmother ("Las dificultades para enterrarlo en sagrado confirmaron el instinto infalible de la dama y dueña de Las Nutrias") who was truly the matriarchal figures of the Turriaga clan.

The second cycle of the narrative recounts the author's return as an adult and professor to his grandmother's home. This brief account includes all of the components of an oral tale. It begins with an *abstract* ("Pasaron algunos años. Ya yo era professor. Un día volvimos a visitar a la abuela") followed by an *orientation* to the situation regarding the grandmother's success with the family ranch ("Las cosas había cambiado mucho. Con la muerte de mi padre la abuela se deshizo de todo el ganado"). The series of incidents that constitute the *complicating action* involve a few anecdotes: driving off the main highway; realizing from a distance that grandmother's house is on fire; arriving at the destination to discover the devastating effects of the fire ("Las arañas de cristal, deshechas. . . . Los muebles, traídos desde Kansas, hechos carbón . . .y se quemaron todos los santos, las reliquias y relicarios, el altar al Santo Niño de Atocha"). The family gathers that night with the grandmother who appeared subdued, more *frágil*, and willing to follow orders ("Lo que tú quieras, mi hijito"). The grandmother disappears into the woods only to be found by the narrator who sees her in a new light ("La vi crecer. Y fue como antes era: recta, alta y esbelta"). The *resolution* of the story is the realization that the grandmother would recover her strength through a mystical communication with the grandfather as she lighted up her cigar ("Vi encenderse la brasa de su puro. Estaba con mi abuelo. . . . Allí se harían las decisiones, se tomarían las determinaciones. Estaba recobrando sus fuerzas espirituales"). In the *coda*, the narrator tells the reader about the happiness he feels knowing that his grandmother would return to herself again ("Mañana sería otro día pero mi abuela seguiría siendo la misma. Y me alegre"). With this the story ends, and the narrator's second journey to his grandmother's home seems to be remembered with the same sense of childhood wonder expressed in the first cycle.

In "Amena Karanova," the reader is guided by the storyteller to the supernatural world of Amena Karanova, a famous European opera singer, and her secretary, Dátil Vivanca. The tale starts with the plane crash at the Albuquerque airport and the miraculous survival of everyone on board including the two mysterious visitors. The narration sequence could be described in terms of Labov's elements of oral stories, but the tale can also be seen in relation to Joseph Campbell's (1949) basic mythic structure recounting the adventures of a "hero" who goes on a journey and is aided by "helpers" to endure the series of trials or "tests." There is a sacred marriage between the hero and a goddess figure, followed by a reemergence from the kingdom of dread in the form of a rescue, resurrection, or threshold struggle. The hero returns to the place of departure and restores the world with the boon that he brings.

This universal plot can be found in both Eastern and Western cultures (Martin 1986: 88–90), and, in the case of this story, we follow the heroine, Amena Karanova, an enchanting woman with a mysterious past ("cuando te ibas, te llevabas una imagen avasalladora e imponente de una mujer luminosa y verde. Una mujer arrogante y aristocrática, de una belleza escultórica y clásica. Suponías que había en ella pasión y violencia, ternura y compasión. Quedabas seguro que traía consigo una tremenda tristeza que escondía un misterio serio"). Amena has traveled with her servant to New Mexico on a quest to find meaning in life after the death of

Damián, her fiancé, in an automobile accident. ("Amena se encontró aturdida y perdida en una noche sin fin, en un espacio infinito, sin atalayas y sin lámparas. Sin voluntad para vivir, sin voluntad para morir"). New Mexico's clear skies and intense sunlight help to transform Amena, and eventually she marries Petronilo Armijo, a local banker, who had acted as her companion in the new environment and helped in building a new home. Dátil continues to serve her mistress ("Pasaba largas horas con Dátil en secretas y misteriosas conversaciones. Era como si le estuviera dando instrucciones, preparándola para algo"), and later she raises Amena's son, Damián, as her own child since Amena dies giving birth. Damián grows up to become a talented painter. Like his mother, there is something about Damián that sets him apart from the rest ("Pero había en Damián un algo que lo diferenciaba de los demás. Llevaba en sí sustancias y esencias misteriosos que él mismo no acertaba en comprender y que a menudo determinaban su conducta o desataban su fantasía"). He is in a sense a resurrection of his mother, and the art he produces is a boon that brings spiritual tranquility to the local people. The portrait of his mother that was donated to Father Nasario's church increases the religious fervor of many persons. ("Llegó a ser que no era nada extraordinario ver a alguna viejita de rodillas ante Santa Amena. El padre Nasario empezó a recibir noticias, y empezó a sonarse por el mundo, que la santa había producido este o aquel milagro.")

The day arrives for Damián to go on his journey. He receives from Dátil a letter that had been written by Amena years before which provides specific instructions on where to go in Europe and whom to see. Damián embarks on his quest to locate Amina Karavelha, a famous opera singer performing in Madrid. The two meet and their friendship and affection grow. Count Barnizkoff, who attempts to maintain his claim over Amina, is rejected ("En ese momento Barnizkoff quiso tocarla, quizás abrazarla. Amina se alzó como una diosa vengativa y lanzó la mirada mortifera, la mirada de fuegos verdes y chispas de oro"). Damián paints a portrait of Amina and attains much fame in Europe. After their marriage, the newlyweds return to New Mexico to live in their enchanted house. There they are welcomed by Dátil and Petronilo. Happiness has returned once again. ("La casa se calentó, se alegró, se sonrió. Volvió a vivir, Volvió a soñar. La casa es el cuerpo, así que el cuerpo nuestro es el alma de la casa. Cuando nuestro cuerpo está ausente, la casa se muere"). Thus the narrative cycle is completed: the hero-son returns from his journey to New Mexico, the "land of enchantment." Unlike other tales, this hero was not tested, interrogated, or attacked. Damián had special powers that he displayed when he painted. In a sense, he and his mother brought beauty to the world through their art, the son as painter and the mother as singer.

ACTORS AND CHARACTERS

Narratives can be conceived as a sequence of events, or fábulas in Roland Barthes's (1966) sense. The characters, together with the sequences of actions, constitute the parts of the whole, and the actors are the agents that perform the different actions (Bal 1985: 25–37). Not all actors are human, and some do not become characters in the story. At one level, characters can be seen as exemplifying various "roles" such as the *quest* or call for adventure in "Mi caballo mago" ("Yo," the narrator, as the "subject" and the wonder horse as the "object"), the *metamorphosis* or coming of age in "Mi abuela fumaba puros" ("Yo," the narrator's childhood memories of his grandmother and subsequent return years later as an adult), and the *search* of Amena and her son, Damián (both are artistic donors, and the people are the recipients of the gifts).

In "Mi caballo mago" there are both human and nonhuman actors. The wonder horse and nature act in humanlike ways. The horse is described as "rey de oriente en su jardín silvestre," "orgullo, fama y arte en carne animal," and "arrogante majestad del campo." Nature reacts during the narrator's first magical encounter with the legendary horse ("De pronto el bosque se calla. El silencio enmudece. La tarde se detiene. La brisa deja de respirar, pero tiembla. El sol se excita"). The father, the ranch hands, and the townspeople are mentioned briefly by the author. The wonder horse as object and the narrator as subject are principal actors in the story. They are the only actors that attain character status in the fabula given their functions, delineations, and roles. The other actants are linked to narrative space, both in human (narrator–father–ranch hands–townspeople) and nonhuman (wonder horse–narrator's horse–nature) terms. The narrator reveals little about himself ("Yo tenía quince años. . . . Escuchaba embobado a mi padre y sus vaqueros hablar del caballo fantasma. . . . Participaba de la obsesión de todos"). The Wonder Horse, in contrast, is described in poetic terms ("Blanco como el olvido"; "Libre como la alegría"; "El caballo mago"; "Cuadro de belleza encendida y libertad varonil"; "Ideal invicto y limpio de la eterna ilusión humana") much like the Platero of Juan Ramón Jiménez (Ulibarrí 1962).

In "Mi abuela fumaba puros," the principal actors are the narrator and his beloved grandmother. The grandfather, don Prudencio, is depicted by the narrator on the basis of stories told about him ("Según entiendo, mi abuelo era un tipazo. Se cuentan muchas cosas de él"). Don Prudencio succeeded in fulfilling a number of social obligations ("Fue entre cívico, social, y político, y padre de familias") but also exhibited strong human tendencies ("pendenciero, atrevido y travieso. Murió de una manera misteriosa, o quizás vergonzosa"). The grandmother is recalled as a portrait ("Silueta negra sobre fondo azul. Recta, alta y esbelta"). She is both human ("estatua animada") and soul ("alma petrificada"). As a woman she had learned to transcend the harsh reality of a rural society ("la abuela había dominado la realidad difícil en que vivió") that demanded so many human responses: anger, insults, consolation, silence, and acceptance ("Dios da y Dios quita, mi hijito. Bendito sea su dulce nombre"). She never shed a tear, and her spiritual strength enabled her to preside over the burial of both husband and son and to endure the conflagration of the family home.

As in the previous story, the narrator discloses almost no information about himself. He explains, for example, the behavior of his grandparents (No creo que él y mi abuela tuvieran un matrimonio idílico en el sentido de las novelas sentimentales donde todo es dulzura, suavidad y ternura. Ambos eran hijos de su tierra y su tiempo). He maintains the narrative sequence with deictic markers of time ("Al pasar el tiempo"; "cuando mis padres se casaron"; "Cuando yo tenía ocho años"; "un día invierno"; "Apenas había entrado y estaba deshelándome"; "Entonces entró mi abuela en acción"; "Pasaron algunos años") and location ("Que volviendo de Tierra Amarilla a Las Nutrias"; "Allí pasaba su largo rato. Los demás permanecíamos en la sala haciendo vida de familia como si nada. Yo crecí en la ventosa loma en el centro del valle de Las Nutrias, con los pinos en todos los horizontes"). The narrator does confess that he was antisocial when he moved away from Las Nutrias to Tierra Amarilla and that he did not understand as a child why his grandmother felt a violent resentment when his father died of a gunshot wound.

The other members of the family (the narrator's mother, brother Roberto, sister Carmen, and uncle Juan Antonio) perform static roles. The uncle brings the bad news about the death of the father, Alejandro. The mother, in turn, reacts to the death by becoming almost hysterical ("Mi madre lloraba desaforadamente, en punto de ponerse histérica. . . . La situación de mi madre rayaba en la locura"). The foreman, Juan Maes, performed his role by bringing a team of horses to help pull the car out of the snow. These actors perform specific functions in the narrative:

Actant/Subject	Function	Object/Receiver
uncle Juan Antonio	informs	the family about the death of the father
the mother	mourns	her husband's death
brother Roberto and sister Carmen	want to visit and	their grandmother
	want to console	their mother
Juan Maes	wants to help	the family pass over the snowy road

The functions that these actors perform serve to contrast the heroic attributes and multiple functions of the grandmother as wife, mother, "gramma," and "madre del clan Turriaga."

"Amena Karanova" includes both supernatural and worldly actors. The supernatural actors are associated with the arts in the areas of music and painting, while the earthly characters are involved with banking, religion, entertainment, and the old European aristocracy. The functions that the different actors perform are outlined below.

Actant/Subject	Function(s)	Object/Receiver
Amena Karanova	wants to find	meaning in life
	wants to find	happiness through marriage with Petronilo
Dátil Vivanca	wants to serve	her mistress, Amena
	wants to raise	Damián, Amena's son
Damián Karanova	wants to follow	his inner artistic voice
	wants to fulfill	his mother's wishes
Amina Karavelha	wants to have	a portrait painted by Damián
	wants to love	Damián
Mandarina	wants to serve	her mistress, Amina
Petronilo Armijo	wants to help	Amena adjust to New Mexico
	wants to make	Amena happy as his wife
	wants to be liked/near	his son, Damián
Father Nasario	wants to place in his church	the portrait of Amena painted by Damián
Count Barnizkoff	wants to have	Amina's love
Virgie Joy	wants to have	a portrait painted by Damián

The two artists, Amena and Damián, search for meaning and fulfillment in life. They are surrounded by sympathetic servants; a caring husband and father, Petronilo; and a responsive priest, Father Nasario, who offers Amena's portrait to his churchgoers. Count Barnizkoff and Virgie Joy want to reap the benefits of others rather than offer their own talents or services.

LANGUAGE AND TEXT

Ulibarrí is both narrator-protagonist in "Mi caballo mago" (CM) and "Mi abuela fumaba puros" (AFP). In both narratives, he is telling personal accounts about his life drawn from a vivid re-creation of childhood experiences, thereby allowing him "to create a rich mixture of fact and fiction" (Tatum 1978: 440). In "Amena Karanova" (AK), the narrator-spectator tells the story, makes use of various direct speech forms to represent the voices of the different actors, and includes letters written by Amena and Damián

Karanova. In all three stories the narrator reports the actions through multiple levels of narration.

Narrator's Text
Pasó el verano y entró el invierno. (CM)
El poetrero era grande. Tenía un bosque y una cañada. (CM)
El aroma del tabaco llenaba la casa. (AFP)
Entonces entró mi abuela en acción. (AFP)
Se estrelló el avión en el aeropuerto de Albuquerque. (AK)
De pronto ella apaga los rayos. (AK)

Summer passed and winter came. (CM)
The pasture was large. It contained a grove of trees and small
    gully. (CM)
The aroma of the tobacco filled the house. (AFP)
That is when my grandmother went into action. (AFP)
The place crashed at the Albuquerque airport. (AK)
Suddenly she turned off the ray, and cut off the electric
    current. (AK)

Narrator's Voice
¡Allí está! ¡El caballo mago! (CM)
¿Qué hacer contigo, Mago? (CM)
No seas tonta. Estarán quemando hierbas, o chamizas
    o basura. (AFP)
¿Quién sabe? (AK)

There he is! The Wonder Horse! (CM)
"What shall I do with you, Mago?" (CM)
"Don't be silly. They must be burning weeds, or sage brush,
    or trash." (AFP)
Who Knows? (AK)

Narrator Quoting Others
Dime, ¿Quién es el más rico de todas estas tierras? (AFP)
"Allí está don Prudencio haciendo sus cosas." (AFP)

"Tell me, who is the richest man in all these parts?" (AFP)
"There's don Prudencio doing his thing." (AFP)

Direct Speech
"Esos son hombres." (CM)
¿Qué pasó? (AFP)

¡La casa de mi granma! (AFP)
Soy Amena Karanova. (AK)
Damián quisiera que me contaras de ella. (AK)

"That was a man's job." (CM)
"What happened?" (AFP)
"Grandma's house!" (AFP)
I am Amena Karanova. (AK)
Damian, I wish you would tell me about her. (AK)

Indirect Speech
Me sentí verdugo. (CM)
Le llamó ingrato sinvergüenza, indino (indigno), mal
   agradecido. (AFP)
Le dijo que venía de una tierra remota y exótica. (AK)

I felt like an executioner. (CM)
She called him ungrateful, shameless, unworthy. (AFP)
She told him that she came from a distant and exotic land. (AK)

Free Indirect Discourse
Ahora seguiría siendo el ideal, la ilusión y la emoción. (CM)
El puro que antes había sido símbolo de autoridad ahora se
   había convertido en instrumento afectivo. (AFP)
Parecía que su misión en la vida era glorificiar a Amina. (AK)

Now he would always be fantasy, freedom, and excitement. (CM)
The cigar that had once been a symbol of authority had now
   become an instrument of love. (AFP)
It seemed that his mission in life was to glorify Amina. (AK)

The narrator tells his own version of the story (narrator's text),
expresses his own involvement in the tale (narrator's voice), and
quotes the words of other actors. He reports the actors' own discourse (direct and indirect speech) and offers nonnarrative comments (free indirect discourse). Thus the narrator is both storyteller
and commentator. Furthermore, examples of actors' personal language are minimal compared to the narrator's text.

Ulibarrí not only tells his fábula but devotes narrative time to
describing some of the actors and objects in the stories. The descriptions vary in terms of discourse patterns, semantic structures,

and language forms (Brown and Yule 1983: 125–52). The descriptions are always presented within the boundary of the orthographic paragraph, and, for the purpose of this analysis, the individual sentences of each paragraph have been numbered and listed sequentially.

In paragraph A, the initial description of the wonder horse follows a pattern of specific attributes (blanco/libre/ilusión/libertad/ . . . y dominada las serranías, 1–6) of overall significance to the narrator (7). Similes (2, 4) and metaphors (5) are used to create a poetic image of the horse. In paragraph B, the narrator tells us about his dramatic encounter with the horse. The horse is situated on high ground surrounded by summer green (4). Then, through a series of metaphors, the horse is depicted as both statue and engraving (5), pride, fame, art in animal flesh (7), a picture of burning beauty (8), an ideal, pure and invincible (9). The metaphors create the impression that the horse as animal beauty is elusive and indescribable.

A
1. Era blanco.
2. Blanco como el olvido.
3. Era libre.
4. Libre como la alegría.
5. Era la ilusión, la libertad y la emoción.
6. Poblaba y dominaba las serranías y las llanuras de las cercanías.
7. Era un caballo blanco que llenó mi juventud de fantasía y poesía.

B
1. Luego mis ojos aciertan.
2. ¡Allí está!
3. ¡El caballo mago!
4. Al extremo del abra, en un promontorio, rodeado de verde.
5. Hecho estatua, hecho estampa.
6. Línea y forma y mancha blanca en fondo verde.
7. Orgullo, fama y arte en carne animal.
8. Cuadro de belleza encendida y libertad varonil.
9. Ideal invicto y limpio de la eterna ilusión humana.
10. Hoy palpito todo aún al recordarlo.

A

He was white.

White as memories lost.

He was free.

Free as happiness is.

He was fantasy, liberty, and excitement.

He filled and dominated the mountain valleys and surrounding plains.

He was a white horse that flooded my youth with dreams and poetry.

B

Then my eyes focus.

There he is!

The Wonder Horse!

At the end of the glade, on high ground surrounded by summer green.

He is a statue.

He is an engraving.

Line and form and white stain on a green background.

Pride, prestige, and art incarnate in animal flesh.

A picture of burning beauty and virile freedom.

An ideal, pure and invincible, rising from the eternal dreams of humanity.

Even today my being thrills when I remember him.

The description of the abuela in C is referential in nature, starting the narrator's recollection that she always dressed in black (1) and that she always kept her hair parted in the middle and combed straight (7), never loose (8). The picture includes the type of blouse (2), skirt to the ankles (3), a cotton apron (5), and bootlike shoes (6). The style here is nominal, with the focus on the clothing items (nouns). In description D, the emphasis is on attributes of the abuela. She was strong (1), never bending or folding due to the circumstances over the years (3), and serious to formal on most occasions (4). A smile, compliment, or caress from her was like precious gold coins (5) that she never wasted (6). In description E, the style is nominal, emphasizing the use of nouns, as in her stature (4), the clothing she wore (5, 6), and her eyes (7) and thoughts fixed elsewhere (Tuson 1980: 217–21). Somewhat like the wonder horse, she was a black silhouette on a blue background (3), an animated statue (9), a petrified soul (10). The three metaphors form a coherent metonymic description of her physical appearance: a black silhouette—an animated statue—a petrified soul.

C
1. Siempre la ví vestida de negro.
2. Blusa de encajes y holanes en el frente.
3. Falda hasta los tobillos.
4. Todo de seda.
5. Delantal de algodón.
6. Zapatos altos.
7. El cabello apartado en el centro y peinado para atrás, liso y apretado, con un chongo (moño) redondo y duro atrás.
8. Nunca la ví con el cabello suelto.

D
1. Era fuerte.
2. Fuerte como ella sola.
3. A través de los años en tantas peripecias, grandes y pequeñas tragedias, accidentes y problemas, nunca la ví torcerse o doblarse.
4. Era seria y formal fundamentalmente.
5. De modo que una sonrisa, un complido o una caricia de ella eran monedas de oro que se apreciaban y se guardaban de recuerdo para siempre.
6. Monedas que ella no despilfarraba.

E
1. Ese primer recuerdo: el retrato.
2. La veo en este momento en al alto de la loma como si estuviera ante mis ojos.
3. Silueta negra sobre fondo azul.
4. Recta, alta y esbelta.
5. El viento de la loma pegándole la ropa al cuerpo delante, perfilando sus formas, una por una.
6. La falda y el chal aleteando agitados detrás.
7. Los ojos puestos no sé dónde.
8. Los pensamientos fijos en no sé qué.
9. Estatua animada.
10. Alma petrificada.

C

She always dressed in black.
A blouse of lace and batiste up front.
A skirt down to her ankles.
All silk.
A cotton apron.
High shoes.
Her hair parted in the middle and combed straight back,
smooth and tight, with a round and hard bun in the back.
I never saw her with her hair loose.

D

She was strong.
As strong as only she could be.
Through the years, in so many situations, small and big
tragedies, accidents and problems, I never saw her bend or fold.
Fundamentally, she was serious and formal.
So a smile, a compliment or a caress from her were coins of
gold that were appreciated and saved as souvenirs forever.
Coins she never wasted.

E

The first memory: the portrait.
I can see her at this moment as if she were before my eyes.
A black silhouette on a blue background.
Straight, tall and slender.
The wind on the hill cleaving her clothes to her body up front,
outlining her forms, one by one.
Her skirt and her shawl flapping in the wind behind her.
Her eyes fixed I don't know where.
An animated statue.
A petrified soul.

The description of Amena stresses her magnetic eyes. Description F can be characterized as an extended metaphor: eyes that hypnotized and immobilized (2), immense green eyes with flecks of gold (3), something wild and untamed (5) lurking inside deep wells (6) and firing flashes and sparks like a vigilant panther (7). Dátil is also described in metaphorical terms when it comes to her eyes and lips (3). Yet description G is more general, listing attributes about her personality (2) and body (4).

F

1. Antes de ver a Amena se la miraba a los ojos.
2. Eran unos ojos que imantaban, que clavaban, que inmovilizaban.
3. Eran unos inmensos ojos verdes con flecos de oro.
4. Un verde volátil, un oro incendiario.
5. Algo silvestre, algo indomado.
6. Estaban refugiados en el fondo de unas cuencas apartes oscuras y hondas.
7. De allí despedían brillos y destellos como una pantera alerta en lo oscuro de su cueva.

G

1. Dátil era bonita.
2. Fresca y lozana como una amenaza.
3. Tenía chispas en los ojos y cerezas en los labios.
4. Carnes y contornos llenos y redondos, en todo sentido atractivos, pero ya en el camino de la gordura.

F

Before anyone saw Amena one looked at her eyes.
They were magnetic.
They hypnotized and immobilized you.
They were immense green eyes with flakes of gold.
A fiery green, an incendiary gold.
Something wild, something untamed.
They lurked inside deep wells, set apart and in darkness.
From there they fired flashed and sparks like a vigilant panther from the shadows of her cave.

G

Dátil was pretty.
As fresh and lusty as an apple.
She had sparks in her eyes and cherries on her lips.
Her flesh and contours were full and round, attractive in every way, but already pointing toward plumpness.

Descriptions H, I, J, and K highlight the setting or the location of objects/actors within narrative space. Description H is referential in nature, enumerating the human and nonhuman elements present in Tierra Amarilla during a high summer day: the forests (2), the cattle (3), the narrator dozing on his horse (4), the cowboys sitting around a campfire (6), and the sun setting behind the narrator (7). The entire scene reflects a deep, harmonious silence (8) according to the narrator. The pattern here is that of particulars to a general observation, but it can also be seen as a series of descriptive statements followed by an evaluation. In description I, the narrator laments the effects of fire on his grandmother's home. The description is encyclopedic in the manner that the items are listed: the crystal chandeliers broken (2), the magnificent sets of tables and washstands with marble tops destroyed (3), the furniture brought from Kansas turned to ashes (4), the bedspreads of lace, crochet, embroidery (5), and the portraits and pictures of the family (6). The listing of the objects and the effects of the fire (deshechas, destruídos, hechos carbón) produce a referential-rhetorical description that connects the objective elements with evaluative predicates. In description J, the house built by Amena is characterized with considerable referential detail: a traditional New Mexican house (2); the outside with adobe, vigas, portales, fireplaces (3); the inside, a palace from the Middle East (4) with patios, fountains, arches, porches, and gardens (5). The flowers are also depicted with various levels of specification: the seeds had been ordered by Amena (7), there were exotic plants and flowers with strange and sensual perfumes (8), and the black roses with flashes of green and intoxicating aroma attracted much attention (9). There were gardens and orchards extending in every direction (10). The narrator concludes his description of the dwelling by comparing it to a place in the *Arabian Nights* (11) or an inheritance, a life not born, one to be lived (12). The description seems to move from the real/concrete to the surreal/abstract.

The description of Damián's studio (K) follows a pattern similar to other accounts. There is a listing of the different elements: the large windows (3), the drapes (4), the blackboard and easel (5), the fireplace (6), an easy chair and a Moroccan leather couch (7), a library of sketching and technique books as well as collections of copies of world-famous paintings (8). The narrator concludes his description with a personal observation about the appropriateness of all the items for a painter not yet born.

H

1. Pleno el verano.

2. Los bosques verdes, frescos y alegres.

3. Las reses lentas, gordas y luminosas en la sombra y en el sol de agosto.

4. Dormitaba yo en un caballo brioso, lánguido y sutil en el sopor del atardecer.

5. Era hora ya de acercarse a la majada, al buen pan y al rancho del rodeo.

6. Ya los compañeros estarían alrededor de la hoguera agitando la guitarra, contando cuentos del pasado o de hoy o entregándose al cansancio de la tarde.

7. El sol se ponía ya, detrás de mí, en escándalos de rayo y color.

8. Silencio orgánico y denso.

I

1. Yo sí me lamenté.

2. Las arañas de cristal, deschechas.

3. Los magníficos juegos de mesas y aguamaniles con sobres de mármol, los platones y jarrones que había en cada dormitorio, distruídos.

4. Los muebles, traídos desde Kansas, hechos carbón.

5. Las colchas de encaje, de crochet, bordadas.

6. Los retratos, las fotos, los recuerdos de la familia.

J

1. La casa fue tomando forma.

2. Por fuera, era una casa nuevomexicana tradicional.

3. De adobe, con vigas y ristras, portales, chimeneas.

4. Por dentro, era un palacio del medio oriente.

5. Patios, fuentes, arcos, portales, jardines.

6. Flores y más flores.

7. Amena había hecho traer semillas de su tierra.

8. Aparecieron en los jardines plantas y flores exóticas, nunca vistas, perfumes raros y sensuales.

9. Lo que más llamó la atención fueron unas rosas negras con destellos verdes y un aroma intoxicante.

10. Las huertas y arboledas se extendían por todos lados.

11. Entrar en esa casa era salirse del mundo de todos los días y entrar en el mundo de las mil y una noches.

12. Era como si Amena no hubiera construido una casa sino una heredad, una vida todavía por nacer, todavía por vivir.

K

 1. Pronto se puso patente el propósito del aposento.
 2. Era un estudio de pintor.
 3. Tenía unos tremendos ventanales que daban al horizonte poniente que inundaban el cuarto de luz y color.
 4. Cortinajes corredizos lo llenaban de misterio y soledad.
 5. Tenía una pizarra y un caballete prestos para utilizar.
 6. En un rincón una chimenea nuevomexicana.
 7. Una butaca y un diván de cuero marroquín.
 8. Una selecta biblioteca de libros de dibujo y técnica, de ilustraciones de las pinturas más famosas del mundo.
 9. Todo lo necesario para un pintor, que aún no había nacido.

H

It was high summer.

The forests were fresh, green, and gay.

The cattle moved slowly, fat and sleek in the August sun and shadow.

Listless and drowsy in the lethargy of the late afternoon, I was dozing on my horse.

It was time to round up the herd and go back to the good bread of the cowboy camp.

Already my comrades would be sitting around the campfire,

playing the guitar, telling stories of past and present, or surrendering to the languor of the late afternoon.

The sun was setting behind me in a riot of streaks and colors.

Deep, harmonious silence.

I

I did lament.

The crystal chandeliers, wrecked.

The magnificent sets of tables and washstands with marble tops.

The big basins and water jars in every bedroom, destroyed.

The furniture brought from Kansas, turned to ashes.

The bedspreads of lace, crochet, embroidery.

The portraits, the pictures, the memories of the family.

J

The house was taking shape.

On the outside, it was a traditional new Mexican house.

Adobe, *vigas*, strings of chile, *portales*, fireplaces.

Inside it was a palace of the Middle East.

Patios, fountains, arches, porches, gardens.

Flowers and more flowers.

Amena had brought seeds from her native land.

Exotic plants and flowers appeared in her gardens never before
     seen, strange and sensual perfumes.

What attracted everyone's attention were the black roses with
     flashes of green and an intoxicating aroma.

The gardens and orchards spread out in every direction.

To enter the house was to leave the world of every day and to
     enter the Arabian Nights.

It was as if Amena had not built the house.

She had created an inheritance, a life not yet born, a life to
     be lived.

K

The purpose of the apartment soon became evident.

It was a studio for a painter.

It had large windows facing the western horizons that flooded
     the room with light and color.

Drawn drapes filled it with mystery and solitude.

It had a black board and easel, ready to use.

There was a New Mexican fireplace in the corner.

An easy chair and a couch of Moroccan leather.

A select library of sketching and technique books, collections
     of copies of the most famous paintings of the world.

Everything necessary for a painter, who had not yet been born.

Descriptions L, M, N, and O illustrate the narrator's descriptive language along with the narrative text. Description L follows a verbal style (Tuson 1980: 221–24) emphasizing movement: *(Yo) sigo* (despacio, palpitante, pensando, admirando, apreciando, 1–6). The narrator uses adverb and participle forms along with a series of gerunds to indicate his conduct as the afternoon advances (7) and his horse enjoys eating his fill (8). In description M, the action sequence is expressed primarily with preterit verb forms: *entró* (1), *le llamó* (2), *tomó* (5), *se entregó* (6), *habló* (8). The abuela's anger is characterized in terms of three metaphors that form a coherent metonymic description of her fury: *una santa ira* (1), *un torrente inacabable* (3), and *una furia soberbia* (4). Here the verb forms and figurative language are combined to describe how the abuela took complete control of the situation. The preterit verb forms are used to indicate completed actions of noncyclic events. In description N, the activities associated with magical qualities of Amina's voice are distinguished with imperfect verb forms, reflecting unbound, continuing actions (*era* una voz mágica/*subía* violenta y *bajaba* tierna. Amina *blandía* su lanza y la voz *retaba*, la bajaba y la voz *acariciaba*; se *alzaba* temblorosa; *descendía* lenta y suave, 3–6).

The end of the performance is captured with a series of metaphors (un feroz alarido, un grito de guerra, un radiante desafío . . . y se quedó inmóvil, como una victoriosa diosa de mármol, 7) and preterit verbs (*terminó, se quedó*). The beginning (empezó a cantar 1) and the end (y se quedó inmóvil, 8) are recorded with preterit forms, while the middle is set with imperfective verbs. Description O establishes an enchanting scene by enumerating the elements, the actors, and the sequence of events through the use of varied verb forms. The scene opens with descriptive expressions about the full moon (1) and the scent of jasmine in the air (2). The verb sequence begins with the imperfect (la orquesta batía rítmos bélicos, 3), followed by present tense forms (los artistas *gesticulan* y *cantan* en el tablado; Damián *desatento* . . . la música *se calla*. *Aparece* La Karavelha en la escena, 4–7), then descriptive expressions (alta, arrogante y majestuosa. Una explosión de aplausos, 8–9), and ending with a gerund construction (Damián *se encontró repitiendo* una y otra vez las palabras, 10) and the actual words of Damián (Esta tiene que ser la mujer más hermosa del mundo entero, 10). The wonder of the moment is dramatized by both narrator and actor. The actions occur in both present and past. Furthermore, the beauty of the night and La Karavelha appear to be timeless, not bound by verb tense or aspect.

L

1. Sigo.
2. Despacio.
3. Palpitante.
4. Pensando en su inteligencia.
5. Admirando su valentía.
6. Apreciando su cortesía.
7. La tarde se alarga.
8. Mi caballo cebado a sus anchas.

M

1. Entró en una santa ira contra mi padre.
2. Le llamó ingrato, sinvergüenza, indino (indigno), mal agradecido.
3. Un torrente inacabable de insultos.
4. Una furia soberbia.
5. Entretanto tomó a mi madre en sus brazos y la mecía y la acariciaba como a un bebé.
6. Mi madre se entregó y poco a poco se fue apaciguando.
7. También nosotros.
8. La abuela que siempre habló poco, esa noche no dejó de hablar.

N

1. Empezó a cantar.
2. La orquesta con ella.
3. Era una voz mágica que un momento subía violenta, y otro bajaba tierna.
4. Amina blandía su lanza y la voz retaba, la bajaba y la voz acariciaba.
5. A ratos se alzaba temblorosa, con gorgoritos rebeldes o sumisos, hasta la ventana abierta de la luna atenta.
6. Descendía lenta y suave, a posarse tierna en el regazo colectivo del gentío.
7. Terminó su actuación con un feroz alarido, un grito de guerra, un radiante desafío que estremeció la tierra y le sacó lágrimas a la luna.
8. Y se quedó inmóvil, como una victoriosa diosa de mármol.

O
1. Noche de luna llena.
2. Olor de jazmín en el aire.
3. La orquesta batía ritmos bélicos.
4. Los artistas gesticulan y cantan en el tablado.
5. Damián desantento, a la expectativa.
6. De pronto la música se calla.
7. Aparece La Karavelha en la escena.
8. Alta, arrogante y majestuosa.
9. Una explosión de aplausos.
10. Damián se encontró repitiendo una y otra vez las palabras que su padre un día dijera: —Esta tiene que ser la mujer más hermosa del mundo entero.

L
I follow.
Slowly.
Quivering.
Thinking about his intelligence.
Admiring his courage.
Understanding his courtesy.
The afternoon advances.
My horse is taking it easy.

M
She went into a holy fury against my father.
She called him ungrateful, shameless, unworthy.
An inexhaustible torrent of insults.
A royal rage.
In the meantime she took my mother in her arms and rocked her and caressed her like a baby.
My mother submitted and settled down slowly.
We did too.
My grandmother who always spoke so little did not stop talking that night.

N
She began to sing.
The orchestra played.

It was a magic voice that one moment rose violently and
   descended tenderly the next.
Amina brandished her lance and the voice threatened.
She lowered it and the voice caressed.
Sometimes it rose tremulously, with rebellious or submissive
   tremors, as high as the open windows of the attentive moon.
It came down slow and easy to rest tenderly on the collective
   lap of her listeners.
She ended her performance with a fierce shout, a battle cry, a
   radiant challenge that shook the earth and made the moon cry.
And she was still, like a triumphant goddess of marble.

O
A full moon.
The scent of jasmine in the air.
The orchestra playing rhythms of war.
The actors singing and gesticulating on the stage.
Damian was in attentive, waiting.
Suddenly the music stopped.
La Karavelha appeared on the stage.
Tall, arrogant, majestic.
An explosion of applause.
Damian found himself repeating over and over again the same
   words his father had said one day: "This one has to be the
   most beautiful woman in the whole world."

CONCLUSION

As storyteller, Ulibarrí brings an orality dimension to his narratives. Two of the stories analyzed incorporate the six basic components of an oral tale. "Amena Karanova" follows the universal
mythic structure recounting the adventure story of a mysterious
hero/heroine who restores the world with his/her gifts as an artist.
The principal characters in these stories seem to be engaged in a
search for meaning by understanding a quest, experiencing a metamorphosis, or engaging in a self-actualization process. Ulibarrí is
the narrator-protagonist in "Mi caballo mago" and "Mi abuela
fumaba puros." Both are personal stories told as oral narratives in
poetic prose. The tale about Amena Karanova takes the reader to a

supernatural world that is also inhabited by earthly persons. Here, reality and fantasy are placed side by side. In his personal stories, human/nonhuman actors appear along with heroic/nonheroic figures.

As narrator, Ulibarrí speaks through many voices. He tells the story, comments on the actions, and quotes or reports the actors' own discourses. At the same time, the narrator's text contains numerous examples of descriptive language. These descriptions are always set within the boundary of the orthographic paragraph and typically include metaphoric expressions. Through these descriptions the voice of the poet becomes evident. Actors like the wonder horse, the abuela, Amena, Dátil, and Amina are described in both literal and figurative discourse. Descriptions of the countryside, a fire-devastated home, Amena's dream house, and Damián's studio follow an enumerative pattern, with a listing of the items and a personal comment by the narrator in some instances. The narrative text itself is crafted with great care, paying special attention to such features as the use of verb forms. Moreover, his narratives transcend the New Mexican landscape and the local color as the reader is taken on a journey that celebrates the human spirit in a poetic world.

WORKS CITED

Bal, Mieke. *Narratology: Introduction to the Theory of Narrative.* Toronto: University of Toronto Press, 1985.

Barthes, Roland. 1966. "Introduction to the Structural Analysis of Narratives." In *Image, Music, Text.* 79–124. London: Collins, 1977.

Brown, Gillian, and George Yule. *Discourse Analysis.* Cambridge: Cambridge University Press, 1983.

Campbell, Joseph. *A Hero with a Thousand Faces.* New York: Pantheon, 1949.

Labov, William. *Language in the Inner City.* Philadelphia: University of Pennsylvania Press, 1972.

Martin, Wallace. *Recent Theories of Narrative.* Ithaca: Cornell University Press, 1986.

Martínez, Julio, and Francisco A. Lomelí, eds. *Chicano Literature: A Reference Guide.* Westport, Conn.: Greenwood Press, 1985.

Tatum, Charles M. Review of *Mi abuela fumaba puros. World Literature Today* 52 (Summer 1978): 440.

Tusón, Jesús. *Teorías gramaticales y análisis sintáctico.* Barcelona: Editorial Teide, 1980.

Ulibarrí, Sabine. *El Cóndor And Other Stories.* Bilingual edition. Houston: Arte Público, 1989.

Ulibarrí, Sabine. *El mundo poético de Juan Ramón.* Madrid: Artes Gráficas Clavileños, 1962.

Ulibarrí, Sabine. *Mi abuela fumaba puros y otros cuentos de Tierra Amarilla.* Berkeley: Quinto Sol, 1977.

Ulibarrí, Sabine. *Tierra Amarilla: Cuentos de Nuevo Mexico.* Quito: Editorial Casa de la Cultura Ecuatoriana, 1964.

FORMAL ASPECTS OF LANGUAGE USE
IN THE WORKS OF SABINE R. ULIBARRÍ

JAMES J. CHAMPION

This computer-aided study is an attempt to characterize selected works of Sabine Ulibarrí by comparing measurable formal aspects of his language with those of other writers in Spanish, both Peninsular and Latin American. Three collections of Ulibarrí's short stories have been chosen for study. These works are *Tierra Amarilla, Mi abuela fumabo puros,* and *Primeros encuentros,* the first two of which (and I believe, by extension, the third) Charles Tatum (1985: 389) says may be compared to works of Spanish and Spanish American *costumbrismo.* All of the stories were rendered into machine-readable form by use of a scanner. Two other collections of short stories, *Los funerales de la mamá grande* by Gabriel García Márquez and *El llano en llamas* by Juan Rulfo, also in machine-readable form, serve as a basis of comparison between more widely known Latin American works and those of Ulibarrí. In addition, comparisons will be made with the figures given in Estelle Irizarry's (1990) statistical study of Peninsular authors. As Irizarry states, "A 'stand-alone' statistical study of a single author or literary text is virtually useless in the absence of data involving similar texts against which to measure and compare the significance of results" (265). Reference will also be made to the figures given in a standard frequency dictionary of Peninsular Spanish (Juilland and

Chang-Rodríguez 1964). Programs to analyze the stories were written in MaxSpitbol 1.2 and run on a Macintosh IIcx. Systat 5.0 was used for the statistics and graphs.

It is not the purpose here to substitute "quantitative analysis" (objectively measured data) for "qualitative analysis" (literary analysis in the traditional sense). Quantitative studies might better be considered as tools, which may serve two purposes: (1) to alert us to aspects of a literary work that merit further attention because of significant variations from linguistic norms (e.g., as in "Mi caballo mago" and "Los penitentes," discussed below), and (2) to provide empirical evidence that may help to reinforce or refute observations arrived at by other means (e.g., the impressionistic view that Ulibarrí consistently uses shorter sentences than, say Gabriel García Márquez or Juan Rulfo).

WORD STATISTICS

The figures included in this section are (1) the total number of words in each story; (2) the number of *different* words (or types); (3) the type-token ratio (*different* words as a percentage of the total); (4) the number of *hapax legomena* (words that occur only once); (5) hapax legomena as a percentage of total words; (6) mean word length; and (7) the standard deviation of word length. Perhaps a simplified example will best clarify at this point the different uses of the terms "type" and "hapax legomena." A list of all the words in a given text may be presented in a number of ways: (1) multiple occurrences of the same word form combined, producing a nonlemmatized word count; (2) all variants of the same base form (lemma) combined, producing a lemmatized word count; and (3) base forms listed *with* their corresponding variants. (See table 1.)

Clearly, the third possibility, the lemmatized list with variants, contains the most information. Such a list is included in Alphonse Juilland and Eugene Chang-Rodríguez's *Frequency Dictionary of Spanish Words* (1964), but, as Irizarry (1990: 268) laments, "The fact that a program for comprehensive lemmatization is not yet available in Spanish makes the course of unlemmatized type-to-

Table 1
Word Counts

Test	1. Non-lemmatized	2. Lemmatized	3. Lemmatized with variants
buena	2 buena	3 bueno	3 bueno
buena	1 bueno	2 en	2 buena
bueno	2 en	6 ser	1 bueno
en	1 era	1 taza	2 en
en	3 es		2 en
era	1 ser		6 ser
es	1 son		1 era
es	1 taza		3 es
es			1 ser
ser			1 son
son			1 taza
taza			1 taza

ken ratios the only one available at present." In the nonlemmatized list in table 1, all of the entries are types; there are five hapax legomena (*bueno, era, ser, son, taza*). In the lemmatized list, all of the entries are also types, but there is only one hapax legomenon (*taza*). The figures in this study are based on a nonlemmatized list (as are those in Irizarry 1990).

As shown in table 2, the length of Ulibarrí's stories varies from a low of 767 words ("Se fue por clavos") to a high of 11,955 ("Hombre sin nombre"). There is some justification for omitting "Hombre sin nombre" from any consideration of Ulibarrí's *costumbrista* stories. Charles M. Tatum (1985: 391) points out it "differs in length, form and content from the author's other fiction. . . . [it] deals with a number of philosophical themes such as life as a dream, the father-son relationship, and the development of the individual personality." Indeed, Theodore A. Sackett (1972: 515), while stressing these same points, refers to "Hombre sin nombre" as a novella. In spite of all this, it is included in this study for the sake of completeness. Tables 3 and 4 provide the same statistics for Rulfo's *El llano en llamas* and García Márquez's *Funerales*.

Table 2
Word Statistics: Ulibarrí

Story	Word Total	Types	Type/ Token	Hapax Legomena	Hapax/ Total	Mean Length	Standard Deviation
(Tierra)							
Caballo	1,906	807	42.34	592	31.06	4.38	2.53
Relleno	2,463	929	37.72	661	26.84	4.51	2.67
Juan P.	2,090	828	39.62	606	29.00	4.51	2.69
Sábelo	1,890	702	37.14	503	26.61	4.27	2.41
Fragua	2,341	903	38.57	661	28.24	4.41	2.57
Hombre	11,955	2,906	24.31	1,948	16.29	4.36	2.65
(Abuela)							
Puros	2,476	976	39.42	723	29.20	4.53	2.70
Brujerías	3,868	1,345	34.77	951	24.59	4.42	2.62
Cirilo	1,397	603	43.16	440	31.50	4.46	2.56
Aguilar	1,780	704	39.55	503	28.26	4.46	2.54
Elacio	1,977	689	34.85	398	20.13	4.61	2.80
Kasa	1,214	516	42.50	360	29.65	4.34	2.49
Mano	2,129	763	35.84	500	23.49	4.40	2.47
Apache	2,496	990	39.66	721	28.89	4.59	2.67
Clavos	676	332	49.11	237	35.06	4.49	2.43
Penitentes	1,628	726	44.59	535	32.86	4.62	2.69
(Encuentros)							
Forastero	1,802	649	36.02	437	24.25	4.30	2.47
Güera	1,559	643	41.24	473	30.34	4.49	2.54
Oso	1,005	485	48.26	352	35.02	4.52	2.60
Adolfo	1,149	465	40.47	320	27.85	4.45	2.56
Nicomedes	1,427	593	41.56	422	29.57	4.42	2.53
Tomás	1,460	595	40.75	421	28.84	4.43	2.51
Se casaron	1,172	431	36.77	277	23.63	4.53	2.65
Mónico	2,392	939	39.26	676	28.26	4.47	2.54
Generosa	1,467	622	42.40	451	30.74	4.50	2.55

In observing the type-token ratios and the hapax legomena as a percentage of total words, some interesting correlations appear. If the three collections of Ulibarrí's stories are combined and ordered by increasing length, an inverse relationship between length of story and type-token ratio, as well as hapax legomena as a percentage of total words, will be observed (see table 5).

While this correlation is not absolute, it is clear at the maximum and minimum values. As shown in table 6 and 7, a similar

Table 3
Word Statistics: Rulfo's *El llano en llamas*

Story	Word Total	Types	Type/ Token	Hapax Legomena	Hapax/ Total	Mean Length	Standard Deviation
Macario	2,072	618	29.83	389	18.77	4.01	2.22
Tierra	1,580	560	35.44	369	23.35	4.19	2.31
Cuesta	3,005	853	28.39	554	18.44	4.16	2.36
Pobres	1,630	581	35.64	386	23.68	4.07	2.28
Hombre	3,147	1,029	32.70	692	21.99	4.16	2.34
Madrugada	1,834	698	38.06	487	26.55	4.24	2.39
Talpa	3,310	932	28.16	589	17.79	4.39	2.47
Llano	5,160	1,453	28.16	945	18.31	4.52	2.52
Diles	2,438	811	33.26	524	21.49	4.18	2.29
Luvina	3,033	982	32.38	649	21.40	4.25	2.30
Noche	1,207	531	43.99	371	30.74	4.39	2.46
Acuérdate	1,121	469	41.84	352	31.40	4.21	2.45
Ladrar	1,311	517	39.44	341	26.01	4.16	2.29
Anacleto	4,291	1,281	29.85	865	20.16	4.24	2.43
Derrumbe	2,379	852	35.81	592	24.88	4.44	2.66
Matilde	2,333	798	34.20	555	23.79	4.29	2.45

inverse relationship also may be observed in the stories of Rulfo and García Márquez.

In all three authors, the relationship between the total number of words, on the one hand, and the type-token ratios and hapax legomena as a percentage of total words, on the other hand, is ap-

Table 4
Word Statistics: García Márquez's *Funerales . . .*

Story	Word Total	Types	Type/ Token	Hapax Legomena	Hapax/ Total	Mean Length	Standard Deviation
Siesta	2,401	839	34.94	607	25.28	4.37	2.52
Un día	878	373	42.48	267	30.41	4.37	2.52
Ladrones	8,229	2,057	25.00	1,299	15.79	4.50	2.53
Baltazar	2,425	860	35.46	623	25.69	4.51	2.50
Viuda	2,192	845	38.55	624	28.47	4.60	2.69
Después	7,915	2,054	25.95	1,335	16.87	4.61	2.77
Rosas	1,620	575	35.49	389	24.01	4.44	2.42
Funerales	5,681	2,069	36.42	1,609	28.32	4.98	3.12

Table 5
Ulibarrí
(in order of ascending word totals)

	Word Total	Type/ Token	Hapax/ Total
Clavos	676	49.11	35.06
Oso	1,005	48.26	35.02
Adolfo	1,149	40.47	27.85
Se casaron	1,172	36.77	23.63
Kasa	1,214	42.50	29.65
Cirilo	1,397	43.16	31.50
Nicomedes	1,427	41.56	29.57
Tomás	1,460	40.75	28.84
Generosa	1,467	42.40	30.74
Güera	1,559	41.24	30.34
Penitentes	1,628	44.59	32.86
Aguilar	1,780	39.55	28.26
Forastero	1,802	36.02	24.25
Sábelo	1,890	37.14	26.61
Caballo	1,906	42.34	31.06
Elacio	1,977	34.85	20.13
Juan P.	2,090	39.62	29.00
Mano	2,129	35.84	23.49
Fragua	2,341	38.57	28.24
Mónico	2,392	39.26	28.26
Relleno	2,463	37.72	26.84
Puros	2,476	39.42	29.20
Apache	2,496	39.66	28.89
Brujerías	3,868	34.77	24.59
Hombre	11,955	24.31	16.29

parent. This relationship must be kept in mind when comparing these figures with the corresponding figures in Irizarry (1990). In that study, the author organized and analyzed a 150,000-word corpus of twentieth-century Peninsular Spanish (randomly selected blocks of 5,000 continuous words, for each of thirty well-known authors). The type-token ratios for the Spanish authors range from a low of 25.6 (Unamuno) to a high of 40.6 (Pérez de Ayala), with an average for all authors of 33.6. Unamuno and Pérez de Ayala also provide the maximum and minimum values for hapax legomena

Table 6
Rulfo's "El llano . . ."
(in order of ascending word totals)

	Word Total	Type/ Token	Hapax/ Total
Acuérdate	1,121	41.84	31.40
Noche	1,207	43.99	30.74
Ladrar	1,311	39.44	26.01
Tierra	1,580	35.44	23.35
Pobres	1,630	35.64	23.68
Madrugada	1,834	38.06	26.55
Macario	2,072	29.83	18.77
Matilde	2,333	34.20	23.79
Derrumbe	2,379	35.81	24.88
Diles	2,438	33.26	21.49
Cuesta	3,005	28.39	18.44
Luvina	3,033	32.38	21.40
Hombre	3,147	32.70	21.99
Talpa	3,310	28.16	17.79
Anacleto	4,291	29.85	20.16
Llano	5,160	28.16	18.31

Table 7
García Márquez's "Los funerales . . ."
(in order of ascending word totals)

	Word Total	Type/ Token	Hapax/ Total
Un día	878	42.48	30.41
Rosas	1,620	35.49	24.01
Viuda	2,192	38.55	28.47
Siesta	2,401	34.94	25.28
Baltazar	2,425	35.46	25.69
Funerales	5,681	36.42	28.32
Después	7,915	25.95	16.87
Ladrones	8,229	25.00	15.79

as a percentage of total words: low 15.64 (Unamuno); high 32.70 (Pérez de Ayala). The average value for this ratio among the thirty authors is 24.18. If we compare the story of Ulibarrí's that comes closest to 5,000 words ("Brujerías," 3,868 words), we find that the figures for these two categories are very close to the average for the Peninsular authors. Similarly, comparing García Márquez's story that comes closest to 5,000 words (Los funerales . . .," 5,681 words), we find that the figures are quite close to the Peninsular average. In contrast, the figure for the story of Rulfo's that is closest to 5,000 words ("El llano en llamas," 5,160 words) is considerably below the Peninsular average, although not as low as the corresponding figure for Pérez de Ayala.

Before looking at the figures for mean word length, it should be noted that in all cases the mode, or most frequently used word length, is two letters. This was noted also by Irizarry in the thirty Spanish authors she studied. The reason is not far to seek. If we consider only the twenty most frequently occurring words in Ulibarrí's combined works, we find that the two-letter words among them (*de, la, el, en, se, no, me, un, mi, lo, yo*) account for 20.08% of total words (the total of *all* two-letter words is 24.48%). The figure for Rulfo's stories (*de, la, el, se, no, en, lo me, le, un*) is 19.01 percent (with a total for *all* two-letter words of 24.74%), while in García Márquez's stories, two-letter words among the twenty most frequently occurring (*de, la, el, en, se, un, no, su, al*) account for a full 23 percent of all words (with a total for all two-letter words of 25.69%). The word-length distribution for these three authors, as seen in figure 1, is similar to that of a 5,000-word sample taken from Cervantes (reproduced in Williams 1970: 139). Indeed, this distribution—a peak at the two-letter word, a decrease, a second peak at the five-letter word, and a final gradual decrease—may be considered typical of literary Spanish.

Although word-length distribution combined with mean word length is more informative than mean word length alone, the figures for word-length distribution are not available in Irizarry (1990). The figures given for Ulibarrí, Rulfo, and García Márquez are for the complete collections of stories (see table 8).

Mean word length in Ulibarrí's stories ranges from a low of 4.27

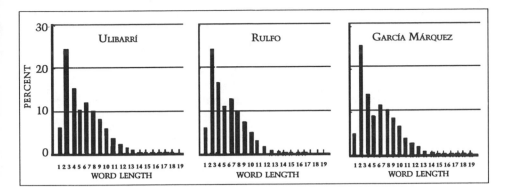

FIGURE 1. WORD-LENGTH DISTRIBUTION.

letters ("Sábelo") to a high of 4.62 ("Los penitentes"), with the average for all his stories taken together at 4.44. The standard deviation is a measure of how much the values vary around the mean. A lower number indicates less variation from the mean. The standard deviation figures for Ulibarrí range from a low of 2.41 ("Sábelo") to a high of 2.80 ("Elacio era Elacio"), with a figure of 2.60 for all stories taken together. Mean word length in Rulfo ranges from a low of 4.01 ("Macario") to a high of 4.52 ("El llano en llamas"), with an average of 4.27 for all stories. The standard deviation ranges from 2.22 ("Macario") to a high of 2.66 ("El día del derrumbe"), with an average of 2.41. For García Márquez, the figures fro the mean word length range from 4.37 ("La siesta del martes" *and* "Un día de estos") to 4.98 ("Los funerales de la mamá grande"), with an average of 4.61. The standard deviation ranges from 2.42 ("Rosas artificiales") to 3.12 ("Los funerales de la mamá

Table 8
Word Length

	Mean	Standard Deviation
Ulibarrí	4.44	2.60
Rulfo	4.27	2.41
García Márquez	4.61	2.71
Peninsular authors	4.5	2.7

grande"), with an average figure of 2.71 for all the stories. Of these three authors, Ulibarrí falls between García Márquez and Rulfo in terms of both mean length of words and the degree of variation from the mean. The mean word length for the thirty Peninsular authors in Irizarry (1990), in which figures are calculated to one decimal place, ranges from a low of 4.1 (Unamuno) to a high of 5.0 (Gómez Ojea *and* Granell), with an average length of 4.5 for all authors. The standard deviation among these authors ranges from a low of 2.3 (Cela) to a high of 3.1 (Granell), with an average standard deviation of 2.7. The word statistics for Ulibarrí and García Márquez are very close to the average figures for the Peninsular authors (with Ulibarrí's figures slightly under and García Márquez's slightly over), while those for Rulfo indicate considerably shorter word length and considerably less variation from the mean. In none of the authors studied here or by Irizarry (1990) is the mean word length ever less than 4.00 or greater than 5.00. Likewise, the standard deviation of word length is never less than 2.20 or greater than 3.20.

SENTENCE STATISTICS

The tables in this section give statistics on (1) mode, the most frequently used sentence length (in number of words); (2) maximum sentence length; (3) average or mean sentence length; and (4) standard deviation, the degree to which sentence length varies from the mean.

As shown in table 9, the most frequent sentence length (mode) for Ulibarrí's individual stories run from a low of 3 (6 different stories) to a high of 9 ("La Kasa KK"). Maximum sentence length ranges from a low of 23 (4 different stories) to a high of 54 ("Sábelo"). Mean sentence length ranges from a low of 6.98 ("Un oso" *and* "Se casaron") to a high of 13.75 ("Juan P."). Standard deviation ranges from a low of 4.36 ("Un oso") to a high of 9.00 ("Juan P.").

In Rulfo's stories, the ranges are (from low to high): mode 4–18; maximum sentence length 34–100; mean 8.48–24.37; standard deviation 6.79–17.22

For García Márquez's stories the ranges are mode 4–35; maximum sentence length 33–192; mean 10.06–33.16; standard deviation 7.04–23.48.

Table 9
Sentence Statistics: Ulibarrí

Story	Mode	Maximum	Mean	Standard Deviation
(Tierra)				
Caballo	4	36	7.45	5.38
Relleno	5	38	11.67	8.11
Juan P.	8	50	13.75	9.00
Sábelo	7	54	12.27	8.96
Fragua	3	53	12.52	9.37
Hombre	7	48	11.60	8.26
(Abuela)				
Puros	4	47	10.40	8.57
Brujerías	4	48	10.34	7.56
Cirilo	5	27	8.22	6.15
Aguilar	(5/6)	38	10.17	7.55
Elacio	(4/7)	31	10.52	6.88
Kasa	9	36	10.15	6.61
Mano	(8/11)	24	10.33	5.41
Apache	8	34	11.86	7.15
Clavos	3	23	7.60	4.86
Penitentes	5	50	11.80	8.38
(Encuentros)				
Forastero	4	44	10.41	6.90
Güera	6	30	10.20	5.88
Oso	3	23	6.98	4.36
Adolfo	3	24	8.62	5.17
Nicomedes	3	23	8.63	5.17
Tomás	3	35	10.07	6.36
Se casaron	(3/6)	23	6.98	4.64
Mónico	6	36	9.06	6.28
Generosa	4	46	9.06	6.32

The sentence-length distributions for the collections of stories by Ulibarrí, Rulfo, and García Márquez, in groups of ten words each (sentences from 1 to 10 words in length, etc.), are given in figure 2.

In order that the reader may appreciate the enormous variety in sentence length in written Spanish prose, I have adapted in table 12 the sentence statistics given by Irizarry (1990: 272), to one decimal place, for the 5,000-word samples of the thirty Peninsular authors.

Table 10
Sentence Statistics: Rulfo

Story	Mode	Maximum	Mean	Standard Deviation
Macario	9	61	16.31	10.74
Tierra	4	37	10.53	7.89
Cuesta	(5/6)	76	16.33	11.22
Pobres	(10/13/17/26)	65	21.75	13.83
Hombre	8	52	11.49	8.09
Madrugada	6	59	15.82	10.01
Talpa	18	82	17.99	13.90
Llano	7	77	16.17	11.80
Diles	5	68	11.63	9.78
Luvina	4	74	11.70	11.02
Noche	6	43	10.01	7.40
Acuérdate	(4/11/24)	63	24.37	15.65
Ladrar	4	34	8.64	6.79
Anacleto	5	66	8.48	6.95
Derrumbe	4	100	18.30	17.22
Matilde	8	76	17.27	12.60

The ranges for the Peninsular authors are mode, 2 (Cela and Espina) to 40 (Cunqueiro); maximum sentence length, 38 (Gironella) to 245 (Solana); mean, 7.2 (Unamuno) to 44.3 (Solana); and standard deviation, 7.0 (Gironella and Matute) to 29.8 (Solana). A summary of the ranges of these values for all authors is given in table 13.

Table 11
Sentence Statistics: García Márquez

Story	Mode	Maximum	Mean	Standard Deviation
Siesta	(5/6)	45	13.27	9.31
Día de estos	5	33	11.11	7.72
Ladrones	5	53	10.94	8.28
Baltazar	4	49	12.24	9.72
Viuda	7	47	17.61	10.58
Día después	14	88	21.31	14.94
Rosas	5	35	10.06	7.04
Funerales	35	192	33.16	23.48

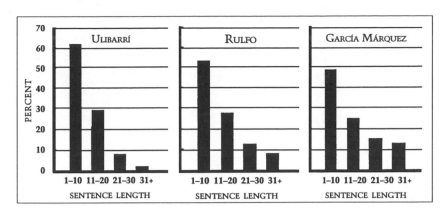

FIGURE 2. SENTENCE-LENGTH DISTRIBUTION.

The mean sentence length and standard deviation for all stories of each author taken together and the mean sentence length and standard deviation for all Peninsular authors is given in table 14.

While the figures given in the section on word statistics for mean word length and standard deviation did to vary a great deal from author to author (the mean always varying between 4 and 5; the standard deviation, between 2.2 and 3.2), the figures for mean sentence length and standard deviation vary considerably. The mean sentence length and standard deviation of García Márquez's stories are very close to the Peninsular averages. The figures for Rulfo's stories show that he uses shorter sentences with less variation from the mean, while the figures for Ulibarrí's stories show not only a much shorter average sentence length but also a consistent use of shorter sentences, that is, much lower variation from the mean. If we look at the sentence distribution percentages in figure 2 above, we se that sentences of from 1 to 10 words make up over 60 percent of Ulibarrí's sentences, those from 11 to 20 words make up nearly 30 percent, those from 21 to 30 words make up a little over 7 percent, and those over 30 make up only 2 percent. If we compare these figures to those of Rulfo and García Márquez, we see a decreasing percentage of sentences of 1 to 10 words long, with a corresponding rise in the use of

Table 12
Sentence Statistics: Peninsular Authors

Story	Mode	Maximum	Mean	Standard Deviation
Ayala	6	91	17.8	15.7
Azorín	14	105	18.3	14.4
Barea	9	49	14.6	9.5
Baroja	14	66	23.3	14.7
Cela	2	158	15.7	24.9
Chacel	9	71	21.2	14.4
Cunqueiro	40	158	37.4	26.0
Delibes	3	67	17.6	12.6
Dieste	4	149	11.4	14.0
Espina	2	83	14.4	13.3
Galvarriato	3	107	13.9	14.5
Gironella	5	38	10.3	7.0
Gomez de la Serna	17	71	17.3	12.3
Gomez Ojea	33	135	32.3	22.1
Goytisolo	3	56	11.7	8.7
Granell	3	168	17.2	16.7
Laforet	9	54	11.3	8.6
Marsé	3	171	15.9	16.7
Martín Gaite	5	63	10.7	9.4
Matute	6	50	9.2	7.0
Miró	10	64	12.4	9.5
Perez de Ayala	9	124	16.9	15.5
Quiroga	5	60	9.9	8.5
Sánchez Ferlosio	9	68	13.9	9.6
Sender	8	71	15.0	11.1
Solana	22	245	44.3	29.8
Torrente Ballester	3	53	10.0	8.1
Unamuno	3	86	7.2	9.4
Valle-Inclán	3	90	14.1	11.3
Zunzunegui	4	49	9.8	7.6

longer sentences. As was true with the word statistics above, sentence-length distributions are not available for the Peninsular authors.

SELECTED WORD FREQUENCY

In Irizarry (1990), the most frequently occurring word and the most frequently occurring initial letter are given for each author. Table 15 summarizes these observations.

Table 13
Ranges of Sentence Statistics

	Mode		Maximum		Mean		Standard Deviation	
	Low	High	Low	High	Low	High	Low	High
Ulibarrí	3	9	23	54	6.98	13.75	4.36	9.00
Rulfo	4	18	34	100	8.48	24.37	6.79	17.22
García M.	4	35	33	192	10.06	33.16	7.04	23.48
Penninsular	2	40	38	245	7.5	44.3	7.0	29.8

Table 14
Cumulative Sentence Statistics

	Mean	Standard Deviation
Ulibarrí	10.31	7.40
Rulfo	13.34	11.25
García Márquez	15.37	13.67
Peninsular	16.5	13.4

Table 15
Most Frequent Word and Initial Letter

Word	Number of Authors	Letter	Number of Authors
de	22	e	13
la	4	l	9
que	2	d	8
y	1		
el	1		

Regarding the initial letters, Irizarry (1990: 271) observes correctly, "The fact that only three letters . . . [are] present in the highest initial position among all the writers is probably a linguistic rather than stylistic attribute, reflecting the high frequency articles ('el,' 'la,' 'los,' and 'las') and the common preposition 'de' [as well as the preposition 'en']." In remarking on the authors whose most frequently occurring word is neither "de" nor one of the definite articles, Irizarry states, "The preference of Cela and Unamuno for 'que' suggests a tendency to explain rather than condense. A clause introduced by 'que' is more explanatory than the more elliptical prepositional phrase introduced by 'de'. . . . dieste's 'y' suggests a tendency to link rather than subordinate, in line with the uncomplicated narrative style of *Historias e invenciones de Félix Muriel* noted by critics."

Given the possibility that the relative frequency of "que," "de," and "y" may be more indicative of some aspects of an author's style than simply the word that is used most frequently, figures have been calculated for the relative frequency of these words in the works of Ulibarrí, Rulfo, and García Márquez. These figures will be compared with one another, as well as with the frequency of these words in the *Frequency Dictionary of Spanish Words* (Juilland and Chang-Rodríguez 1964). In this work, a sample of a half million words (the "lexical universe"), taken equally from five genres (or "lexical worlds") of written Peninsular Spanish, was analyzed. These genres are (1) plays, (2) novels and short stories, (3) essays, (4) technical literature, and (5) journalistic literature. The figures I shall use for comparison are those of the total sample as well as those of the novels and short stories. In all cases the figures for "de" include the occurrences of "del; the figures for "y" include the occurrences of "e"; and those for "que" include the conjunction as well as the pronoun (which were originally counted separately in Juilland and Chang-Rodríguez 1964). (See table 16.)

The first column of figures indicates that in the lexical universe of the *Frequency Dictionary of Spanish Words*, the sum of occurrences of "de," "que," and "y" account for 13.56 percent of *all* words. This number is rather high, since it includes essays and technical and journalistic literature, the figures for which are con-

Table 16
"De," "que," and "y" as Percent of Total Words

	FDSW (all)	FDSW (novels, stories)	Ulibarrí	Rulfo	García Márquez
de	7.03	6.58	4.81	5.08	6.63
que	3.54	2.61	2.93	4.06	2.49
y	2.99	3.22	3.55	3.28	3.01
Total	13.56	12.41	11.29	12.42	12.13

siderably higher than those for the literary genres. In the lexical world of novels and short stories, occurrences of these three words account for 12.41 percent of all words. The corresponding figures for Ulibarrí, Rulfo, and García Márquez are similar, with the figure for Ulibarrí being somewhat lower than the others. The distribution of these three words relative to one another reveals considerable variation between sources. In the *Frequency Dictionary of Spanish Words* (novels and short stories as well as the total sample), the occurrences of "de" are double those of "que" or "y," as they are also in the stories of García Márquez. While not double in the stories of Ulibarrí or Rulfo, "de" is still by far the most frequently occurring word, due to its multiple uses (see, e.g. Gili Gaya 1979: 251–53, where six major categories are listed). This makes all the more striking Irizarry's reference above to Cela and Unamuno, both of whom use "que" more frequently than "de," and to Dieste, who uses "y" more frequently than "de." This variation may be seen more clearly in table 17, where the figures repre-

Table 17
"De," "que," and "y" as Percent of ("de" + "que" + "y")

	FDSW (all)	FDSW (novels, stores)	Ulibarrí	Rulfo	García Márquez
de	52	53	43	41	55
que	26	21	26	33	20
y	22	26	31	26	25

sent the percentage of occurrence of each of the three words relative to one another (rounded off to whole numbers).

Again, we find the distribution figures for García Márquez's stories much closer to the Peninsular average, in this case to the corpus of the *Frequency Dictionary of Spanish Words,* while the figures for Ulibarrí and Rulfo are at considerable variance. Ulibarrí uses "de" some 10 percent less than the Peninsular sample for novels and stories, while using both "que" and "y" approximately 5 percent more each. Rulfo uses "de" some 12 percent less than the Peninsular sample for novels and short stories, but in his case, the difference is made up almost entirely by a very high figure for "que." It must be emphasized that these figures are for the *collections* of stories by Ulibarrí, Rulfo, and García Márquez and thus indicate only the total distribution. Further analysis will show a great deal of variation among stories by the same author. It is at the level of the individual story that the distribution and relative frequency of these function words may be stylistically significant. Table 18 presents the figures for each of these three function words as a percentage of total words, the cumulative total as a percentage of total words, and the occurrences of each word as a percentage of the total of the three words (i.e., the percentages relative to each other, rounded off to whole numbers), for each of Ulibarrí's stories as well as for each of the three volumes.

As we read down each of the columns, we find that "de" as a percentage of total words ranges from a low of 3.24 ("Se fue por clavos," the shortest of all the stories) to a high of 6.71 ("Don Tómas Vernes"); "que" ranges from a low of 1.58 ("Don Tomás Vernes") to a high of 3.76 ("Hombre sin nombre," mentioned above as not only the longest of the stories but also considered possibly of a different genre); "y" ranges from a low of 1.88 ("Se casaron . . .") to a very high 5.35 ("Mi caballo mago"). The cumulative total for the three words ranges from a low of 8.76 ("Un oso") to a high of 12.31 ("Hombre sin nombre"). As a percentage of the total of the three words, "de" ranges from a low of 33 ("Los penitentes") to a very high 58 ("Don Tomás Vernes"); "que" ranges from a very low 14 ("Don Tomás Vernes") to a high of 35 "Se fue por clavos"); and

Table 18
Distribution of "de," "que," and "y" in Ulibarrí

	Percent of Total Words				Percent of ("de" + "que" + "y")		
Story	de	que	y	Cumulative	de	que	y
(Tierra)	4.84	3.34	3.79	11.97	40	28	32
Caballo	4.93	1.84	5.35	12.12	41	15	44
Relleno	4.87	2.76	3.25	10.88	45	25	30
Juan P.	5.07	3.16	3.64	11.87	43	27	30
Sábelo	4.18	3.12	3.49	10.79	39	29	32
Fragua	5.08	3.33	3.89	12.30	41	27	32
Hombre	4.84	3.76	3.71	12.31	39	31	30
(Abuela)	4.76	2.75	3.53	11.04	43	25	32
Puros	5.37	2.30	3.63	11.30	48	20	32
Brujerías	4.86	3.05	3.75	11.66	42	26	32
Cirilo	4.08	3.15	3.79	11.02	37	29	34
Aguilar	4.83	2.81	2.98	10.62	46	26	28
Elacio	4.96	1.67	3.54	10.17	49	16	35
Kasa	5.27	2.06	3.87	11.20	47	18	35
Mano	4.60	3.33	3.01	10.94	42	30	27
Apache	5.05	2.48	3.37	10.90	46	23	31
Clavos	3.24	3.24	2.79	9.27	35	35	30
Penitentes	3.87	3.62	4.17	11.66	33	31	36
(Encuentros)	4.82	2.48	3.18	10.48	46	24	30
Forastero	4.38	3.22	3.33	10.93	40	29	30
Güera	5.71	2.50	4.62	12.83	45	20	36
Oso	3.88	1.89	2.99	8.76	44	22	34
Adolfo	3.57	3.48	2.96	10.01	36	35	30
Nicomedes	4.34	1.96	3.29	9.59	45	20	34
Tomás	6.71	1.58	3.36	11.65	58	14	29
Se casaron	4.86	2.39	1.88	9.13	53	26	21
Mónico	5.14	2.17	3.18	10.49	49	21	30
Generosa	4.09	3.14	2.52	9.75	42	32	26

"y" ranges from a low of 21 ("Se casaron . . .") to an extremely high 44 ("Mi caballo mago").

The general frequency pattern for Ulibarrí is the same as that for novels and short stories in the *Frequency Dictionary of Spanish Words* and for García Márquez: "de" is by far the most frequent, followed by "y" and then "que." The frequencies for Rulfo invert "que" and "y." We shall note the exceptions to this general frequency pattern in Ulibarrí. In two of the stories ("Mi caballo mago" and "Los penitentes"), "y" is the most frequently used word. In no case is "que" the most frequently used word, although in one very short story ("Se fue por clavos") "que" and "de" occur an equal number of times. In addition, in five stories ("Hombre sin nombre," "Mano Fashico," "Adolfo Miller," "Se casaron . . . ," and "La hermana Generosa"), "que" is used more frequently than "y." I do not believe that much is to be made of this inversion of "que" and "y." However, when "y" is used more frequently than "de," this deviates so widely from the norm that it would seem to merit further attention. Can it be that in "Mi caballo mago" and "Los penitentes": the preponderance of the conjunction "y" "suggests a tendency to link rather than subordinate, in line with . . . uncomplicated narrative style," as stated by Irizarry with reference to the writings of Dieste? Can it be that a high frequency of "y" is indicative of children's speech or the speech of the uneducated, as suggested by Samuel Gili Gaya (1979: 276): "El pleonasmo de *y* es la forma infantil y popular de las narraciones. En estas primeras fases del lenguaje, la conjunción *y* sirve además para expresar muchas relaciones que más tarde se expresarán con otros medios"? This point is stressed by Nila Gutiérrez Marrone (1978: 32, 40) in analyzing Rulfo's stories. However, of the three stories the author points out as having a high incidence of "y" ("Macario," "Es que somos muy pobres," "El paso de Norte"), only "El paso de Norte" has a figure much above normal (4.9%), while "Acuérdate" (with a figure of 4.6%) is not even mentioned. Only in "El paso de Norte" does the figure for "y" exceed that of "de." Returning to Ulibarrí, the narrative point of view of "Mi caballo mago" is that of a young adolescent, perhaps still in his "primeras fases del lenguaje." The narrative perspective of "Los penitentes," however, is that of an older man who is a writer and *not* an uneducated person. Nor, in this case, I believe, does the high frequency of "y" indicate "a tendency to link rather than subordinate," at least not at the phrase level. At this point "quantitative analysis," having pointed out deviations from the norm that may be worthy of further investigation, leaves open the possibility of alternative explanations.

CONCLUSION

Numerous quantitative measurements, at the word, sentence, and lexical level, have been calculated in an attempt to characterize selected writings of Sabine Ulibarrí, by comparing these data with those of other writers of Spanish, both Peninsular and Spanish American. Other measurable phenomena, such as richness of vocabulary and *true* type/token ratios, which depend on vocabulary lemmatization, await a comprehensive program to carry out these tasks.

WORKS CITED

García Márquez, Gabriel. *Los funerales de la mamá grande*. Buenos Aires: Editorial Sudamericana, 1973.

Gili Gaya, Samuel. *Curso superior de sintaxis española*, 12th ed. Barcelona: Bibliograf S.A., 1979.

Gutiérrez Marrone, Nila. *El estilo de Juan Rulfo: Estudio lingüístico*. New York: Bilingual Press, 1978.

Irizarry, Estelle. "Stylistic Analysis of a Corpus of Twentieth-Century Spanish Narrative". *Computers and the Humanities* 24 (1990): 265–74.

Juilland, Alphonse, and Eugene Chang-Rodríguez. *Frequency Dictionary of Spanish Words*. The Hague: Mouton, 1964.

Rulfo, Juan. *El llano en llamas*. 2d ed. México: Fondo de Cultura Económica, 1970.

Sackett, Theodore A. Review of *Tierra Amarilla*. *Modern Language Journal* 56 (1972): 515–16.

Tatum, Charles M. "Ulibarrí, Sabine (1912–)" in *Chicano Literature: A Reference Guide*, ed. Julio A. Martínez and Francisco A. Lomelí, 385–95. Westport, Conn.: Greenwood Press, 1985.

Ulibarrí, Sabine R. *Mi abuela fumaba puros*. Berkeley: Quinto Sol, 1977.

———. *Primeros encuentros*. Ypsilanti, Mich.: Bilingual Press, 1982.

———. *Tierra Amarilla*. Albuquerque: University of New Mexico Press, 1971.

Williams, C. B. *Style and Vocabulary: Numerical Studies*. New York: Hafner Publishing Co., 1970.

SABINE R. ULIBARRÍ'S ESSAYS: A CRITICAL DIALOGUE WITH DIFFERENCE

Francisco A. Lomelí

> *Let the essay avow itself* almost *a novel: a novel without proper names.*
> —Roland Barthes

Sabine Ulibarrí's long-standing literary career defies any single epoch as well as any one genre. His writings exemplify a presence couched within the unique and continuous Hispanic literary tradition particular to New Mexico. In fact, often serving as a link with the past, he also ponders inevitable changes and transformations in a Hispanic society that has survived marginalized and abandoned. His literary production aims to ground itself in a specific place (New Mexico) and an ethnos (Hispanic) as two suns of his system of discourse and rhetoric, in other words, his basic reference points of experience and reality.

Ulibarrí does not speak out alone. Along with other important southwestern voices—Fray Angélico Chávez, Fabiola Cabeza de Baca, Cleofas M. Jaramillo, Rafael Chacón, Roberto Vialpando, Secundino Baca, and many others—he forms part of a broad constellation of writers who serve as a transitional linkage between the territorial days (before 1912) and (post) modern times. As an early accomplished poet (*Al cielo se sube a pie*, 1961, and *Amor y Ecuador*, 1966) and a splendid short fiction writer (*Tierra Amarilla:*

Cuentos de Nuevo México, 1964, and *Mi abuela fumaba puros/ My Grandma Smoked Cigars*, 1977), Ulibarrí has achieved distinction for his sensitive portrayals of a region's soul and ethos at a time when it was not yet fashionable or readily promoted. Although he precedes what came to be termed the Chicano literary renaissance of the 1960s, he has also directly contributed to it, partly through his short fiction but more through a steady essayistic production. It is my contention that the latter, rarely acknowledged by critics, must be considered an essential component of his overall oeuvre, thus accounting for a variegated authorship of delving into the spirit, the passion, and the imagination of a people. His repeated incursions in the essay conjure up the image of either a visionary or a quixotic madman who confronts social phenomena the way a surgeon approaches the operating table. While recognizing that the essay is perhaps the most fleeting of genres, he nonetheless attempts to place it in the forefront.

To adequately understand Ulibarrí's recourse in the essay, some preliminary comments are necessary. It is not uncommon to find the essay ignored as a genre in the study of literature, for its perception brings to mind what Robert G. Mead refers to as a presumably "inferior genre," a genre that does not match the others in literary merit. While many anthologies even tend to exclude the essay as a regular representative entry, most formal attempts to classify literature view it as organically unclassifiable or as terra incognita. A black sheep or outcast within the literary genres family, often it is not even recognized as a peripheral part of that family,[1] particularly as of late when traditional genres matter less or where intergeneric hybridization is commonplace. The essay's fate, however, rests much on the type of interest it generates in terms of immediacy, impact, and timing. Fundamentally at the root of the problem is the very issue of its definition and conceptualization.[2] General variant descriptions are usually offered, but consensus is rarely reached. Critics are more apt to describe what an essay is not rather than what it is. An epistemological approach inevitably denotes a type of Pandora's box in that the term "essay" represents more what René Wellek labels a "generic institution" instead of a single prosaic form. On closer examination, the essay, what Xavier Villaurrutia (1940: 104) calls "una literatura de ideas" (a literature of ideas), consists of a hybrid construct—what Alfonso Reyes terms "the centaur of the genres" (Oviedo 1990: 12)—that, according to José Luis Martínez in *El ensayo mexicano moderno* (1958), ranges from the article and the critical study to the monograph and the treatise. Somewhere in between this vast spectrum of approaches and methodologies emerges one notion or another of the essay, depending on the reader's reception and grasp of the subject. Perhaps part of its inherently polemical quality is ascribed to its elastic, flexible, and exploratory nature; that is, the essay is many things at once. No wonder José Miguel Oviedo (1990: 13) classifies it as antidogmatic, asystematic, and with some frequency heretical, but he also adds, "El ensayo es una forma *dialogante*, un pensamiento que quiere ser comunicación abierta, tanto con el lector como con el mundo histórico al que pertenece" (16; The essay is a *dialoguing* form, a thought that wishes to be open communication, as much with the reader as with the historical place to which he forms a part).

As to its actual origins in the Renaissance, including the usage of the word *essay*, credit is first attributed to Michel de Montaigne in his *Essais* from 1589. Yet Francis Bacon has observed an irrefutable fact: "The word is late [in literary history], but the thing is ancient" (Martínez 1958: 8). With all its possible definitions, there seems to be little debate as to its diverse range and moldability. Perhaps Oviedo, in *Breve historia del ensayo hispanoamericano* (1990), best synthesizes the apparent polemics with regard to its intrinsic makeup: "El ensayo, aunque definible, parece no tener límites. Género camaleónico, tiende a adoptar la forma que le convenga, lo que es otro modo de decir que no se ciñe a una forma establecida" (11; the essay, although definable, seems to have no limits. A chameleon genre, it tends to adopt the form that best suits it, which is another way of saying that it does not restrict itself to a single established form). The essay, then, lends itself as a medium to expound on a topic that demands a certain vantage point or position; it is by definition didactic, original, and reflective in its composition. And by implication, a specific opinion is delineated with either partisanship in mind or at least a definite hypothetical prospectus.

Ulibarrí's essays, then, operate much within these parameters, except that he also offers other twists. His essays comprise a pivotal aspect of his agenda to recover part of the Hispanic literary presence as he experienced it while living in northern New Mexico. At the same time, his motive involves an active reassessment of what it means to be Hispanic in a social ambience that has either been oblivious to their presence or does not possess the necessary tools to understand them. From his writings emanate a creative spirit tempered by the pragmatic desire to effect change in ideology and perception, for the good of cultural interaction. While indulging in cultural comparative analyses and some theoretical/philosophical questions, there is the underlying inducement to spur a new sensibility about Hispanics outside his ethnic group and within it. If at times he seems mildly lofty or oppositional, his essays require a qualification: his chosen field of discourse entails, first, a quixotic didacticism about cultural politics in the broadest sense of the word and, second, a profound attempt at searching for thyself, much in the vein of José Ortega y Gasset, Miguel de Unamuno, Aurelio Espinosa, Walt Whitman, and Octavio Paz. He insists on this search to establish that Hispanics do in fact belong within the social matrix of the United States instead of being viewed as newcomers to it. What emerges is a foundation for better understanding to document what a Hispanic is within a larger American historical context of permanence and continuity.

Part of the reason for the limited recognition and dissemination of Ulibarrí's essays is explained in terms of his minimal interest to publish them—suggesting that they immediately become part of the public domain. Most exist in mimeograph form with few published exceptions,[3] and his main collection, "One Voice of Juan Hispano (A Collection of Lectures on Hispanic Themes)," has principally existed as a manuscript in progress. The functionality of this collection, along with other independent essays, is determined by their specificity to a given situation or request. Therefore, one key consideration is that Ulibarrí's essays are deeply rooted in a Hispanic oral-intellectual tradition, which stipulates a dynamic interaction of forensics, polemics, cultural/political exchanges, a parabolic function, and editorial duels as widely evident in early Hispanic newspapers. If part of the initial motive is rooted in stirring new reflections about a particular subject, a didacticism is often complemented by a sublimely confrontational style and tone. Well lodged in this oral tradition of playing out discord and perspectives of difference,[4] Ulibarrí, however, does not dichotomize between oral and written literatures. Except for a few anthologized samples of his essays, the bulk of his essayistic production remains unpublished and generally uncataloged. But this does not diminish their intrinsic value, because the majority of his essays are cultural disquisitions whose effectiveness is already field-tested in lecture tours nationally and abroad—receiving much enthusiastic and favorable acclaim as unforgettable pieces of public discourse.

His essays usually target a specific event (i.e., a conference, symposium, lecture series, rally, issue, etc.), and, therefore, they represent a topical landmark by probing into established thought as it relates to culture, history, and politics by Chicanos and/or Hispanics. If at times he proposes to be provocative, at other times he wishes to raise dust or at least attempt to reduce rhetoric and misconceptions to their bare bones. Ulibarrí never appears complacent or resigned to accept conditions as they might exist, but neither is he openly discontent or bitter. His writings aim to fill in gaps; that is, he bridges cultural interaction for the sake of attaining a new synthesis of comprehension. Besides emanating as manuscript versions or temporal pieces, a partial explanation for their exclusion from critical discourse is that Ulibarrí's essays directly correspond to the arena of oratory as public deliveries or performance, a tradition reminisced by Hispanics with high esteem but currently on the decline. Their intent is to address a specific situation or respond to a particular need, as a spokesperson, a performer, an agent of exchange, a catalyst, and a thinker or even a visionary. Viewed in a larger context, his writings also add to the long-standing legacy of debunking myths or rectifying historical distortions, or in other cases, as purely intellectual reflections. As part of a generation prior to the Chicano movement, he represents an important link to the past as it overlaps into the present by contributing to the ongoing review and analysis of contentious issues, using the essay as a medium and forum to discuss topics of concern. He does not invite controversy, but he does not avoid it either for he seeks truth, appeals to reason, and ultimately wills a new social order.

Ulibarrí's "One Voice of Juan Hispano"[5] is a varied compilation of fourteen essays but certainly not an exhaustive one in proportion to his lifetime activity in the genre. It features some of his most memorable lectures, which have endured changes and modifications, depending on the time and occasion. However, he also has to his credit numerous other loose essays that exist in mimeograph form or xerox copies, which he generously shares with friends and interested parties. "One Voice of Juan Hispano" came about simply as an effort to cluster a series of lectures once an essayistic corpus was forming; it is not the result of a deliberate selection process. Because the collection, as a preliminary assemblage, continues unpublished, its primary objective is to propose representative essayistic samplings of diverse topical concerns. The body of essayistic work comes together more as a manageable text or working draft. Most of all, the collection serves well as a testimony to his combative spirit, *inquietud* (restlessness), and commitment to the ideas espoused in the essays.

"One Voice of Juan Hispano" encompasses a wide range of subjects and concepts, covering four basic areas: Hispanic culture, cultural politics, education, and philosophy and literature. While the author posits an "everyman's" vantage point, stemming from the "Juan Hispano" label, he likewise proposes to define a firmly—but not dogmatic or doctrinaire—nationalistic perspective in tone, modality, and composition. His essays correspond well to the parameters of the genre, but the finality is not strictly essayistic in and of itself for they must be judged essentially as pertaining to oratory or performances. The feature of "one voice" serves to accentuate the personal focus, which is typical of the essay. As Pilar

A. Sanjuan (1954: 9) observes, "one element that remains constant in all the definitions of essay . . . is subjectivity, the author's point of view." In the case of Ulibarrí, it must be emphasized that his prosaic writings form part of oral tradition; his essays are, first, meant to be heard and then read. Verification rests in that his presentations have become noteworthy as speeches and, less so, as written expositions. The principal category to which they belong is found in José Luis Martínez's breakdown of the essay into ten central categories in his capital study, *El ensayo mexicano moderno*. Although Ulibarrí's hybrid essayistic production relates to various categories as outlined by Martínez, such as "el ensayo interpretatiro" (the interpretive essay) or "el ensayo expositivo" (the expositional essay), one classification embraces his writings better than any other: "el ensayo-discurso u oración . . . como expresión de los mensajes culturales y civilizadores" (the essay-speech or oration . . . as an expression of cultural and civilizing messages) in which the essayist is a buffer or guard keeper of culture. As Martínez points out, "Formalmente oscila entre la oratoria del discurso y la disertación académica, pero lo liga al propiamente llamado ensayo la meditación y la interpretación de las realidades matcriales o cspiritualcs" (Formally, it oscillatcs bctwccn thc art of public speaking of a speech and the academic dissertation, but meditation and interpretation of material and spiritual realities link it fittingly to the so-called essay).[6]

Ulibarrí furthcrmorc manages to transcend the limitations of a single classification because, in most cases, his objective revolves around the composition of a public declaration, better known as a manifesto, that is, a forum for broadcasting a new vision of how things might be. Directly involving himself in the whirlwinds of controversy and polemics, he recognizes full well not to acquiesce to contrary views or to retreat. For that reason, his recourse is not diplomatic double-talk or discretely and pleasantly rhetorical dilutions; instead, he prefers to dynamically engage in differing critical dialogues to aspire to a new synthesis of understanding. Confrontation is preferable to silence; the unflinching pen is better than the indecisive posture. Most of all, he dwells on enouncing opinions with incisive or witty observations so as to rethink ideological questions. He might not always possess a unique theoretical platform for dissecting Hispanic issues, but he certainly sheds new light on how to perceive cultural happenings and modes of thought. Ulibarrí's essays embody a renewed attempts at disseminating ideas in the best tradition of Juan Luis Vives, Michel Montaigne, Francis Bacon, Miguel de Unamuno, Mariano-José de Larra, Octavio Paz, Octavio Romano, and others. His essays are a tribute to his people, for he functions as a knowledgeable spokesperson for Hispanics, being both jury and inquisitor, both leader and follower, both advocate and devil's advocate. His writings aim to stir, teach, provoke, rally, instruct, guide, and, above all, affirm dignity, self-respect, and create a higher awareness of issues proper to Hispanics. In that sense, he offers philosophical therapy at the same time that he intimates a deep conviction toward self-regeneration. Much like his favorite literary figure, Don Quixote, he tries to mend wrongs and undo the snags of injustice, while suggesting a path of redemption.

The majority of the essays in "One Voice of Juan Hispano" are characterized by their brevity, generally between four and eight pages, implying that their intentions are direct and pungent for quick consumption. Their composition denotes a quick reading— or listening—in one sitting, with the exception of "Sor Juana, the Woman" and "The Magic of Don Juan," which are both article-length essays of thirteen to fifteen pages that entail carefully argued observations within the traditional confines of literary criticism. The latter two consist of more in-depth exposés of the complex nature of a literary figure and a literary archetype, respectively. Both essays are constructed from the point of view of interpretation and analysis to closely examine and decipher enigmas. Every angle rests on original observations and conclusions. Although the expository style resembles a literary essay, the highly subjective presence of a critical reader leads us to believe that these two writings conform to the "ensayo interpretativo," as described by Martínez. That is, they deal with actual reading, and, therefore, the exercise is purely intellectual with a peripherally extraliterary application. With respect to the famous Mexican nun of the seventeenth century, Sor Juana Inés de la Crux, Ulibarrí comments, "Sor Juan is fascinating because of her duality, her multiplicity. She is a personality of many dimensions and proportions, many sides, of many and fleeting shades. She was, and continues to be, an enigma, full of contradictions, mystery and interrogations" (1958: 13).

It is in the shorter essays, however, where Ulibarrí best exhibits his flair for eloquence, biting wit, and unwavering assertions in well-focused prosaic treatments of single subjects. By consistently setting out to define and defend Hispanic causes or issues, he insists that his audience/reader give credence to a Hispanic perspective as a way of promoting intercultural dialogue and exchange so as to negotiate or mediate differences from a position of strength instead of weakness. His style, charged with energy and vigor, vibrates in an effort to appeal to empathy and rational understanding, while carefully avoiding cultural demagoguery or self-righteousness. He resorts at times to flights of poetic registers to make his points that much more attractive and sensorially convincing. Logic and common sense are well balanced vis-à-vis the obstacles of prejudice and bigotry. His central thrust is to meticulously dismantle contradictions instead of indicting gratuitously. In a real sense, Ulibarrí deconstructs myths and stereotypes to see them for what they are: false and self-perpetuating assumptions or smoke screens that distort or obfuscate truth.

One of his favorite topics is language and how it contains and conditions a people's view of the world. In "Differences and Similarities Between the Hispanic and the Anglo-American Cultures," the author emphasizes how idioms in language "will reveal the inner life, the secret reality and the privacy of the people who speak it. The language is the best conductor of cultural values" (1). Although the examples provided in this essay might lead to arbitrary selections, the illustrations fulfill a purpose of demonstrating how certain ordinary idiomatic expressions contrast dramatically from one language to the other, thus revealing a fundamentally different rate of speed. English appears to stress speed (i.e., "run to the bank," "run down to the neighbor's," etc.), whereas Spanish seems to accentuate a less hectic speed through the multiple idioms containing the verb *andar* or a metonymic connection between "to walk" and "to be" ("anda muy bonita"/She is pretty, "no anda bien"/not being well). These examples actually purport to be tricky because they do not always relate to movement or a rate of speed. Nonetheless, Ulibarrí proceeds in this essay to carefully trace the history of the mestizo and how Moorish, Indian, and African bloods contributed to the formation of a new composite in the Americas. To explain divergent views from Anglo-Americans, he at times utilizes Unamunian argumentation, such as the Hispanic tragic sense of life, or Octavio Pazian interpretations to highlight the relationship between life and death as two complementary phases of the same thing. The listener/reader receives poignant cultural comparisons in an unforgettable abridged form.

Since language encapsulates much of his philosophical and pragmatic bent, this topical groundwork serves as a common denominator in most of his essays. So much hinges on its continuity for Hispanics. As he points out in "Language and Culture,"

> The language, the Word, carries within it the history, the culture, the traditions, the very life of a people, the flesh. Language is people. We cannot conceive of a people without a language, or a language without a people. The two are one and the same. (1)

Language represents such a fundamental constant in Ulibarrí's efforts to define culture that, he claims, everything must be done to preserve it for it contains the secret of cultural meaning. As one of his principal concerns, he states, "If the language goes, the culture goes with it. This is precisely the spiritual crisis of the minorities of the United States" (2), to which he adds,

> Each language is a unique vision of the world. All of the history of a people is synthesized in its language. It is the novel in which a people has deposited its laughter and tears, its triumphs and its failures, its aspirations and disappointments, its attitudes, thoughts, prejudices and beliefs. The language is the living current that joins the individual to a culture, a history, a vital reality. The language gives the individual an identity and quality. (3)

Its survival then depends on education wherein the meeting of differences is best ironed out for the good of society. Consequently, an adamant and uncompromising defender of bilingual education emerges evoking education in general as the instrument for change and mediation. In the foreword to *La fragua sin fuego/No Fire for the Forge* (1971), he notes,

> I submit that ignorance and stupidity are criminal and infinitely unAmerican. Human beings are not refrigerators and cannot be forced into the same mold. Viva la diferencia! . . . Take us as we are. We'll be glad to do the same for you. New Mexico will be the richer for it. (4–8)

Another important area of discourse where Ulibarrí excels is in discussing, and unmasking, stereotypes and caricatures as pernicious figments of cultural conflict. A meticulous and deliberate approach befits the highly charged and emotive topic in order to unravel their elusiveness. Above all, he proposes that stereotypes and caricatures often defy critical thinking as modes of convenience, which becomes a simplistic response in dealing with difference. He stipulates that these relieve the person of the responsibility of thinking by succumbing to easy and quick images as configurations of untruths and fabrications.

> The fact that these images may be, and often are, essentially untrue, deceptive and usually malicious is never investigated. These images frequently carry a built-in perversion, discrimination or bias. They make the purveyor feel superior, and the victim inferior. They appear in the guise of something innocuous, or friendly, or funny. ("EDUCATION AND STEREOTYPES AND CARICATURES," 1)

Again, his answer lies in education wherein new alternatives might be sought to alleviate and deflate a long tradition of pitting one group against another. This power play requires a renewed sense of egalitarianism from which the Hispanic will directly benefit. These changes would then have an impact on children's habits as well as their relationship to a learning environment. Therefore, the institutions would no longer serve as homogenizing factories but rather as agents of intercession or compromise for the sake of translating differences for children. As is evident, this New Mexican writer does not simply analyze a given situation; he indulges in proposing solutions to specific problems.

Ulibarrí also treads on sensitive topics, for example, in his essays "The Spanish Woman" and "Hispanic Individualism." The data presented might be questionable in its accuracy, but it makes enjoyable reading for the curious. While avoiding any polemics or more current revisionism by feminists, he manages to make succinct assessments of highly complex social phenomena by grounding his comments on Spain. Not developing the idea to its maximum possibilities, he does not venture into prescribing Hispanic women's roles in today's society. Instead, he opts for concluding how religion has directly shaped Spanish culture: "One would almost dare to say that Spain is more Marian than Christian" ("The Spanish Woman," 4). It would have perhaps been more enticing to sociologically apply this cultural value to peoples in a locally recognizable setting, although the associations are implied. His comment "Spain comes pretty close to being a matriarchy" ("The Spanish Woman," 5) is at the very least provocative and contains an ideological point worth examining further, given that he seems to turn the patriarchal system on its ear. Men, instead of appearing strong and virile, occupy the status of a satellite in the family organization, at times approaching the quality of wimps who are unable to handle minimal household chores. In "Hispanic Individualism," Ulibarrí again places his subject in Spain, leaving it unsaid as to its concrete relevance to Hispanics in the Americas. He prefers to examine original Iberian roots from a philosophical stance rather than specifics to people in this continent, perhaps hinting that constants remain as cultural determinants and that their new variants are too complex to adequately unravel into totally new entities. This is the selection process of a thinker who chooses his topics and develops an ideology of culture. Through the power of association we are to appreciate a legacy of racial mixtures and syncretic deities. The intimate experience of miscegenation with indigenous peoples and of African origin only seem to augment Hispanic complexity, diversity, and differences into a true melting pot, almost to the point that it is virtually impossible to reach a single classification. In other words, they defy any Eurocentric concept of ethos.

Therefore, the author in many of his essays alludes more to Hispanic antecedents as unique in comparison with the rest of Europe, and he concentrates less on how different Hispanics have become by leaving it understood. He covers controversial points related to "national character" à la Octavio Paz; however, he is careful not to become a victim of pitfalls inherent in that approach. Nonetheless, he evaluates general trends and interprets their meaning without depending on empirical information to prove his observations. For example, in "Spanish Catholicism," he incisively observes, "even the atheists in Spain are Catholic. Catholicism is more than a religion, it is a way of life" (1). His perspective leans toward highlighting constants and common denominators that still remain as factors conditioning our way of seeing the world. For that reason, it is necessary to emphasize the fact that he is more of a thinker and a poet than a sociologist.

On close review of Sabine Ulibarrí's essays, we discover a vantage point of unforgettable exposés that permit reflection by rethinking and reformulating concepts toward culture and Hispanics in particular. Sometimes fiery or feisty and other times patiently didactic, his essays lead the reader/audience through a new mental path of evaluating history and social behavior. He is adept at mapping out valuable strategies of viewing Hispanic culture as an important—but different—element in American society. Pride glows throughout a firm but rational resistance. He resists facile rhetoric laden with political jargon; instead, he pursues the means of persuasion through careful analyses. He alludes to a people's long-standing presence, durability, and resilience vis-à-vis social changes, conquests, and onslaughts. In addition, he shows the path toward change without making that process become a one-way road toward unconditional assimilation. Ulibarrí then taps into common sense, historical consciousness, and cultural-political rights. As a reminder of what we have been, he emphasizes retaining the essence of our ethos. Finally, he provides an essayistic testimony that although certain institutions (e.g., *sociedades literarias,* or literary associations) are things of the past, that he has fulfilled a role of informant, conscience, troubadour, critic, spokesman, and role model who has tried to fill a void. If the Hispanic voice has not been as prevalent as before, he now sets out to demonstrate how to relive that tradition by manifesting small dosages of a spirit filled with *inquietud* and commitment for his people, thus reclaiming part of ourselves in the process. Ulibarrí's essays, his person, his message, and his ideas embody the cultural philosophy of a New Mexican Hispanic whose time in history has always been now.

NOTES

1. To confirm this impression, one might review such works as René Wellek and Austen Warren's *Theory of Literature*, Rafael Lapesa Melgar's *Introducción a los estudios literarios*, Charles Tatum's *Literatura chicana*. The general finding is a penchant for overlooking the essay—or at least downplaying it—as if it does not form part of the five traditionally established genres. For a more ample discussion, consult Robert G. Mead, Jr.'s *Breve historia del ensayo hispanoamericano* in conjunction with Peter G. Earle's and Robert G. Mead, Jr.'s *Historia del ensayo hispanoamericano*.

2. Given the divergent views on the nature of the essay, Enrique Anderson Imbert opts to avoid the tempting pitfalls of a definition thus: "Como no creo en los géneros tampoco creo en las definiciones. Una aproximación escolar sería: el ensayo es una composición en prosa, discursiva pero artística por su riqueza en anécdotas y descripciones, lo bastante breve para que podamos leerla en una sentada, con un ilimitado registro de temas interpretados en todos los tonos y con entera libertad desde un punto de vista muy personal (1946: 120; Since I don't believe in genres neither do I believe in definitions. A scholastic attempt might be: the essay is a composition in prose, discursive but artistic for its richness in anecdotes and descriptions, sufficiently brief so as to read it in one sitting, with an unlimited register of themes interpreted from all angles and with total freedom from a very personal point of view).

3. The published essays are as follows: "La lengua: Crisol de la cultura," in Marie Esman Barker's *Español para el bilingüe*; "Cultural Heritage of the Southwest," in Philip D. Ortego's *We Are Chicanos*; and his foreword to *La fragua sin fuego/No fire for the Forge*.

4. This term, generally understood in various ways, here is utilized according to the concepts proposed by Jacques de Derrida (1973: 141) in "Differánce" when he states, "We shall designate by the term differánce the movement by which language, or any code, any system of reference becomes 'historically' constituted as a fabric of difference. . . . Differánce is what makes the movement of signification possible only if each element is said to be 'present,' appearing on the stage of the presence, is related to something other than itself but retains the mark of a past element and already lets itself be hollowed out by the mark of its relation to a future element."

5. Any reference to specific essays contained within this collection will be referred to with their corresponding pagination by individual article because the unpublished manuscript lacks consecutive pagination. The essays contained are as follows: 1. "Differences and Similarities Between the Hispanic and the Anglo-American Cultures"; 2. "The Spanish Woman"; 3. "Hispanic Individualism"; 4. "The Hispano: A Case of Names and Identity"; 5. "Spanish Catholicism"; 6. "Language and Culture"; 7. "Education and Stereotypes and Caricatures"; 8. "A Land and a People"; 9. "Foreign Language Teaching: Who Gives a Damn?"; 10. "The Language Teacher"; 11. "Children and a Second Language"; 12. "Hispanic Literature in the U.S.A."; 13. "Sor Juana, the Woman"; and 14. "The Magic of Don Juan."

6. *El ensayo mexicano moderno* (México: Fondo de Cultura Económica, 1958), 10–11. The author offers the following categories: (1) ensayo como género de creación literaria (the essay as a genre of creative writing); (2) ensayo breve, poemático (the brief, poetic essay); (3) ensayo como fantasía, ingenio o divagación (the essay as fantasy, ingenuity, or digression); (4) ensayo-discurso u oración (the essay-speech or oration); (5) ensayo interpretativo (the interpretive essay); (6) ensayo teórico (the theoretical essay); (7) ensayo de crítica literaria (the essay of literary criticism); (8) ensayo expositivo (the expository essay); (9) ensayo-crónica o memoria (the chronicle-essay or memoir); and (10) ensayo breve, periodístico (the brief, journalistic essay).

WORKS CITED

Anderson Imbert, Enrique. "Defensa del ensayo." In *Ensayos*. Tucumán, Arg.: Los Tollers Gráficos Miguel Violetta, 1946. Pp. 119–24.

Clemente, José Edmundo. *El ensayo*. Buenos Aires: Ediciones Culturales Argentinas, 1961.

Derrida, Jacques de. "Differánce." In *Speech and Phenomena and Other Essays on Husserl's Theory of Signs*. Translated by David B. Allison. Evanston: Northwestern University Press, 1973. Pp. 129–60.

Earle, Peter G., and Robert G. Mead, Jr. *Historia del ensayo hispanoamericano*. México: Ediciones de Andrea, 1973.

Lapesa Melgar, Rafael. *Introducción a los estudios literarios*. Edición Cátedra. Madrid: 1974.

Martínez, José Luis. *El ensayo mexicano moderno*. México: Fondo de Cultura Económica, 1958.

Mead, Robert G., Jr. *Breve historia del ensayo hispanoamericano*. México: Manuales Stadium, 1956.

Ortego, Philip D. *We Are Chicanos*. New York: Washington Square Press, 1973.

Oviedo, José Miguel. *Breve historia del ensayo hispanoamericano*. Madrid: Alianza Editorial, 1990.

Saldívar, Ramón. *Chicano Narrative: The Dialectics of Difference*. Madison: University of Wisconsin–Madison, 1990.

Sanjuan, Pilar A. *El ensayo hispánico: estudio y antología*. Madrid: Editorial Gredos, 1954.

Sifuentes, Roberto. "Essay." In *A Decade of Chicano Literature (1970 1979): Critical Essays and Bibliography*, by Luis Leal et al. Santa Barbara, Calif.: Editorial La Causa, 1982. Pp. 57–64.

Tatum, Charles. "Sabine Ulibarrí." In *Chicano Literature: A Reference Guide*, ed. Julio A. Martínez and Francisco A. Lomelí, Westport, Conn.: Greenwood Press, 1985. Pp. 385–95.

Ulibarrí, Sabine R. "One Voice of Juan Hispano (A Collection of Lectures on Hispanic Themes)." Unpublished manuscript.

———. "Cultural Heritage of the Southwest." In *We Are Chicanos*, ed. Philip D. Ortego, 14–20. New York: Washington Square Press, 1973.

———. Foreword. *La fragua sin fuego/No Fire for the Forge*. Cerrillos, N. Mex.: San Marcos Press, 1971. Pp. 2–8.

————. "La lengua: crisol de la cultura." In *Español para el bilingüe*, by Marie Esman Barker. Skokie, Ill.: National Textbook Co., 1971. Pp. 27–33.

Villaurrutia, Xavier. *Textos y pretextos*. México: La Casa de Madrid, 1940.

Welleck, René and Austen Warren. *Theory of Literature*. New York: Harcourt Press, 1956.

Zum Felde, Alberto. *Indice crítico de la literatura hispanoamericana: Los ensayistas*. México: Editorial Guaranía, 1954.

VUELO DE COMBATE

Era tiempo de muerte. Era tiempo de tristeza y llanto. El ángel de la muerte volaba loco sobre la tierra, descendiendo al azar a besar la frente de un inocente y joven militar.

El río de cuerpos inundaba los cementerios y otros sepulcros incógnitos y los llenaba de sangre, huesos y carne. Ese angel y ese río despedían un aroma que pervadía el mundo entero e intoxicaba a las gentes con su esencia pungente y pudiente.

Casi no había madre que no tuviera un hijo ya muerto o peligrosamente pendiente de un hilo sobre el oscuro abismo del aniquilamiento en tierras lejanas y desconocidas. Una esposa, un marido. Una chica, un novio. Una mujer, un hombre.

Era tiempo de vida. Era tiempo de alegría y risa. Todo el mundo se divertía. La gente bailaba y cantaba como nunca antes al son y al compás de una orquesta celestial. La vida se hizo sueño, ilusión, fantasía. Se gozaba y se saboreaba cada momento que el destino nos daba por si acaso se agotaran, por si acaso despertáramos. Cuando se vive de emociones la vida se hace novela, drama, poema.

Era tiempo de guerra. El pueblo estaba en función de guerra. No había hombre, mujer o niño que no anduviera fulminado por los rayos, destellos y explosiones de bombas y artillerías en los campos, cielos y mares de batalla allá lejos. No había americano que no llevara en sus narices el hedor de la muerte. Y ese olor enciende el espíritu, enardece la sangre y aviva los sentidos. Nunca se vive tanto, nunca el sentimiento sube tan alto, nunca florece la sensación como en tiempo de guerra. Amar y morir. Cada soldado, cada marinero, cada aviador, se hizo poeta. Las cartas de amor que se escribieron. Las cartas de amor que se recibieron. Las pasiones se hicieron palabra. El amor se hizo alma, se hizo poema.

Yo, que le tengo horror a la guerra, yo, que odio y aborrezco la matanza de seres humanos, recuerdo con nostalgia y añoranza aquellos tiempos. Quisiera sentir con aquella intensidad el temblor de mi vida, el estremecimiento y el bullir de mi existencia como entonces. Quisiera ser otra vez lo que en aquellos días fui. Quizás el desastre, el naufragio humano, es necesario para que la vida alcance su máximo apogeo. Acaso, cuando la muerte está presente, la vida se levanta, se afianza, se afirma y grita.

Estaba muy oscuro. Eran las dos de la mañana. La niebla ocupaba cada hueco del mundo de Wellingborough en Inglaterra donde estaba nuestra base aerea. El frío y la humedad se filtraban por la ropa, por la carne, hasta el tuétano. Desfilábamos sin prisa y en silencio hacia la cafetería a tomar nuestro desayuno.

Después nos reunimos en un gran salón con un tremendo mapa de Europa en el frente. Le llamaban a esta sesión orientación. Un oficial con un apuntador nos indicó la trayectoria de nuestro vuelo, nos apuntó los sitios donde podríamos esperar contra-ataque, y nuestra destinación. Era Berlín. Cada avión llevaría seis bombas de mil libras cada una. Era el 20 de junio de 1944.

Pasamos a una bodega donde recogimos nuestro equipo de combate, luego, al avión. Era necesario revisar todos los instrumentos, la operación de las ametralladoras, el funcionamiento de cada manivela. Todo tenía que estar en orden.

Luego, esperar. Desterraríamos a las seis. Todo onírico. Todo oscuro. El tremendo avión gris parecía grotesco y fantasmagórico. Nosotros, en nuestros abultados trajes de combate, parecíamos fantasmas. El mundo, envuelto en ráfagas y olas de niebla y negrura, con luces que casi no iluminaban, parecía un paisaje de un planeta esperando su Génesis. El silencio gobernó nuestras actividades, cada quien sumergido en sus propios pensamientos, temores y vulnerabilidades. Una vez acabadas éstas, surgió la animada charla. Bromas, chistes, burlas, insultos. Hay que acudir al escándalo y a la extravagancia para ahuyentar la duda, el terror y el pensamiento.

El destierre estaba lleno de aprensión. Los aviones desterraban en la oscuridad a intervalos de treinta segundos. Si uno se averiara sería una matanza general. Nosotros acurrucados en el pequeño departamento del radio, cada uno acojinando con su cuerpo a otro compañero por si hubiera un choque. Silencio otra vez. Otra vez las cavilaciones. El frío que llevábamos dentro no tenía nada que ver con el frío externo.

Pronto tomamos altura. Cada quien tomó su posición en el avión. Yo bajé a mi globo girador de plástico transparente con sus dos ametralladoras, calibre 50. Enchufé mi traje de combate. Me puse mi máscara de oxígeno. Disparé unos tiros para ver si mis armas funcionaban; el intenso frío a 35,000 pies de altura puede congelar la grasa e inutilizar la pieza. Todos hicieron lo mismo. Después vino la comunicación. Cada miembro de la tripulación informó por el *intercom* que todo en su posición estaba en orden.

¡Qué soledad tan sola! Fuera del avión, fuera de la tierra, fuera del tiempo. Lanzado por el espacio como cometa errante por fuerzas fuera de mi control. Arriba, sobre las nubes, el mundo está iluminado, aunque no haya salido el sol. Por encima un cielo infinito más azul que el azul. Por debajo una geografía desconocida y movediza, hecha de nubes, blancas, negras y grises, con sus montañas, sus valles, sus riscos y cañones. A lo lejos, extraños y cambiantes horizontes.

Nuestro escuadrón formó una punta de flecha y se dirigió al rendezvous, un punto exacto en el mapa del aire. Allí acudirían los otros escuadrones de diferentes bases aéreas, identificados por una letra de molde en la cola. Acudirían también los aviones de caza que nos acompañarían por una tercera parte del vuelo. Fueron llegando, una a una, las puntas de flecha y fueron formando una inmensa punta de flecha, amenazadora y mortífera, las pequeñas flechas escalonadas, a diferente nivel, para evitar así el fuego cruzado.

Cruzamos La Mancha y entramos en terreno enemigo. Nuestros aviones de caza se encargaban de los ataques de aviones enemigos. Nosotros a salvo. Contemplábamos sus escaramuzas como un espectáculo deportivo. Veíamos como a veces explotaba un avión en el aire, como descendía otro a espantosa velocidad, dejando una estela de humo negro, camino a estrellarse. Alguna vez un solitario paracaídas que flotaba lentamente hacia el suelo. Aplaudíamos cuando la víctima era enemiga. Llorábamos cuando era nuestra. No creo que se nos ocurriera que el enemigo fuera ser humano.

Muy pronto esos aviones de caza tuvieron que arrendarse por falta de gasolina; y nos quedamos solos. Nuestra salvación estaba ahora en nuestros manos. Los ojos abiertos y alertas escudriñaban el espacio sin fin en busca de un puntito en la lejanía que pudiera ser una amenaza y un peligro. Los alemanes se escondían en acecho detrás de un monte de nubes y nos saltaban cuando menos esperábanos. Nos atacaban de la dirección del sol para que nos deslumbrara. De pronto oíamos, "¡Bandidos a las seis arriba (o abajo)!" Las direcciones estaban marcadas por el reloj. La nariz del avión era las doce, la cola era las seis.

Es muy difícil ser valiente en sangre fría. No verle la cara al enemigo, no desata las corrientes de tu venganza. Nosotros estábamos obligados a sacar el coraje de quién sabe dónde para confrontar una abstracción mortífera.

Cayeron muchos aviones, muchos nuestros, muchos de ellos. Cuando caía uno de los nuestros, el que le seguía entraba y llenaba el hueco que dejaba. La formación, inmensa punta de flecha, seguía intacta, implacable, inexorablemente, hacia su destinación.

El B-17, nuestro bombardero, era grande y gris. Se movía por el aire lento, digno y bello. Sus líneas y contornos eran toda una sinfonía, una armonía, una majestuosa amenaza. Parecía estar fijo en el espacio, mas dejaba detrás cuatro largas y blancas estelas de vapor movedizo. Mil aviones dejaban cuatro mil estelas, un cielo azul a rayas blancas.

Cuando el ataque de los aviones enemigos terminaba (por falta de gasolina), empezaba el tiroteo de la tierra. Nos disparaban cañonazos que lanzaban proyectiles de metal que explotaban en el aire a la altura determinada por ellos, llenando el cielo con miles de pedacitos de metal asesino. Nosotros podíamos ver las bocanadas de humo negro, pero no podíamos oír la explosión ni oler el humo. Lo que si podíamos oír era la metralla pegándole al avión y perforándolo. Sonaba como granizo en un tejado de metal. Al pasar por esto un trozo de metal perforó el suelo del avión, buscó la zona vulnerable entre la barba y la garganta de un joven ametrallador, y evadiendo el delantal de hierro, el casco de hierro, penetró y lo mató.

Sentí el batacazo en el lado. Una metralla, tamaño de mi puño, le dio a mi paracaídas que llevaba a mi lado con tanta fuerza que me desmayó. Yo creí que me había muerto en esa rápida clarividencia que viene al instante de morir. Cuando no contesté al llamado del *intercom* mis compañeros bajaron y me sacaron. Desperté dentro del avión. Incrédulo. Confundido. Me palpé todo el cuerpo esperando estar gravemente herido. Nada. No tenía nada. El feroz golpe me desinfló los pulmones y me quitó los sentidos. Volví a mi sitio.

A las entradas de Berlín volvieron los bandidos. Una bala de 20 milímetros penetró el casco de hierro del piloto por el lado izquierdo, le batió los sesos, y salió por el lado derecho. El motor número tres recibió un cañonazo y se encendió. Las llamas llegaban hasta mi globo de plástico transparente. ¡Y aún no entrábamos en la pista del blanco, aún llevábamos seis bombas de mil libras cada una!

Por el *intercom* el co-piloto nos presentó las dos alternativas que teníamos: abandonar el avión en paracaídas o poner el avión en picada para ver si la velocidad del viento apagaba el fuego. A todos nos habían dicho, y lo teníamos muy presente, que lo más terrible para un aviador americano que aterrizaba en *festung Europa* eran las mujeres, ancianos y niños. Por ese motivo cada uno de nosotros llevaba una 45 automática. Yo llevaba una daga fajada en la pierna entre la rodilla y el tobillo. Caer en las manos de esas feroces fieras era mucho más espeluznante que una muerte instantánea, limpia y digna. Si cayéramos en manos de los militares estaríamos a salvo. Había convenios internacionales que nos protegían. Cada uno, uno por uno, votó: "Ponerlo en picada." La suerte estaba jugada. No importaba que aviones de esa camada no se ponen en picada.

Luego había que decidir qué hacer con las bombas. Alguien dijo, "Vamos a dejarles un recuerdo que no olviden nunca." Otro dijo, "Vamos a buscar el vecindario más elegante." Nadie se opuso. Todos de acuerdo. Así lo hicimos. Ningún remordimiento. Ahora me pregunto, ¿Qué le pasa a los pensamientos y sentimientos de los hombres cuando están en el mismo umbral de la muerte?

El avión descendió con una velocidad espantosa. El aparato temblaba y se sacudía con un estruendo que parecía que se iba a despedazar. Nosotros en silencio, sin palabras, sin respiración, sin pensamientos siquiera. Cuando el co-piloto lo sacó de la picada fue como una explosión. Parecía que por un instante quedamos suspendidos en el aire. Luego, vacilando, se enderezó. El fuego se apagó.

Nuestras penas no habían terminado. En el descenso le pegaron al motor número cuatro del mismo lado. Funcionaba pero se calentaba y era necesario apagarlo hasta que se enfriara. En estas condiciones no pudimos conseguir altura y nos quedamos a un nivel apenas sobre los árboles.

Todavía en Berlín recibimos un cañonazo directo del temido 88 de los alemanes en al ala del lado derecho. Rompió la arboladura principal del ala. Lo único que la sostenía era la piel de aluminio. Cortó cables tambíen. De modo que muchos elementos e instrumentos dejaron de funcionar. El agujero tenía un metro de diámetro. Eramos un elefante mortalmente herido. Botamos por la ventana todo lo que había suelto, todo lo que se podía arrancar, para aligerar el peso.

Allí estábamos casi incapacitados en tierra enemiga a unas novecientas millas de la Mancha Inglesa y de los White Cliffs de Dover. Estábamos todos convencidos que de ninguna manera podríamos llegar a esa tierra de promisión. ¿Qué hacer? Lo discutimos y decidimos renguear hasta donde pudiéramos y hacer el mayor daño posible.

No es posible describir el miedo al que no lo ha sentido. Acaso es algo muy individual y personal. Para mí fue como una especie de fiebre que me consumía y me agotaba, que me roía y me carcomía por dentro como una enfermedad rabiosa. Ya pasado, me dejaba suelto, vacío y débil. Creo que es más pensamiento que sentimiento. En momentos de combate desaparece el miedo por completo. Entonces el sentimiento se encarga de la situación. El pensamiento hace cobardes. La emoción hace héroes.

Cuando un avión está alto en el cielo, se puede ver desde lejos. Cuando vuela sobre los árboles, no se ve hasta que está encima. El nuestro volaba casi de lado. Volábamos tan bajo que éramos invisibles. El radar no nos podía localizar.

Al volar sobre un pueblo o una ciudad barríamos los tejados con nuestras ametralladoras, nueve instrumentos de muerte de calibre 50. Así mismo con los barcos residenciales del Rhin.

Llegamos a una avenida bordeada de hileras de árboles. Iba marchando un escuadrón de soldados. No nos vieron hasta que estábamos sobre ellos. Las ametralladoras entraron en acción. Yo me reía como un loco. Tenía la absurda impresión que eran títeres y que se doblaban cuando alguien les cortaba la cuerda. No puedo ahora justificar o explicar la irracionalidad y la locura que se apoderó de mí y de mis compañeros. ¿Es que la vida estaba ya vendida y que ahora tocaba cobrar? No sé.

Entre tanto seguíamos adelante hacia el oeste, hacia la lejana Inglaterra. Muy despacio, el avión no podía más. En silencio. No había qué decir, o no hallábamos cómo decirlo. Por la radio oíamos a los alemanes, histéricos, discutiéndonos. Nos habían calificado como un elefante enloquecido que iba sembrando muerte y destrucción por el continente.

Llegó el momento en que se nos acabó la munición. La habíamos malgastado creyendo que no llegaríamos hasta aquí. De pronto oímos por el *intercom:* "*¡Nueve bandidos a las seis!*" No teníamos con qué defendernos. Había llegado el fin.

Yo creía que en el momento de la muerte le llega a uno una clarividencia, una lucidez mental, que le permitiría, al fin, alcanzar un conocimiento del misterio de la vida. Creía que entonces me vendrían pensamientos profundos y nobles. Nada de eso ocurrió. Lo que pasaba por mis mentes era una tonada sentimental, una conversación inócua, un día de campo, un batido de leche, una hamburguesa. Todo frívolo y trivial.

¡Qué tremenda decepción!

Inesperadamente oímos por el radio en acento indiscutiblemente americano:

"*Amiguito a amigote, pierdan cuidado. Nosotros los llevaremos a casa.*"

Tienen que ser las palabras más dulces que yo he oído en mi vida. Por la ventana vimos a seis aviones P47. Uno se posó en la punta de cada ala y el tercero adelante. Los otros tres pasaron a trabarse con los nueve bandidos.

Cruzamos La Mancha apenas a flor del agua. Los barcos de los Franceses Libres, avisados de nuestro problema, estaban listos para recogernos si cayéramos. Nosotros otra vez apelotonados en el compartimiento del radio. Gimiendo, quejándose, como llorando, como alma agonizante, nuestro querido y herido avión subió sobre los riscos de Dover como a gatas. Aterrizó de panza porque el tren de aterrizaje estaba averiado. Aunque no lo vimos, a medida que el avión iba resbalando y arrancándose la piel por el pavimento de la pista de emergencia, una camioneta inglesa iba a toda velocidad a nuestro lado.

No recuerdo qué hicieron los demás. Yo me bajé y besé el suelo. Luego me apoyé en el avión, ahora tranquilo, porque me sentía mareado y débil. Durante todo el trance del combate fui dueño de mí mismo. Ahora sentía que mis facultades y capacidades se me iban. Me fueron cogiendo temblores que me sacudían todo el cuerpo. Sentí nacer dentro de mí una inquietud, una histeria, que amenazaba estallar en llanto o alarido. Lo que más me agobiaba era el terror de hacer el ridículo. Para usar una frase vulgar de esos días, "*No sabía si cagar o hacerme ciego.*"

En estas angustiosas circunstancias se personó un inglés con un vaso grande lleno de whiskey y me dijo, "*Bebételo todo.*" Ese inglés, si no me salvó la vida, me salvó la sanidad y mi amor propio.

Nos llevaron a nuestro cuartel. Allí en el tablero estaba la lista de las bajas del día. Allí aparecían nuestros nombres. Habían visto nuestro avión descender encendido y no vieron paracaídas, y así informaron. Ya nos habían dado por perdidos. ¡Qué raro es ver tu nombre en la lista de muertos! En realidad, parecía que yo comtemplaba la lista desde el otro mundo.

Me tumbé en mi catre boca arriba. No sentía ni frío ni calor. No tenía hambre ni sed, ni sueño. No oía nada. No veía nada. No me dolía nada. Cuando el espanto, el susto y el terror es tanto que ya el cuerpo y el intelecto no pueden más, viene, gracias a Dios, la inconsciencia. Me veo en la lejanía del recuerdo como si yo fuera otro, como si fuera desde otro mundo.

Era tiempo de vida y muerte. Tiempo de llanto y canto. Era tiempo de guerra. Fue un pedazo de la historia, ya en órbita en el espacio de la memoria. Sólo existe en el recuerdo y en la palabra escrita.

¿QUIÉN ERES?

Si olvidas de donde vienes,
¿sabes, tú, a donde vas?
Si has perdido tu pasado,
¿dónde está tu porvenir?

Si eres hombre sin historia,
serás hombre sin futuro.
Si reniegas de tus padres,
¿qué esperarás de tus hijos?

Si no tienes parentesco
con tu familia y tu pueblo,
cuando ríes, ríes solo,
cuando lloras, lloras solo.

Un presente solitario,
sin ayer y sin mañana,
Sin parientes, sin compadres,
sin amigos, sin hermanos.

Qué solo estás en el mundo,
perdido en la niebla blanca.
Solo, con tu culpa a cuestas
y tu soledad a solas.

NUEVO MÉXICO NUESTRO

Tierra que me vio nacer,
me ha visto vivir
y me verá morir,
me enseñó a querer.

Tierra llena de risa,
de llanto y encanto,
de promesa y desencanto,
de rosas y de espinas.

Tierra de cielos altos y limpios,
horizontes lejanos y místicos,
de suelo bravo y agreste,
de vientos secos y fuertes.

Sol que calienta o quema,
nubes que cobijan o asustan,
calor en las cañadas,
fríos en las alturas.

Se viste de oro de día,
se pone plata de noche.
El alba lleva muchas luces,
la tarde, cien mil colores.

Un mundo entre cielo y suelo,
entre este y oeste un hemisferio,
en conjunto un universo
que ha sido y es todo nuestro.

En el seno de la montaña,
en el corazón del valle,
en el regazo del llano,
mi cariño duerme y sueña.

Pino, piñón y posole,
chile, chicharrón y atole,
empanadas y frijoles,
urracas, chinchontes, flores.

No me quitan las veredas
del recuerdo y sentimiento
a mi Tierra Amarilla,
a la tierra ama mía.

Corridos, alabados,
inditas, coplas y versos,
canciones de mi pasado,
cantos de mi porvenir.

Tierra nuestra, consagrada
en amores y dolores,
regada de sangre hispana,
de lágrimas y sudores.

Muchas veces en la brisa
de alguna noche tranquila
hay susurros y murmullos,
y suspiros imprecisos.

Son las voces de los viejos
que perduran en el viento.
Tienen tanto que decirnos
para el tiempo en que vivimos.

Escucha, nuevomexicano,
la voz de tus antepasados,
te viene a través de los años,
lastimera y envuelta en llanto.

"No te olvides
ni te entregues.
No te dobles
ni te dejes.
Levántate, y anda.
Atrévete, y manda."

La voz sale de la tierra,
sube sola la alta sierra.
Baja triste al hondo valle,
a decirte lo que vales.

ASESINO DE LA LUNA

Por un ojo de la luna
se me fue el jilguero.
Por el otro, engañado,
se me fue el lucero.

Por las mismas sendas van
los toros del amanecer
y las golondrinas.

Por una rendija
de su sonrisa
se me fueron mis amores.

Conejito sorprendido
anda y dile a mi familia
que soy lunicida.
Bestiecita, asustadita,
anda y dile a la policía
que la luna sobre La Puerta del Sol
ya no es la misma.

Luna, luna, luna, luna,
luna de la lunería
no te escapas de mi puntería.

FANTASÍA EN Z MENOR

Ven conmigo a la cocina.
Tú haces las tortillas,
yo pico la carne
para el chile colorado.

La olla de frijoles
hierve alegre en la estufa.
Los aromas familiares flotan
en el íntimo recinto nuestro.

Tú me cuentas traviesa
tus aventuras y mentiras,
entre risas y desvíos.
Yo me río y te cuento las mías.

Suben vapores olorosos
de los platos campesinos.
Por el cuerpo fluye sabroso
el calor ingenuo del vino tinto.

A la mesa divagamos;
un viaje a alguna parte inventamos.
Real o ficticio, no importa,
lleno de quimeras y venturas.

Después, una antigua película
con ropa ya fuera de moda
y vocabulario ya olvidado;
recuerdos, burlas y risas.

Ya ves, no pido demasiado,
me conformo con muy poco.
Pero piénsalo bien despacio;
no quiero poco, lo quiero todo.

LANGUAGE AND CULTURE

In the beginning, and it is so today. The language, the Word, carries within it the history, the culture, the traditions, the very life of a people, the flesh. Language is people. We cannot even conceive of a people without a language, or a language without a people. The two are one and the same. To know one is to know the other. To love one is to love the other.

We are gathered here to consider this dual unity, this single duality, a people and their language, in danger of coming apart. This threatened split infinitive has become a national problem. A wedge has been driven between the Hispano and his language. As a result the Hispano is floundering in confusion, and his language is dying on the vine. A dynamic and aggressive Anglo culture has come between him and his past and is uprooting him from the soil, cutting him off from his ancestors, separating him from his own culture. Very little is being done to facilitate his transition from the culture of his forefathers, whose voice is silent, to the culture of the majority, whose voice makes his laws and determines his destiny.

As his language fades, the Hispano's identity with a history, with a tradition, with a culture, becomes more nebulous with each passing day. His identity as an Anglo is not yet in sight. There is no assurance that such an identity is possible, or even desirable. A man is what he is, and if he isn't all of that, he isn't much of anything. In terms of the national interest, our greatest natural resources are our human differences, and it behooves us to cultivate those differences. It is one thing to homogenize milk, it is quite another thing to homogenize the citizenry. It would appear, therefore, that a loyal, productive and effective Hispano citizen, proud of what he is and of what he has to give, has more to offer his country than a de-Hispanicized, disoriented Anglo with dark skin, a mispronounced name, and a guilty conscience to boot.

From the standpoint of the preservation of our natural resources, every attempt must be made to save the Spanish language. It is the instrument that will make the English language available to the Spanish-speaking child through well-trained bilingual teachers. The voice of America must be multilingual if it is to be understood around the world. The best bilinguals in Spanish and English are coming out of the Spanish-speaking Southwest. This human resource, which our government and industry are utilizing most effectively, must not be allowed to dry up. For better or for worse, our destiny is inextricably interwoven with the destiny of our Spanish-speaking friends to the south.

If we wish to hold on to the cultural heritage of the Southwest, we must preserve the Spanish language. If the language goes, the culture goes with it. This is precisely the spiritual crisis of the minorities of the United States. They are losing their native language, and with the language they are losing a certain consciousness of their own existence. They are losing something of their vital polarity, something of their identity. They find themselves somewhat uprooted, somewhat disoriented. A manner of being, a way of life, forged slowly since the beginning of history is lost with the loss of the language. Until a new consciousness is forged through and by the newly acquired language, these minorities will remain somewhat disoriented.

In Spanish we say, "He who speaks two languages equals two people." He equals two because, in fact, he is two people, with different points of view, different ways of focusing on reality, life and death.

Each one of his languages is the mold of the thinking, the very being of a people. Each language has its own and peculiar way of interpreting phenomena. Each language is a unique vision of the world. All of the history of a people is synthesized in its language. It is the novel in which a people has deposited its laughter and its tears, its triumphs and its failures, its aspirations and disappointments, its attitudes, thoughts, prejudices and beliefs. The language is the living current that joins the individual to a culture, a history, a vital reality. The language gives the individual an identity and quality. Each language is so unique that translation is impossible. "Me gustan las mujeres," does not mean "I like women." Each language has its own internal logic, its own hidden activation, that is impossible to transfer to another language.

The language carries within it what a people are: The English language reveals what the English-speaking people are. From the beginning of their history these people have marched constantly and consistently in the direction of democratic socialism. The process has culminated in our time in the socialistic democracies of England and the rest of the English-speaking countries. The slogan for these peoples has been and continues to be: "The greatest good for the greatest number."

The individual has surrendered his hegemony to the social welfare. The family is the smallest social group, composed of several individuals who all defer to a chief, historically, the father (in our days this is debatable). The family, now the individual, enters a larger social group, which we'll call the district, which also has its chief. The district enters the city, with its mayor. The city enters the county, the county the state, the state the federation, each one with its chief. In all cases the individual submits to the group and the chief. Everything perfectly organized and regulated.

This social process occurs in the very same manner in the English language. The word is the social group that corresponds to the family, and here too, the individuals defer to the majority and to the chief. For example, the word is not IN-TER-EST-ING. It is IN-ter-est-ing. The word enters the sentence, the next social group, and each sentence has its key word. The sentences enters the paragraph, which also has its key sentence. The paragraph enters the chapter, the chapter the book. Perfect linguistic socialism. This can be carried to a ridiculous extreme in popular speech: "Did you eat yet, Joe?" "Not yet, did you?" becomes "Jeet jet Jo?" "Nojet, Jew?" Punctuation is organized, regular and practical, as is the life of the people.

Let us now look at the Spanish-speaking peoples. If there were a single word (which there isn't) that could define the social, private and public life of these peoples, that word would have to be AN-ARCHY. The history of civil war, social and political conflict. Neither the individuals nor the groups have ever wanted to submit their personal rights to any hierarchy. Traditionally the individuals have always risen against all discipline, and the Hispanic truth of all time has been and is PUBLIC DISORDER.

The very same thing happens in the language. Every sound, every syllable, every word, every sentence, that is, every individual, demands and receives individual attention in the Spanish language. Look at the word we examined in English before. Now it is IN-TE-RE-SAN-TE. Perfect linguistic individualism. Spanish punctuation is equally anarchistic, as are the Spanish-speaking peoples.

The French people are cultured, intellectualistic, elegant, exquisite, well organized. Their language reflects the very same characteristics. The skin of the Italian is full of music, and his language is a symphony.

To demonstrate the loyalty the language has to the spirit of the people who speak it, let us examine what happens in a single point of view, that attitude toward time:

In Spanish a watch WALKS.

In English a watch RUNS.

In French a watch MARCHES.

In German a watch FUNCTIONS.

Let us approach the Spanish language to see what we can find of cultural heritage, of human warmth, in it. Spanish subjectivism is well known. We know the Hispano functions impulsively and emotionally. What else is the subjunctive but a subjective and personal posture before reality? The subjunctive exists only in the mind of the individual who has the right to evaluate and adjust reality according to his own feelings. The subjunctive has practically disappeared from most of the modern languages, but it continues stronger than ever in Spanish.

The exaggerated use of the reflexive is another case in point. It is an approaching, a personalizing, a humanizing, and embracing of actions—look at the difference there is between "Murió mi padre" (which communicates information only) and "Se murió mi padre" (which adds the human element). Consider the truly emotional impact and human involvement in "Se me murió mi padre." "Me gradúo en junio" (I graduate myself in June) is a completely personal and individualizing point of view. Here the individual gives himself the responsibility and the credit, and why not? The opposite happens too: "Se me cayó el libro" (The book fell itself on me). Here the responsibility is rejected and the book is blamed.

The use of the diminutive in Spanish is an altering and a humanizing of the reality that surrounds us, a modification according to our own design. "Chico" is already a diminutive. "Chiquito" does not mean the object is smaller. It now carries emotional content. "Chiquitito" imbues the object with personal values. The diminutive is truly a personal vision of reality.

The Spanish language reflects the religious reality of the people. An immense number of religious expressions rise out of Hispanic thought to enter the language. Dios mío, Ay Dios, Adiós, Vaya con Dios, Válgame Dios, Si Dios quiere, Sea Dios servido, Por Dios, Ave María Purísima, Por los Santos Nombres. The words "God" and "Jesus Christ" are not bad words in Spanish. There are no euphemisms in the Spanish language for these words. In English we do not dare say, "My God!" or "Jesus Christ!" We are forced to use euphemisms. "My Gosh!" or "Jiminy Christmas!"

The individualistic character of the Spanish language is manifest in expressions like: "Yo me llamo Juan," my name is what I want it to be. It's a philosophical posture. "Nos ponemos el sombrero" (we put on the hat, that is, each one, one hat).

Hispanic humor is evident in words like "salsipuedes" (blind alley—come out if you can), "aguafiestas" (party pooper—fiesta dampener), "hasmerreír" (laughing-stock—make me laugh), "Trotaconventos" (matchmaker—one who trots from convent to convent). The satirical is patent in the names given to doctors: "matasanos" (killer of the healthy), "matavivos" (killer of the living), Dr. "Sangrías" (Dr. Bleeder). To take an oath in Spanish is "protestar" (to protest). I have to do it, but I don't have to like it. A tightwad is a "codo duro" (hard elbow). You could hardly get tighter than that.

Hispanic taboos are also in the language. You have to be very careful about how you use the words "padre, madre, hijo, tía, pan." Being so sacred in the culture, they lend themselves to blasphemy. It is curious to see the many evasions there are for pregnant women: she is in an "interesting state," she is "embarrassed," she is "strapped," she is "waiting," she is "fat." The act of birth is called "dar a luz" (bring forth into the light).

The sensuality of the Hispano is found in expressions like "disfrutar el momento" (pick the fruit of the moment), "saborear la conversación" (taste or savor the conversation), "sufrir un examen" (suffer an examination).

The cordiality and courtesy so traditional in Spanish life embraces us with expressions like "Mi casa es suya" (My house is yours), "a sus órdenes" (at your service), "su servidor" (your servant), "mande usted" (command me).

The Hispano projects the self and identifies it with nature. He says "Amanecí en la fiesta" (I dawned at the party), "Anochecí trabajando" (I nighted working). To dawn and for night to fall are natural phenomena. He humanizes them. And the opposite: "Está queriendo llover" (It is wanting to rain). To want, the act of willing is a human phenomenon. The Hispano attributes it to nature.

ANNOTATED BIBLIOGRAPHY OF SABINE REYES ULIBARRÍ

Teresa Márquez

PRIMARY WORKS

Al cielo se sube a pie. Madrid: Alfaguara, 1966. 65 pp. In this collection of love poems, Ulibarrí explores time and space. Some of his poetry can be viewed as protests against social structures that keep man oppressed, even though the author has stated that he has no political agenda.

El alma de la raza. Albuquerque: Minority Group Cultural Awareness Center, College of Education, University of New Mexico, 1964. Various pagination. This volume is a compilation of nine lectures presented by Sabine Ulibarrí, in 1970, at the Cultural Awareness Institute, University of New Mexico. His lectures address various topics: differences and similarities between the Spanish-American and the Anglo-American cultures, stereotypes and caricatures, language, Hispanic individualism, Spanish Catholicism, and Spanish women.

"Amena Karanova." *El Cóndor and Other Stories*. Houston: Arte Público, 1989. Reprint. *Short Fiction by Hispanic Writers of the United States*, ed. Nicolás Kanellos, 233–56. Houston: Arte Público, 1993. Amena, an opera diva from a distant and exotic country, lands in Albuquerque by accident and under the guidance of her friend and companion, Datil, begins to build a new life. Amena marries a Hispanic banker but dies giving birth to a son. Ulibarrí uses magic and mystery to bring about a happy conclusion to this story of miracles and life in Hispanic New Mexico.

Amor y Ecuador. Madrid: Ediciones José Porrua Turanzas, 1966. 80 pp.
Ulibarrí's poetry focuses on Ecuador, time and space, and love and
women. His love poems are an attempt to capture the ideal,
symbolized by woman, who in his view represents sensuality,
purity, beauty, and essence. His poems also express concern over the
treatment of the indigenous people in Ecuador and protest the
church's abandonment of man in his time of need.

"El amor y el profesor, o los hijos de la flor." *Hispania* 53 (1970): 25–27.
This is Ulibarrí's presidential address delivered at the Fifty-first
Annual Meeting of the American Association of Teachers of Spanish
and Portuguese in Chicago, 1969. Ulibarrí speaks about the changes
and teaching "flower children." He offers suggestions on how to
inspire and motivate the new generation through language and
literature.

The Best of Sabine R. Ulibarrí: Selected Stories. Edited by Dick Gerdes.
Albuquerque: University of New Mexico Press, 1993. 528 pp. This
collection of bilingual stories, which includes some that have been out
of print or available in Spanish only, is set mainly in the Southwest,
although some of the stories also reflect the author's experiences in
Ecuador. The stories, furthermore, reveal Ulibarrí's art in blending
fantasy and realism as he delves into the human spirit.

El Cóndor and Other Stories. Bilingual Edition. Houston: Arte Público,
1989. 224 pp. The eleven short stories in this collection deal with
the supernatural, love, jealousy, witches, technological fantasy,
murder, and intrigue. In the title story, "El Cóndor," the protagonist,
Professor Garibay, and his mistress carry out a plot to help and
protect the indigenous people who have been marginalized and
disenfranchised for centuries in Ecuador.

"Crepúsculo." In *Al cielo se sube a pie.* Madrid: Ediciones Alfaguara,
1966. 11. Reprint. *Chicanos: Antología histórical y literaria.* Comp.
Tino Villaneuva. México: Fondo de Cultura Económica, 1980. 368
pp. Poem. In this poem Ulibarrí evokes sad yet romantic feelings. He
creates a colorful, vivid image of dawn.

"Cultural Heritage of the Southwest." In *We are Chicanos: An
Anthology of Mexican-American Literature,* ed. Philip D. Ortego,
11–20. New York: Washington Square, 1973. Ulibarrí suggsts
education is the answer to the problems faced by the Hispano
students who start school with several language and cultural
disadvantages. He further suggests that teachers learn the native

language. Last, Ulibarrí recommends the Hispano learn about his culture, his history, and the many contributions of the Hispano community to the United States.

"Desde un rincón ecuatoriano." *Hispania* 52, no. 2 (1969): 275–76. In this report, Ulibarrí describes the activities of the Centro de Estudios Andinos in Quito, of which he is the director and which is administered by the University of New Mexico. He explains that students, enrolled through the university, take classes in Historia del Brasil, Literatura Ecuatoriana, and La comunicación de Masas, for example, and earn credit toward their degrees.

"Don Nicomedes." In *Primeros encuentros/First Encounters*. Ypsilanti, Mich. Bilingual Press/Editorial Bilingüe, 1982. Pp. 38–45. Reprint. *Ceremony of the Brotherhood*, ed., Rudolfo A. Anaya and Simón J. Ortiz, 84–88. Albuquerque: Academia, 1981. Reprint. *Nuestro* 10, no. 2 (1986): 63–64. Four young Anglo cowboys attempt to humiliate an old Mexican cowboy but instead learn a firm lesson from don Nicomedes about respecting other people and their cultures.

"Dos caras." In *El Cóndor and Other Stories*. Bilingual Edition. Houston: Arte Público, 1989. Pp. 139–48. Reprint. *Cuentos de los Estados Unidos*, ed. Julián Olivares, 165–71. Houston: Arte Público, 1992. Two close friends, one well-to-do and one who must work for his successes, share similar life experiences but become bitter enemies after an attempted murder by the well-off friend because of jealousy. The friend survives the attempted murder and on his recovery, plans revenge.

"Flow of the River/Corre el río." In *Flow of the River/Corre el río*, ed. Carol Guzmán, Richard Kuhn, and Donna Pierce, 6–13. Albuquerque: Hispanic Culture foundation, 1988. Ulibarrí uses the Rio Grande as a background to relate the history and settlement of New Mexico. He briefly describes, in English and Spanish, the lives of the Hispanos, their music and religion, their coexistence with the Native Americans, their traditions, and the twentieth-century's impact on those traditions.

Foreword. *La fragua sin fuego/No Fire for the Forge*. Collected, edited, and translated by Ulibarrí. Cerrillos, New Mex.: San Marcos, 1971. Pp. 2–8. In this foreword, Ulibarrí addresses fellow New Mexicans who know little about Hispanos—their lives, beliefs, values, feelings, and aspirations—and who make no attempt to understand the Hispano culture. He speaks of Hispanos as a conquered people who have lost their language, the symbol of their culture. Ulibarrí urges Nuevo Méxicanos to "mix" but not melt into the "American melting pot."

Forcword. *Sueños Dreams*. Edinburg, TX.: University of Texas-Pan American, 1995. 105 pp. Ulibarrí hopes this work reflects some pattern or at least achieves a semblance of unity in his attempt to develop and elaborate the fragments of his dreams into dream stories. Ulibarrí believes dreams are important to self image and play a role in how life is viewed.

"La fragua sin fuego/No Fire for the Forge." *La fragua sin fuego/No Fire for the Forge*. Collected, edited, and translated by Ulibarrí. Cerrillos, New Mex.: San Marcos, 1971. Pp. 9–24. Told from a nine-year-old boy's view, this story is about the town's blacksmith, Edumenio. A loner and a complex man, Edumenio lives outside the town's social life and is more at ease with the village's children who visit his shop. Edumenio marries a beautiful young woman on one of his many mysterious trips to the city. The town thinks of his new wife as "one of those women." The people's cruelty in their treatment of Edumenio and his beautiful young wife causes the breakup of their marriage.

La fragua sin fuego/No Fire for the Forge. Collected, edited, and translated by Ulibarrí. Cerrillos, New Mex.: San Marcos, 1971. 66 pp. Written by Ulibarrí's students in a creative writing class, this collection of short stories and poems is about dreams, love, folktales, childhood memories, and life in New Mexico. The title story, "La fragua sin fuego," is by Ulibarrí.

"The Gallant Stranger." *Primeros encuentros/First Encounters*. Ypsilanti, Mich.: Bilingual Press/Editorial Bilingüe, 1982. Pp. 2–11. Reprint. *Nuestro* 10, no. 2 (186): 59–61. An accidental weeklong visit by a soul-weary and tired gringo cowboy enriches and influences the life of a Hispano family in northern New Mexico. The narrator recalls the family's memories of the gracious and gentle stranger who was the talk of the community, long after his departure, for his mysteriousness and generous repayment for their hospitality and generosity.

Governor Glu Glu and Other Stories/El gobernador Glu Glu y otros cuentos. Tempe, Ariz.: Bilingual Press/Editorial Bilingüe, 1988. 153 pp. Mysterious men who perform great deeds of charity, city rabbits, people of a mystic valley, an unwanted lamb and his fate, a bold woman's actions, a mother's smothering love and its effects, a young Indian woman's death by love, and love's devastating impact on a young lover are the subjects of this bilingual collection of short

stories. In the title story, "Governor Glu Glu," Ulibarrí presents a
humorous tale of a man who gossips.

"Hombre sin nombre." In *Tierra Amarilla: Cuentos de Nuevo México*.
Quito: Editorial Casa de la Cultura Ecuatoriana, 1964. Pp 51–101.
Tierra Amarilla: Stories of New Mexico/Cuentos de Nuevo México,
1st ed. Albuquerque: University of New Mexico Press, 1971. Pp. 84–
176. 7th printing 1984. Pp. 84–167. Reprint. *Mosaico de la vida:
Prosa chicana, cubana y puertorrigueña*. Comp. Francisco Jiménez.
New York: Harcourt Brace Jovanovich, 1981. Pp. 79–85. First
published in Spanish and later translated into English, this novelette
explores the depths of a young man's psyche as he searches to regain
his self-identity after his return to his hometown to write the
biography of his father. He soon finds himself besieged by doubts
and dreams. He falls into a coma, and although he survives the
ordeal, he emerges a changed man.

"Juan P." In *Tierra Amarilla: Cuentos de Nuevo México*. Quito:
Editorial Casa de la Cultura Ecuatoriana, 1964. Pp. 33–41. *Tierra
Amarilla: Stories of New Mexico/Cuentos de Nuevo México*. 1st ed.
Albuquerque University of New Mexico Press, 1971. Pp. 36–61. 7th
printing 1984. Pp. 36–51. Reprint. *Mosaico de la vida: Prosa
chicana, cubana y puertorriqueña*. Comp. Francisco Jiménez. New
York: Harcourt Brace Jovanovich, 1981. Pp 116–22. A once wealthy
and proud family is reduced to poverty and shame because of an
indelicacy accidentally committed by one of the family members
while attending a funeral. During a brief silence in the funeral
service, one of the sisters breaks air, startling the whole
congregation by its force and loudness. Afterward the family is
marginalized, their lives are dramatically changed, and in the
process, they acquire a nickname, "The Frater Family."

"La lengua: Crisol de la cultura." *Hispania* 54 (1959): 319–22. Reprint.
Español para el bilingüe, ed. Marie Esman Barker, 27–33. Skokie,
Ill.: National Textbook, Co., 1976. In this essay, Ulibarrí discusses
several issues dealing with language: the function and importance
of language in the Hispanic culture, some language differences in
the English-speaking culture, the loss of language and the
significance of the loss for minorities in the United States, reality
as reflected through the use of the diminutive adjective in
Spanish, humor, religion, taboos, and sensuality as expressed in
the Spanish language.

"The Little Heavenly Horse: Children's story/Cuento para niños." *De Colores* 4, nos. 1–2 (1978): 116–20. A violent storm keeps Benito, the young protagonist, from falling asleep. The next morning on the way to his fishing hole he discovers a flying horse, thrown off course by the storm. Benito and the flying horse, which he has named Star, become friends. Star meets a herd of horses and wants to join them but is not accepted. Hurt and bruised, Star returns to Benito. One day two other flying horses land: they are Star's parents. Benito is sad to see his friend leave but knows Star must rejoin his family.

"Mexican Literature and Chicano Literature: A Comparison." *Proceedings of the Comparative Literature Symposium: Ibero-American letters in a Comparative Perspective*, ed. Wolodymyr T. Zyla and Wendell M. Aycock, 149–67. Lubbock: Texas Tech Press, 1978. Ulibarrí and Gerdes discuss Mexico's presence in and its influence on Chicano literature through culture, traditions, values, history, and themes. Both agree that Mexican ties are based on the pre-Columbian period, Hispanic values, and the Mexican revolution of 1910. Most Chicano fiction, they explain, either uses the 1910 revolution and selected aspects of Chicano life in the Southwest or rejects Mexican references and focuses on contemporary Chicano reality. They discuss specific novels by Miguel Méndez and Mariano Azuela, in terms of parallels. Finally, Ulibarrí and Gerdes discuss the polemics of regional and universal literature including code switching, universality of poetry, Mexican influences, and paradoxes in and parallels between Mexican and Chicano poetry.

Mi abuela fumaba puros/My Grandma Smoked Cigars. Berkeley: Quinto Sol, 1977. 167 pp. "My Grandma Smoked Cigars," the title story in this collection of bilingual short stories, sets the tone for the rest of the stories about traditions, families and relatives, folktales, the customary practice of nicknaming the village's inhabitants, and life in general in northern New Mexico, as secluded from outside influences.

Mi abuela fumaba puros/My Grandma Smoked Cigars. *El Grito del Sol*, no. 2 (1977): 9–32. In this excerpt from the book by the same title, the narrator begins his story about his grandparents by telling a few tales about his "quarrelsome, daring, and prankish" grandfather. However, the narrator soon shifts his attention to his grandmother, "a straight, tall, and slender woman" who got in the habit of smoking cigars after her husband's death. The narrator develops a loving portrait of a grandmother, who through determination and a strong personality manages to keep the family intact during times of personal loss and grief.

El mundo poético de Juan Ramón. Madrid: Artes Gráficas Clavileño, 1962. 285 pp. In this study Ulibarrí proposes to examine Juan Ramón Jiménez's entire body of poetry as though it were a single unit of work, a long poem. He analyses its creation, evolution, and maturation without attempting to break down Jiménez's work into phases, as done by other critics. Ulibarrí further proposes to identify those elements characteristic of Jiménez's poetry and to demonstrate that the literary methods used by the poet remain the same as those in his early work. He also attempts to explain how each method fits into the total work. In the first part of the book, Ulibarrí endeavors to show the various creative methods used by Jiménez. The second part deals with images and symbols used by the poet, and the third part is a synthesis of the results of Ulibarrí's investigation.

"My Grandma Charged Interest." *Visions of New Mexico* (Winter 1988/89): 20–23. Ulibarrí's recollections of his maternal grandmother who loved fine, elegant things. An emancipated women with intelligence and tact, she was a successful salesperson, who also lent money to friends and acquaintances, and, of course, charged interest.

"My Grandma Smoked Cigars." In *Mi abuela fumaba puros/My Grandma Smoked Cigars*. Berkeley: Quinto Sol, 1977. Pp. 14–29. Reprint. *El Grito del Sol Collection: An Anthology*, ed. Octavio I. Romano-V., 175–84. Berkeley: TQS, 1984. Reprint. *Mexican American Literature*, ed. Charles Tatum, 175–83. Orlando: Harcourt Brace Jovanovich, 1990. An English translation of "Mi abuela fumaba puros." The narrator recalls his fond memories of the grandmother, a strong and dominant woman who through sheer determination helps the family survive several tragedies. Her cigars are a symbol of her power.

"My Uncle Cirilo." In *Mi abuela fumaba puros/My Grandma Smoked Cigars*. Berkeley: Quinto Sol, 1977. Pp. 58–67. Reprint. *El Grito del Sol Collection: An Anthology*, ed. Octavio I. Romano-V., 185–91. Berkeley: TQS, 1984. The narrator's Uncle Cirilo is the sheriff of Río Arriba county, where he maintains the peace without much effort. Don Cirilo is feared and respected by everyone and is the only one who can discipline a roomful of mischievous school children who have played an unusually hurtful trick on their teacher, a nun.

"My Wonder Horse." In *Tierra Amarilla: Stories of New Mexico/ Cuentos de Nuevo México*. Albuquerque: University of New Mexico Press, 1977. Pp. 2–17. Reprint 1984, 2–17. Reprint. *Voices: An Anthology of Nuevo Méxicano Writers*, ed. Rudolfo A. Anaya, 1–6. Albuquerque: El Norte publications, 1987. Albuquerque University of New Mexico Press, 1988. Pp. 1–6. Reprint. *Mexican American Literature*, ed. Charles Tatum, 167–74. Orlando: Harcourt Brace Jovanovich, 1990. "Mi caballo mago" in the original Spanish version, this tender and bittersweet short story reveals the pains suffered by the young protagonist as he struggles through a difficult and challenging time in his rite of passage to become a man.

"Panoramic View of Chicano Culture. *"Hispanic Health Services Research" NCHSR Research Proceedings Series*. U.S. Department of Health and Human Services. DDHS Publication no. (PHS) 80-3288. 1980. Pp. 14–16. Ulibarrí addresses the differences and similarities between the Spanish-Mexican and the Anglo-American cultures at a conference held in Albuquerque, New Mexico, September 5–7, 1979. Culturally, Ulibarrí explains, the United States is European, while Spanish America, including the Southwest, is a mixture of European, African, and Indian in its blood and culture. In regard to attitudes and views on life, the Anglo-American projects an "epic sense of life" in contrast to the Hispano-American's "tragic sense of life." Another difference, continues Ulibarrí, is the psychological need for the Hispano-American to communicate his personal beliefs, hopes, and values, while for the Anglo-American reason controls the emotions. One other difference is in philosophy: in the United States, the philosophy is scientific, in Hispano American countries, the philosophy is poetic. However, both the Anglo-American and the Hispano-American share "the same noble and heroic concept of man, the same humanistic vision of life."

Primeros encuentros/First Encounters. Ypsilanti, Mich.: Bilingual Press/Editorial Bilingüe, 1982. 87 pp. Using humor and irony, Ulibarrí explores the intercultural experiences of Anglos, Hispanos, and Indians in northern New Mexico in this collection of short stories. For example, love conquers cultural differences in the stories "Blondie" and "A Bear and a Love Affair." In "Monico," a young Hispano teacher is mentored by a Native American, a respected leader of his pueblo.

"Profesor de pie." In *Al cielo se sube a pie*. Madrid: Ediciones Alfaguara, 1966. Pp. 40–41. Reprint. *Chicanos: Antología histórica y literaria.* Comp. Tino Villanueva. México: Fondo de cultura económica, 1980. P. 370. Poem.

Pupururú. México, D.F.: Sainz Luiselli, 1987. 117 pp. A bilingual collection of Ulibarrí's versions of traditional children's fairy tales.

Review of Recuerdos de los viejitos: Tales of the Rio Puerco, by Nasario García. *New Mexico Historical Review* 64, no. 1 (1989): 101–2. García's book, according to Ulibarrí, allows the people of Rio Puerco to tell their stories in their own voice, which provides a certain authenticity. Furthermore, Ulibarrí informs the reader that García develops an artistic tapestry of living history as he skillfully blends in the people, the landscape, the relationship between the Navajos and the Nuevo Mexicanos, their joys and sorrows and their humor and superstitions. Ulibarrí informs us that García's work is in contrast to the many books written about Hispanos from the outside, and he hopes others will be inspired to record the many stories that wait to be told.

Spanish for the First Grade. Edited by members of the Workshop on the Teaching of Spanish in the Elementary School, under the direction of Sabine R. Ulibarrí. Albuquerque: Department of Modern and Classical Languages and College of Education, University of New Mexico, 1955. Rev. 1957. 180 pp. Designed as a guide for teachers of Spanish in elementary schools, this manual is intended to help students become familiar with "spoken" Spanish. The eighteen lessons developed and the songs and games included are directed to children from the first to the third grade. A vocabulary list and an annotated bibliography of syllabi and guides, texts, and reference and source materials complete the guide.

Sueños Dreams. Edinburg, TX.: University of Texas-Pan American, 1995. 105 pp. This new collection of ten short stories explore themes familiar in Ulibarrí's previous works: love, miracles, dreams, loyalty, and good and evil. These dream stories, in Spanish with English translations, take place mostly in rural northern New Mexico.

"They Got Married." In *Primeros encuentros/First encounters.* Ypsilanti, Mich.: Bilingual Press/Editorial Bilingüe, 1982. Pp. 58–65 Reprint. *Nuestro* 10, no. 2 (1986): 61–62. A young couple marries despite family objections. She is a gringa, he is a Mexican. Problems of cultural differences and misunderstandings arise, causing pressures on the young couple. In the end, only after their children are grown are the families able to become friends.

"Tiene cruz y no es cristiano." In *El Cóndor and Other Stories*. Bilingual
Edition. Houston: Arte Público, 1989. Pp 125–38. Reprint. *Cuentos
hispanos de los Estados Unidos*, ed. Julián Olivares, 156–64. Houston:
Arte Público, 1992. Camilo wakes us and discovers he is in the middle
of a tornado. His mattress lands in the middle of town, exposing him
totally naked. A cross, mysteriously burned on his back during the
tornado ride, has given Camilo strange electrical powers that he uses to
amuse himself until he prays to be free of his supernatural gifts.

Tierra Amarilla: Cuentos de Nuevo México. Quito. Editorial Casa de la
Cultura Ecuatoriana, 1964. 102 pp. The stories in this collection are
about life and the people in northern New Mexico, as remembered
by the author: "Mi caballo mago," "El relleno de Dios," "Juan P., "
"Sábelo," and "Hombre sin nombre." (In Spanish).

Tierra Amarilla: Stories of New Mexico/Cuentos de Nuevo México.
Comp. Thelma Campbell Nason. Albuquerque: University of New
Mexico Press, 1984. 167 pp. 1993 ed., 214 pp. This bilingual version
of the original collection of short stories in Spanish includes an
additional cuento, "Forge without Fire." In "My Wonder Horse,"
Ulibarrí tells a bittersweet story of a young man's rites of passage;
"The Stuffing of God" is a delightfully humorous tale of a
community's experiences with a priest who mangles the Spanish
language and of his influence on the young protagonist; "The Frater
Family," or "Juan P." expresses the author's feelings about his
village's harsh and cruel treatment of a once wealthy and proud
family; don José Viejo, a former shepherd with a razor sharp tongue,
befriends the young protagonist in "Sábelo" and tells him amazing
stories; in "Forge without Fire," the town's blacksmith is run out of
town by the village's reaction to his new young wife. "Hombre sin
nombre," considered a novelette rather than a short story, is a dark
tale of a young man's search for self-identity.

"Two Young Artists and the Portrait of an Old Man." Review of *River
of Traps*, by William de Buys and Alex Harris. Albuquerque:
University of New Mexico Press, 1990. Mirage (Spring 1991): 15.
Ulibarrí commends de Buys and Harris for their sensitive and
perceptive portrayal of Jacobo Romero, a longtime resident of El
Valle, an isolated village in northern New Mexico, who taught them
the lore, traditions, complexities, and intricacies of life and survival
in New Mexico. Ulibarrí asserts Romero's portrait "should hang in
every New Mexican museum as a work of art" because it is a
portrait painted in pictures and words.

Ulibarrí Speaking on Hispanics [video recording]. Albuquerque: Educational Television Division, IDEA Center, University of New Mexico, 1988. 1 videocassette (VHS) (12 min.) Sci., col. Ulibarrí reads a poem to Flamenco dancing by Eva Encinas accompanied by guitarist Joseph Dow.

[Un día . . .] *Al cielo se sube a pie.* Madrid: Ediciones Alfaguara. 1966. P. 20. Reprint. *Chicanos: Antología histórico y literaria.* Comp. Tino Villaneuva. México: Fondo de Cultura Económica, 1980. 369 pp. Poem.

Ulibarrí, Sabine R., and Dick Gerdes. "Una misma cultura, dos distintas literaturas: La mexicana y la chicana." *El Grito del Sol* 3, no. 4 (1978): 91–115. In this article, the authors explore the significance of the relationship between Chicanos and Mexicans from a literary perspective. They discuss whether Chicano literature is part of the Mexican, Latin American, or American litrature and provide examples of parallels in Chicano and Mexican literatures. Ulibarrí and Gerdes find that Chicano literature either uses the Mexican revolution as a point of departure and then describes certain aspects of Chicano life in the Southwest or totally rejects references to Mexico and focuses on contemporary Chicano reality. Various Chicano novels are discussed or mentioned as the authors explore the polemics of regional and universal literatures as related to Chicano literature. In conclusion, they agree that Mexican history, Mexican art, and Mexican literature are represented in Chicano literature.

"Witcheries or Tomfooleries?" *Mi abuela fumaba puros/My Grandma Smoked Cigars.* Berkeley: Quinto Sol, 1977. Pp. 32–55. Reprint. *Tierra: Contemporary Short Fiction of New Mexico,* ed. Rudolfo A. Anaya, 32–41. El Paso: Cinco Puntos, 1989. The narrator records accounts of encounters with witches, La Llorona, owls, hexes, the devil himself, and healers that have become part of Tierra Amarilla's folklore.

"The Word Was Made Flesh: Spanish in the Classroom." *Aztlán: Anthology of Mexican American Literature,* ed. Luis Valdéz and Stan Steiner, 295–97. Ulibarrí explains how the Spanish-speaking child, already disadvantaged on entering school because of economic and social circumstances, is predestined to failure and eventually will become a dropout. He recommends that the school program, designed to make an Anglo of the Hispano student, instead should educate him in his own culture and history and teach him about the Hispano contributions to this country.

SECONDARY WORKS

Anaya, Rudolfo A. Introduction. *Mi abuela fumaba puros/My Grandma Smoked Cigars*, by Sabine R. Ulibarrí. Berkeley, Quinto Sol, 1977. Pp. 8–9. Anaya comments on Ulibarrí's creative abilities in combining the oral tradition and "his personal approach to the idea of story." He comments on the author's characterizations, imagery, and use of time and space in developing a world since past, which is filled with humor, joy, and tragedy.

Armas, José. "Chicano Writing: The New Mexico Narrative." In *Contemporary Chicano Fiction: A Critical Survey*, ed. Vernon E. Lattin, Binghamton, N.Y.: Bilingual Press/Editorial Bilingüe, 1986. Pp. 32, 34, 36–7, 40. In this overview of New Mexico narrative, Armas quotes from selected works by Ulibarrí and describes the author as a strong promoter of the Spanish language.

———. "Hispanic Contributions Outweigh Recognition. *Albuquerque Journal*, 13 June 1993, B 3. Armas quotes Ulibarrí's comment on Hispanics' role in the military and Hispanic contributions to the nation: "Hispanics make lousy Anglos, but damn good Americans."

Barrera, Rosalinda B., Olga Liguori, and Loretta Salas. "The Vital Role of Mexican-American voices and Perspectives." *Teaching Multicultural Literature in Grades K–8*, ed. Violet J. Harris, 218–225. Norwood, Mass.: Christopher-Gordon, 1993. This chapter is a discussion of Chicano writers and children's literature. The authors discuss Ulibarrí's *Pupurupú: Cuentos de niños/Children's Stories*, a collection of animal tales and variations of well-know stories. Four stories are highlighted for their story lines and character development: "El patito Tito," "Caballito del cielo," "Pupurupú," and "Pulín y Miga." The authors also observe that the Spanish versions of the stories are richer linguistically because of Ulibarrí's humor, subtlety, and rhythm.

Bosch, Rafael. Review of *Al cielo se sube a pie. Hispania* 46 (1963): 669. Bosch attributes Ulibarrí's poetic vision to the influence of Juan Ramón Jiménez, the Spanish poet, although he believes Ulibarrí's poetry reflects his own poetic temperament and character. One of Ulibarrí's poetic characteristics, Bosch explains, is his propensity for the use of symbolic language that is precise, concrete, and passionate.

Bruce-Novoa, Juan. "Magical Realism." Review of *El Cóndor and Other Stories. American Book Review* 11, no. 6 (1990): 14. Bruce-Novoa escribes Ulibarrí's collection of short stories as a "peculiar mixture of . . . personal antecedents—a peculiar and somewhat uneasy mixture." He also describes the location of the stories, New Mexico, as "superfluous and distracting," a locale that does not enhance the development of the stories. The result, observes Bruce-Novoa, is a forced effort to place New Mexico into universal literature, achieved through plot twists and information unnecessary to the development of the stories. This literary style reflects Ulibarrí's strength as an oral-tradition storyteller, according to Bruce-Novoa. He also mentions Ulibarrí's mixture of the fantastic and realism but finds it distracting when Ulibarrí feels compelled to explain his stories too much. Bruce-Novoa concludes that Ulibarrí has created "an interesting, if not altogether successful, synthesis of New Mexico oral tradition and mainstream magical realism."

Chávez, Fray Angélico. Review of *Tierra Amarilla*. "Southwestern Bookshelf," *New Mexico Magazine* 49, 11–12 (1971): 64. Chávez recommends Ulibarrí's collection of "droll and tender tales about northern New Mexico" to parents interested in their children's bilingual education and suggests schools should have copies for supplemental reading. Further, Chávez lauds Nason's introduction for providing "a much-needed ethnic and historical instruction for . . . readers."

Davison, Ned J. Review of *El Mundo poético de Juan Ramón: Las últimas noticias* (Aug. 1 1963). Davison recommends Ulibarrí's study to students of Juan Ramón Jiménez's work and to students of modern poetry. He praises Ulibarrí for his systematic and penetrating analysis of the poet's use of symbolism. Davison also discusses Ulibarrí's investigation of Juan Ramón's use of the adjective and verb and symbols such as the rose, water, gold, woman, and the "I" as multiple symbolism.

Del Amo, Javier. Review of *Tierra Amarilla. Mundo Social* (Dec. 1965): 37. Del Amo makes terse comments on the conflict between the Hispanic and Anglo-American cultures in New Mexico. He briefly explains the plots of "Mi caballo mago," "Sábelo," and "Hombre sin nombre."

Duke dos Santos, María I. "Las Heroínas de Ulibarrí." In *Culturas hispanas de los Estados Unidos de America*, ed. María Jesús Buxo Rey and Tomás Calvo Buezas, 609–13. Madrid: Agencia Española de Cooperación International, 1990. The author explores the development and function of the female characters in several of

Ulibarrí's works: "La hermana generosa," "Fragua sin fuego," "Hombre sin nombre," and "Mi abuela fumaba puros." According to Duke dos Santos, Ulibarrí's female characters serve as background in the development of his male protagonists and often are viewed through the protagonists' eyes, limiting the reader's knowledge of their thoughts or feelings. For example, Duke dos Santos finds that the story "La hermana generosa" does not focus on a female character but on a male protagonist who recalls his memories of a nun who helped him adapt to school while living away from home. Although in "Mi abuela fumaba puros" Ulibarrí develops his fullest and strongest female character, Duke dos Santos finds she is viewed only from the young protagonist's perspective.

"En el cielo de los mexicanos . . ." *El Hispano* 27 (28 August–3 September, 1992): 1. Ulibarrí's statement about Zapata and Villa is featured on the front page of this Spanish-language newspaper: "En el cielo de los mexicanos, brillan dos estrellas: Emiliano Zapata y Pancho Villa. Sus hazañas son monumentos y montañas. Sus palabras son sagradas, dignas del alma del mexicano. . . . Como dijo Zapata: 'Es mejor morir de pie, que vivir de rodillas.'"

"Five Chosen to Receive University Honors." *University of New Mexico Campus News* 24, no. 16 (1989): 1. This news release highlights Ulibarrí's honor as recipient of the Regents' Meritorious Service Medal; it also gives a brief biography of Ulibarrí's accomplishments.

García, Reyes. "Notes Toward an Ethnometaphysics." In *Multiethnic Literature of the United States: Critical Introductions and Classroom Resources*, ed. Cordelia Candelaria, 69–91. Boulder: University of Colorado, 1989. García proposes in his work on ethnophilosophy that philosophy as quest in the Southwest becomes autobiography. As example, García mentions Ulibarrí's "Hombre sin nombre," a story in which "the memory of a literary and literal self" resembles the young writer, the protagonist in search of his identity as he writes his father's biography. García also comments on Ulibarrí's stories and his ability to recreate the cultural ambiance of rural northern New Mexico with images of traditions and times long past.

García-Saez, Santiago. Review of *Mi abuela fumaba puros y otros cuentos de Tierra Amarilla/My Grandma Smoked Cigars and Other Stories of Tierra Amarilla*. *Hispanic Journal* 4, no. 1 (1982): 46–47. García-Saez proclaims Ulibarrí master of the "cuento costumbrista chicano" and master in how he manipulates time in his short stories. Furthermore, he recognizes Ulibarrí's ability to transport his readers to a world filled with clear and precise imageries, full of color and the brilliance of rural life in northern New Mexico. Ulibarrí's stories, adds García-Saez, reflect a mixture of the Spanish and indigenous cultures.

————. Review of *Primeros encuentros/First Encounters. Hispanic Journal* 6, no. 1 (1984): 197–98. According to García-Saez, this collection of nine short stories reaffirms Ulibarrí's place as one of the best storytellers in the literature of the Southwest. He believes Ulibarrí wrote these narratives to reflect his perspectives of the Mexican-American, Anglo and Native American cultures, to honor those teachers who influenced his early life.

González, Angel. [Foreword.] *Al cielo se sube a pie*. Madrid: Ediciones Alfaguara, 1966. Pp. 7–8. González states that Ulibarrí's work represents the efforts of an old culture to reaffirm itself and survive in a hostile environment, that he sees the Spanish language in a precarious position because it is more of a university language rather than a community language, and that he attempts to salvage the Spanish language and its cultural implications at a time when it is not conducive to "live in Spanish and write in Castilian."

González-Berry, Erlinda Viola. "*Tierra Amarilla:* Costumbrismo "Lyrical, Evocation, Dramatic Experience in Chicano Literature in Spanish Roots and Content." Ph.D. dissertation, University of New Mexico, 1978. This study explores the literary modes, costumbrismos, and the picaresque used by nineteenth- and early twentieth-century Spanish American writers as adapted to the Chicano experience in Ulibarrí's collection of short stories, *Tierra Amarilla*. González-Berry states Ulibarrí's use of these literary forms is his way of linking with the cultural foundation severed by colonization, in attempts to recover some of the cultural identity "displaced by time, space, and historical events." Furthermore, she believes Ulibarrí's focus on cultural themes and motifs is an effort to record, salvage, and mystify a way of life that has all but disappeared.

Gurpequi Palacios, José Antonio. "Influencia de Clarín en Ulibarrí: Oviedo en Nuevo Mexico." *Culturas Hispanas de los Estados Unidos de America*, ed. María Jesús Buxó Rey and Tomás Calvo Buezas, 617–25. Madrid: Agencia Española de Cooperación Internacional, 1990. The author summarizes selected narratives by Ulibarrí and Clarín as he compares similarities in their work.

"Honran a Educadores Mexico-Americanos." *El Hispano News* 22, no. 41 (1988): 1. News brief announcing Ulibarrí's selection as one of four national educators featured in a calendar that includes pictures, short biographies, and summaries of professional activities of those honored.

Irizarry, Estelle. "Los hechos y la cultura en los EE. UU." Review of *Mi abuela fumaba puros. Nivel* (Dec. 1978): [pp?] Irizarry points out Ulibarrí's lack of references to the injustices and abuses committed against Chicanos and to the absence of defensive and offensive attitudes in his work. She discusses several of Ulibarrí's more interesting characters and explains how he draws on the anecdotes and jokes of his childhood and on the people of Tierra Amarilla. Irizarry additionally perceives that he refrains from being judgmental. She concludes that with *Mi abuela fumaba puros*, Chicano literature has reached maturity.

Leach, Leah. "Dr. Sabine Ulibarrí tells the Grandfather's Stories." *Las Vegas Daily Optic*, 28 April 1978, 8. Ulibarrí, invited to be a speaker in "The New Mexico Experiences In Creative Exposition" series spnsored by Highlands University, talks about his writing, his family and the people of northern New Mexico, the past, and other influences on his work.

Leal, Luis, and Pepe Barrón. "Chicano Literature: An Overview." *Three American Literatures*, ed. Houston A. Baker, Jr., 9–32. New York Modern Language Association, 1982. Sabine Ulibarrí is acclaimed as one of the most successful authors to write in Spanish.

Lefkoff, Joan. Introduction. *Governor Glu Glu and Other Stories*. Tempe, Ariz.: Bilingual Press/Editorial Bilingüe, 1988. Pp. 7–8. Lefkoff praises Ulibarrí for his characterizations, humor, poetic language, and imagination. She observes that his characters, although ordinary people, find themselves in uncommon situations, in "a world of illusion," mystery, and magic. Ulibarrí, comments Lefkoff, creates "stories of dreams and realities in the best of literary tradition."

Lerat, Christian. "Lumière et Ombres du Souvenir dans *Tierra Amarilla de Sabine Ulibarrí*." In *Escritures Hispaniques Aux Estats-Unis: Memoire et Mutations*, ed. Yves-Charles Grandjeat, Elyette Andouard-Labarthe, Christian Lerat and Serge Ricard, 67–80. Marseilles: Publications de l'Universite de Provence, 1990. This essay is a discussion and analysis of selected stories in Ulibarrí's collection of short fiction: "My Wonder Horse," "The Stuffing of the Lord," "The Frater Family," "Get That Straight," and "Forge

Without Fire." Ulibarrí's place as a writer in New Mexico's letters and regional literature is discussed as well.

———. "Le Retour Aux Sources de Sabine Ulibarrí dans *Tierra Amarilla*." In *Multilinguisme et Multiculturalisme en Amerique du Nord: Temps, Mythe et Histoire,* ed. Jean Beranger, Jean Cazemajou, Jean-Michel Lacroix and Pierre Spriet, 33–43. Bordeaux: University of Bordeaux Press, 1989. Lerat discusses Tierra Amarilla as a place and as a source of influence on Ulibarrí's fiction. He further discusses the question of Ulibarrí's work as regional literature. Several of the short stories in the collection are discussed and analyzed.

Lomelí, Francisco. "Contemporary Chicano Literature, 1959–1990: From Oblivion to Affirmation to the Forefront." In *Handbook of Hispanic Cultures in the United States: Literature and Art,* ed. Francisco Lomelí. 86–108. Houston: Arte Público, 1993. Ulibarrí's Tierra Amarilla is described as a work that depicts a sense of continuity and history in rural northern New Mexico, preserves a regional identity, and abounds with humor. *Mi abuela fumaba puros,* Ulibarrí's other collection of short stories, is viewed as humoristic and folkloric.

Lomelí, Francisco A, and Donaldo W. Urioste. Review of *Tierra Amarilla: Stories of New Mexico/Cuentos de Nuevo México. Chicano Perspectives in Literature,* by Francisco A. Lomelí and Donaldo W. Urioste. Albuquerque: Pajarito, 1976. P. 55. The authors briefly assess the six stories in *Tierra Amarilla,* commenting that each represents a phase in the narrator-protagonist's maturation. The stories, they conclude, are characterized by their timelessness and humor.

———. Review of *Al cielo se sube a pie. Chicano Perspectives in Literature,* by Francisco A. Lomelí and Donaldo W. Urioste. Albuquerque: Pajarito, 1976. Pp. 34–35. Lomelí and Urioste see evidence of Juan Ramón Jiménez's influence on Ulibarrí's poetry, poetry that "expresses the essential qualities of an object without ornaments." They also detect evidence of influence from the French Parnassian and symbolist poets. Both concur that Ulibarrí's work falls within the poetic tradition of Spain.

———. Review of *La Fragua sin fuego/No Fire for the Forge. Chicano Perspectives in Literature,* by Francisco A. Lomelí and Donaldo W. Urioste. Albuquerque: Pajarito, 1976. P. 70. This brief review describes the stories and poetry as "sincere, sensitive and sentimental," varying in theme and style, that reflect the writer's "nostalgic recollections of childhood experiences."

"LUISA NMLA." *New Mexico Library Association Newsletter* 9, no. 1 1981): 8. News release announcing Ulibarrí's appearance as guest speaker at the program meeting of the Library Usage/Information Services to Spanish-speaking Americans (LUISA), on "The Spanish Woman."

Lyon, Fern. Review of *Mi abuela fumaba puros*. *New Mexico Magazine* 56, no. 2 (1978): 33. Lyon briefly describes Ulibarrí's work of ten tales concerning memorable people in the author's childhood as funny, tragic, and moving.

Márquez, Antonio. "Into the Mainstream: Sabine Ulibarrí's 'Hombre sin nombre.'" *Hispanorama Schwerpunkt: Chicanoliteratur* (Feb. 1990): 98–103. This critical study identifies Ulibarrí's story as a psychological novella: complex, ambiguous, and modern. Márquez explores Ulibarrí's use of the phantasmagoria, identity crisis, and Jungian archetypes—shadow, anima, and animus. He further explores the author's use of the Doppelgänger, poetic tropes, images of the life-death cycle, and literary clichés in what he thinks is Ulibarrí's effort to move beyond *costumbrismo* and enter the mainstream of world literature.

———. "Leroy V. Quintana's Return and Search for the Center." In *The History of Home*, by Leroy V. Quintana. Tempe, Ariz.: Bilingual Press/Editorial Bilingüe, 1993. Pp. 7–8. In this introduction to Quintana's collection of poetry, Márquez explains the history of New Mexico literature and its place in Chicano literature. He quotes Ulibarrí's description of New Mexico writers' attachment to the land and their cultural heritage.

Martínez, Elsie C. "*Tierra Amarilla*." Review of *Tierra Amarilla. El Hispano* 22, no. 50 (1988): 4. Martínez states that Ulibarrí's works stands throughout time, that he handles language with aplomb, and that each story can be considered as fantasy or reality. His work, she adds, is picaresque, sad, enigmatic, and maintains the reader's interest.

Meier, Matt S. and Feliciano Ribera. "The Chicano Cultural Renaissance." In *Mexican Americans/American Mexicans: From Conquistadors to Chicanos* by Matt S. Meier and Feliciano Ribera. New York: Hill, 1993. Pp. 233–48. Rev. ed. of *The Chicanos*, 1972. The authors mention Ulibarrí as an "outstanding practitioner" of the short story, a genre favored by several Chicano writers.

Mi abuela fumaba puros/My Grandma Smoked Cigars. Carta Abierta 10 (Dec. 1977): 5. Juan Rodríguez mentions the publication of Ulibarrí's book.

Mi abuela fumaba puros/My Grandma Smoked Cigars. Review. *Rio Grande Writers Association* 8 (Feb. 1978): 5. Reviewer recommends Ulibarrí's collection of bilingual short stories to serious students of Chicano literature and calls attention to the author's character sketches and depiction of rural lifestyles.

"Mid-Year Title VII Directors Conference." *Southwest Bilingual Education Training Resource Center Newsletter* 1, no. 5 (1978): 1–2. This article highlights Ulibarrí's talk, "Differences and Similarities Between the Spanish-Mexican and the Anglo-American Cultures," presented at a conference of educators. Ulibarrí focuses on the country's political relations with Mexico and Latin America and its educational system.

Moesser, Alba Irene. "Sabine Ulibarrí." "La literature méjico-americana del suroeste de los Estados Unidos." Ph.D. dissertation, University of Southern California, 1971. Pp. 228–67. Moesser proposes to analyze Ulibarrí's work as it stands among Chicano authors to demonstrate that his work can be classified as Mexican-American literature. She believes he has produced a body of proper literary work that shows the influence of the Hispanic culture. Ulibarrí's poetry, observes Moesser, follows contemporary form and does not adhere to forms imposed by precepts and customs. His use of time and space identify his work with superrealism. And his other literary characteristics reflect tendencies typical of vanguard and postvanguard literature.

Moiser, Pat. Review of *Primeros encuentros/First Encounters*. *Revista Chicano-Riqueña* 10, no. 4 (1982): 69–70. Moiser states Ulibarrí's writing style, based on the oral tradition, either enhances the text or causes an irritating looseness. She adds that the author appears to scrutinize the impact of his literary characters "on himself as narrator and on each other, searching out or badly stating their significance to him and to the cultures they represent." Moiser further comments that Ulibarrí's stories are filled with brief sentences, sentence fragments, and rhetorical questions and editorial comments that tend to be intrusive. Moiser concludes that Ulibarrí does not allow the reader to reach his or her own deductions about universal or personal insights to be gained from the cultural encounters.

Nason, Thelma Campbell. Foreword. *Tierra Amarilla: Stories of New Mexico*. Albuquerque: University of New Mexico Press, 1971. Pp. vii–x. Nason describes Tierra Amarilla and the descendants of the

Spanish colonists who brought their Hispanic heritage and
Catholicism to northern New Mexico. Their isolation, she claims,
produced a fierce independent spirit and traditions that greatly
influenced Ulibarrí's work. Nason states three reasons why he
should write his stories: his focus on a way of life since past, a need
to record the Hispanic heritage of the region, and his need to provide
an understanding of the region and its problems.

Nemes, Graciela P. Review of *El mundo poético de Juan Ramón*.
Hispania 47 (Mar. 1964): 199–200. Nemes cites Ulibarrí's study for
its direct and concise approach in analyzing the work of poet Juan
Ramón Jiménez. She notes his objective to explore Juan Ramón's
poetry as a single unit of work, without including analyses of other
critics' work. Ulibarrí's footnotes, adds Nemes, further enrich the
reader's knowledge of Juan Ramón's literary accomplishments. (This
review is in Spanish).

Prjevalinsky Ferrer, Olga. Review of *El mundo poético de Juan Ramón*.
Modern Language Journal 48 (1964): 59–60. This reviewer praises
Ulibarrí's study of Juan Ramón Jiménez as a fine and penetrating
work, exact, precise, and methodical and based on modern stylistic
theories. She claims Ulibarrí is never pedantic and his language is
that of an erudite scholar. Further, Prjevalinsky Ferrer suggests that
Ulibarrí's work be read, that if she were to propose conclusions or
suggest objectives demonstrated in his work it would be intrusive.

———. Review of *Al cielo se sube a pie*. *New Mexico Quarterly* 32
(1962–63): 238–39. Prjevalinsky Ferrer uses the following elements
to review Ulibarrí's poetry: "lyrical adjectivation," the absence of
"verbal forms," "decorative representation," "coloration," rhythm,
and "the play upon words." She describes his work as "static poetry,"
poetry that transfers moods through "lyrical adjectivation" and in
which nouns are deprived of "substantivity." She finds that Ulibarrí's
lack of "verbal forms" contributes to "a state of feeling" and to a
condition in which "the adjective carries out the greatest poetical
function." Finally, Prjevalinsky Ferrer believes his work may be partly
influenced by one of Luis de Góngora's poems and that Ulibarrí's poem
"Dios carcelero" links him to other important Spanish poets.

Quintana, Inez. "El norte de Nuevo México visto por Sabine Ulibarrí."
El Hispano, 9 September 1988, 3. Quintana briefly reviews
Pupurupú, a collection of children's stories, and *Governor Glu Glu*,
a group of stories that reflect aspects of New Mexican Hispanic life.

She comments that his children's stories contain specific lessons and his other stories tend to be critical of certain aspects of society.

Ramírez, Arturo. Review of *Mi abuela fumaba puros/My Grandma Smoked Cigars*. *Caracol* (Feb. 1978): 7. Ramírez provides succinct observations of Ulibarrí's attempts to preserve a way of life and of his efforts to continue the traditional folklore of New Mexico. He describes the collection of stories as autobiographical, narrated in the first person from the perspective of an adult recalling his childhood. Ramírez also comments on the author's characterizations, humor, color, and language in "Brujerías o tonterías?," "Mi tío Cirilo," and "Mi abuela fumaba puros."

Rocard, Marcienne. "The Children of the Sun: Chicanos as Precursors of a New World." In *The Children of the Sun: Mexican-Americans in the Literature of the United States*, Marcienne Rocard. Trans. Edward G. Brown, Jr. Tucson: University of Arizona Press, 1989. Pp. 281–91. Rocard uses one of Ulibarrí's quotes in her discussion of the pluralism of Mexican-Americans: "It is one thing to homogenize milk; it is quite another thing to homogenize the citizenry."

Ramos, Charles. Review of *Tierra Amarilla*. *Southwestern American Literature* 2 (Spring 1972): 60. Ramos review captures the essence of Ulibarrí's work: a sensitive loving portrayal of Nuevo Mexicanos and of a way of life long past. Ramos focuses on the main qualities of the short stories in this collection.

Rodríguez, Juan. "El desarrollo del cuento chicano." In *The Identification and Analysis of Chicano Literature*, ed. Francisco Jiménez, 58–67. New York: Bilingual Press/Editorial Bilingüe, 1979. Rodríguez's brief review of Ulibarrí's short stories notes his humor, seriousness, and nostalgia.

Ruiz, Reynaldo. "Sabine R. Ulibarrí." *Dictionary of Literary Biography*, ed. Francisco A. Lomelí and Carl R. Shirley, 260–67. Detroit: Gale, 1989. Ruiz describes Ulibarrí's northern New Mexico, his family, and the influences on his life and work. He explores the author's major works: *Al cielo se sube a pie, Tierra Amarilla, Amor Y Ecuador, La fragua sin fuego, Mi Abuela fumaba puros, Primeros encuentros*, and *El Cóndor and Other Stories*. Ruíz points to Ulibarrí's poetry and his use of imagery, language, and themes such as love, identity, and the spiritual world. He also comments on the author's regional focus, the northern New Mexico spirit and soul, and the integration of childhood experiences into his work.

"Sabine Ulibarrí (1919–   )." *The Hispanic Almanac: From Columbus to Corporate America,* ed. Nicolás Kanellos, 438–39. Detroit: Visible Ink, 1994. This almanac includes a brief essay on Ulibarrí's life as a short story writer, poet, and essayist. The essay provides a list of awards received and books published. A summary analysis notes Ulibarrí's language, style, and themes, and describes his works as "among the most direct and accessible to broad audiences."

"Sabine R. Ulibarrí." *Hispanic Heroes: Portraits of New Mexicans Who Have Made a Difference,* ed. Rose Díaz and Jan Dodson Barnhart, 15. Albuquerque: Starlight, 1992. This brief biographical essay covers Ulibarrí's childhood in Tierra Amarilla, his education, his military service, and his creative works. His teaching, emergence as a spokesperson during the Chicano movement, and appointment to the Royal Academy of the Spanish Language are noted as well.

"Sabine R. Ulibarrí." *Cuentos hispanos de los Estados Unidos,* ed. Julián Olivares, 154–55. Houston: Arte Público, 1993. This biographical sketch focuses on Ulibarrí's early life in Tierra Amarilla, his military and teaching careers, and his literary works. Also included are Ulibarrí's views on Hispanic literature in the United States.

"Sabine R. Ulibarrí." *Short fiction by Hispanic Writers of the United States,* ed. Nicolás Kanellos, 23. Houston: Arte Público, 1993. This short biography highlights Ulibarrí's years in Tierra Amarilla, his studies at the University of New Mexico and the University of California, Los Angeles, his military service during World War II as a gunner, and his teaching career at the University of New Mexico. His writing style is briefly described and his books are listed.

"Sabine Ulibarrí Honored in Mentor's Name." *Mirage* (Winter 1993): 22. This article features Ulibarrí for the award bestowed by the University of New Mexico Alumni Association. The Zimmerman Award is for significant contributions to the university or the New Mexico. His background, creative works, teaching and military careers, and other awards received are mentioned.

"Sabine Ulibarrí." *Mexican American Literature,* ed. Charles Tatum, 165–66. Orlando: Harcourt Brace Jovanovich, 1990. Tatum's brief biography of Ulibarrí covers his allegiance to his Mexican-American heritage, his education, his military service and teaching career. Last, the focus is on the themes, characterizations, and language common in Ulibarrí's work.

Sackett, Theodore A. "A Look at Books." Review of *Tierra Amarilla: Stories of New Mexico. The Albuquerque Journal*, 14 May 1971, C 10. This review considers Ulibarrí's book an important re-creation of a way of life rapidly disappearing and one that offers insights into "the origin, identity and values of Spanish and Mexican Americans." The prose, vision, perspectives, language, forms, ideas, and style characteristic of his work are noted as well.

————. Review of *Tierra Amarilla. Modern Language Journal* 56, no. 8 (1972): 515–16. In this review of Ulibarrí's bilingual edition of five stories and a "novella," Sackett notes the author's poetic portrait of life in a small village in northern New Mexico, filled with details of customs, values, and landscape. Sackett further comments on Ulibarrí's use of language, form, ideas, and style and the influences of the Spanish literary tradition. He also observes that while the short stories and the novella are linked by locale and poetic style, the stories reflect remembrances of a childhood filled with memorable characters while the novella reflects the author's intellect. With this collection, Sackett concludes, Ulibarrí gives valuable insights into the Spanish and Mexican-American culture.

"Simposio en honor al Profesor Sabine Ulibarrí." *El Hispano*, 29 April 1988, 5. Brief announcement of the symposium to be held in honor of Ulibarrí at the University of New Mexico.

Stavans, Ilan. "At War With Anglos." In *The Hispanic Condition: Reflections on Culture & Identity in America* by Ilan Stavans. New York: Harper Collins, 1994. Pp. 61–91. Stavans mistakes Ulibarrí for a Chicana writer in his discussion of literary history and Latina authors who write in English. He mentions Ulibarrí's well-known work, *Tierra Amarilla*.

Summers, Monica. "Ulibarrí Wins Zimmerman." *University of New Mexico Campus News* 28, no. 3 (1992): 1. This news release announces Ulibarrí's receipt of the highest award bestowed by the UNM Alumni Association for his contributions to the university or to the state of New Mexico.

"Symposium in Honor of Ulibarrí Seeking Scholars." *University of New Mexico Campus News* 23, no. 11 (1988): 8. A call for papers on Ulibarrí's prose and poetry for a symposium is announced. The symposium is organized by Rowena A. Rivera and Alfred Rodríguez, professors in the university's Modern and Classical Language Department.

Tatum, Charles M. Review of *Mi abuela fumaba puros*. *World Literature Today* 52, no. 3 (1978): 440. Tatum views Ulibarrí's stories as a series of sketches of people who influenced his childhood: the grandmother who smoked cigars, the fearless Uncle Cirilo, Elacio, the biology teacher, and other family members, friends, and acquaintances. He also observes that Ulibarrí draws on local legends and superstitions to create a rich "tapestry" of memories mingles with fiction to portray a way of life that has practically disappeared.

————. "Sabine Ulibarrí: Another Look at a Chicano Literary Master." *Pasó por aquí: Critical Essays on the New Mexican Literary Tradition, 1542–1988*, ed. Erlinda Gonzáles-Berry, 231–41. Albuquerque: University of New Mexico Press, 1989. Tatum explores *Tierra Amarilla*, *Mi abuela fumaba puros*, *Primeros encuentros*, *Pupurupú*, *El Gobernador Glu Glu*, *Al cielo se sube a pie*, and *Amor Y Ecuador*. He identifies several major themes in Ulibarrí's prose: childhood memories, humor, personalities, legends, encounters with the Anglo culture, and the fantastic. In his poetry, Tatum finds other themes: love, woman as lover, uprootedness, abandonment, and disillusionment, for example. He attributes Ulibarrí's Spanish-speaking environment, literary Spanish, academic training, and the study of Spanish literary masters to his mastery of the Spanish language in his works and to his place in Chicano literature.

————. "Ulibarrí, Sabine (1919–   )." *Chicano Literature: A Reference Guide* ed. Julio A. Martínez and Francisco A. Lomelí, 385–95. Westport, Conn.: Greenwood, 1985. Tatum presents a brief biography and short analyses of *Al cielo se sube a pie* and *Amor y Ecuador*. In these works, Ulibarrí focuses on "uprootedness, solitude, the tragic consequences of progress and life as a transitory state." Moreover, he observes that the author's poetry is "filled with color, finely rendered images, and language carefully selected and appropriate to the content." He compares Ulibarrí's prose to *costumbrismo* and finds that his use of local legends and popular superstition creates a mixture of fact and fiction.

————. "Sabine Ulibarrí." *Mexican American Literature* ed. Charles Tatum, 165–66. Orlando: Harcourt, Brace Jovannovich, 1990. This is a brief biographical essay in which Tatum focuses on Ulibarrí's early background, his education, his military and teaching careers, and his literary work.

"Today's Books." Review of *Tierra Amarilla: Stories of New Mexico.*
Long Beach (Calif.) *Press Telegram,* 10 Nov. 1972. This review
explains the nature of Ulibarrí's stories.

Townsley, Richard. Introduction. *Primeros encuentros/First*
encounters. Ypsilanti, Mich.: Bilingual Press/Editorial Bilingüe,
1982. Pp. vii–viii. Townsley describes Ulibarrí's stories about Tierra
Amarilla and the foreigners who arrive with their own cultures. The
stories, Townsley points out, are from the perspectives of children, now
adults, and reflect the author's humor, compassion, and curiosity.

"Ulibarrí, Sabine R(eyes) 1919– ." *Hispanic Writers: A Selection of*
Sketches From Contemporary Authors, ed. Bryan Ryan, 463–64.
Detroit: Gale Research, 1991. This selection offers information on
Ulibarrí's life, his career as a teacher, awards received, works in
progress, published works, and critical sources.

"Ulibarrí Stories Pure Delight." Review of *Mi abuela fumaba puros.*
New Mexican, 6 November 1987, 22. Ulibarrí is commended for his
delightful portrayal of the Hispanic people of Tierra Amarilla in this
collection of short stories, filled with tragedy and humor. The
review singles out the lead story, "Mi abuela fumaba puros" and
"Witcheries or Tomfooleries?"

Urioste, Donaldo W. "Costumbrismo in Sabine R. Ulibarrí's *Tierra*
Amarilla: Cuentos de Nuevo México." Missions in Conflict: Essays
on U.S.–Mexican Relations and Chicano Culture, ed. Renate von
Bardeleben, Dietrich Briesemeister and Juan Bruce-Novoa, 169–78.
Tübingen: Narr, 1986. Urioste examines "Mi caballo mago," "Juan
P.," and "La fragua sin fuego," short stories that reflect the
"traditional cuadros de costumbres." He concentrates on Ulibarrí's
use of language, irony, caricatures, and humor and points to his
critical view of Tierra Amarilla and its inhabitants. These stories,
Urioste perceives, are more serious and melancholic, nostalgic
depictions of the customs and traditions of a certain past.

———. "The Process of Escape in Sabine R. Ulibarrí's *Tierra Amarilla:*
Cuentos de Nuevo México." In "The Child Protagonist in Chicano
Fiction." Ph.D. dissertation, University of New Mexico, 1985. Pp.
150–84. Urioste explores the use of the child protagonist in "Mi
caballo mago," "El relleno de Dios," "Juan P.," and "La fragua sin
fuego." He explains that these narratives reflect the adult narrator's
memories of childhood experiences and bittersweet recollections of
the past. Ulibarrí's interest in childhood, Urioste further explains, is

a form of sanctuary from the adversities of adulthood and a way of reverting to an age of innocence and youth. In "Mi caballo mago," Urioste discerns Ulibarrí's use of the child protagonist as a way of achieving an understanding and appreciation of "hope, liberty, and the ideal," while in "El relleno de Dios," he offers a sympathetic and understanding picture of his community. However, in Ulibarrí's last two stories, Urioste observes a critical perspective of life in the child protagonist's community.

"Video of Ulibarrí Honors the Man and His Works." *University of New Mexico Campus News* 23, no. 25 (1988): 8. This news release announces the production of a video, "Ulibarrí: Ese Señor de voz hispana," in which Ulibarrí reads selected unpublished poems.

Zamora, Joe. "National Recognition: Dr. Sabine Ulibarrí." *Reflexiones* 1, no. 3 (1988): 8. This bilingual article notes Ulibarrí's national recognition as one of twelve Hispanic educators who have made significant contributions to the field of education.

Zimmerman, Marc. Review of *Tierra Amarilla: Stories of New Mexico, Mi abuela fumaba puros y otros cuentos de Tierra Amarilla, Primeros encuentros, The Condor and Other Stories,* and *El gobernador Glu Glu y otros cuentos. U.S. Latino Literature: An Essay and Annotated Bibliography,* by Marc Zimmerman. Chicago: MARCH/Abrazo, 1992. Pp. 105–6. Zimmerman briefly describes the nature and contents of Ulibarrí's books.

Zuleta Alvarez, Enrique. "Sabine R. Ulibarrí: Escritor hispano y americano." *Tierra amarilla: Cuentos de Nuevo Mexico,* by Sabine R. Ulibarrí. Quito: Editorial Casa de la Cultura Ecuatoriana, 1964. Pp. 9–12. Zuleta Alvarez presents a poetic and romantic portrait of New Mexico and its links to Spain. He also presents a sketch of Ulibarrí's accomplishments as scholar, teacher, and writer of poetry, criticism, and short narrative, such as the collection of short stories in *Tierra Amarilla.*

CONTRIBUTORS

Bruce-Novoa is professor and chair of the Department of Spanish and Portuguese, University of California Irvine. He has taught at Yale, Trinity U, Mainz, Erlangen-Númberg, Harvard, Pennsylvania, and Colorado. He is author of: *Chicano Authors: Inquiry by Interview, Chicano Poetry: A response to Chaos, Retrospace: Collected Essays on Chicano Literature and Literary History, La sombra del caudillo: versión periodistica, Inocencia perversa/Perverse Innocence,* and has two books of short stories and a novel in press.

James J. Champion is professor of Spanish and Linguistics at Southwest Texas State University. He received his Ph.D. in Romance Linguistics from the University of Michigan at Ann Arbor. His current research interests include interactive video and computer applications to Spanish.

Santiago Daydí-Tolson is Professor of Spanish and Portuguese at the University of Wisconsin-Milwaukee where he teaches contemporary Spanish, Latin American and Chicano literature. His publications include *El último viaje de Gabriela Mistral, Five Poets of Aztlán, Voces y ecos en la poesía de José Angel Valente, The post-Civil War Spanish Social Poets, Vicente Aleixandre: A Critical Appraisal.*

Patricia de la Fuente has a doctorate in Comparative Literature from the University of Texas at Austin and another in Continuing Adult Education from Texas A&M University. She teaches in the English Department at the University of Texas-Pan American and publishes on Mexican-American literature and poetry. Since 1985, she has been director of the UT-PA Press.

275

María I. Duke dos Santos is professor of Spanish and Portuguese, Coordinator of the Graduate Spanish Program, and Spanish Division Coordinator at East Texas State University. She has taught at Southwest Texas State University, the University of Texas at Austin, Texas Woman's University and Louisiana State University. Publications and research interests include Hispanic literature written in the United States and Latin American literature and cinema.

Gene Steven Forrest is associate professor of Spanish Language and Literature at Southern Methodist University in Dallas, Texas. His research, involving primarily the nineteenth- and twentieth-century Spanish novel, has resulted in numerous papers and published articles in journals in the U.S. and abroad on writers such as Benito Pérez Galdós, Emilia pardo Bazán, Juan Goytisolo, Miguel Delibes, and Juan Marsé.

María Herrera-Sobek, professor of Spanish at the University of California Irvine, is the author of *The Mexican Corrido: A Feminist Analysis, Northward Bound: The Mexican Immigrant Experience in Ballad and Song,* and *Reconstructing a Chicano/a Literary Heritage: Hispanic Colonial Literature of the Southwest.*

Wolfram Karrer is professor of American Literature at the University of Osnabrück, Germany. His publications in literary history, Black literature, Chicano literature, twentieth century authors and literary theory include *The African American Short Story, 1970 to 1990.*

Luis Leal is professor emeritus (University of Illinois, Champaign-Urbana), now at the University of California, Santa Barbara. His extensive published works have been compiled in *Luis Leal: A Bibliography with Interpretative and Critical Essays* (1988). In 1991 he received the Aztec Eagle, the highest decoration offered by the Mexican government "for outstanding contributions."

Francisco A Lomelí, professor of Spanish and Portuguese and Chicano Studies at the University of California at Santa Barbara, has published numerous articles and books in Latin American literature and Chicano studies. *La novelística de Carlos Droguett: Poética de la obsesión y el martirio, Handbook of Hispanic Cultures in the United States: Literature and Art, Dictionary of Literary Biography* (vols. 82 and 122), "*Chinigchinich*: An Early California Text in Search of Context," "Los mitos de la mexicanidad en la trilogía de Rodolfo Usigly," and "A Literary Portrait of Hispanic New Mexico: Dialectics of Perception."

Teresa Márquez is director of the Government Information Department and bibliographer for Chicano studies at the University of New Mexico General Library. She also is the founder of CHICLE (Chicano Culture and Literature Exchange), and electronic listserve available on the Internet, devoted to the discussion of literature, art, music and theater.

Arnulfo G. Ramirez is chair of the Department of Foreign Languages and Literatures and professor of Spanish and Linguistics at Louisiana State University. He has taught at the University of California at Los Angeles, University of Thessaloniki, Greece, Stanford University, the State University of New York at Albany, and the University of Madrid. Major publications include *Bilingualism Through Schooling, El español de los Estados Unidos: El lenguaje de los hispanos, Literacy Across Languages and Cultures*, and *Creating Contexts for Second Language Acquisition: Theory and Methods.*